The Word

There is Power in the Spoken Word of God

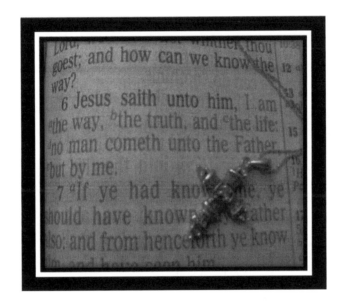

Reaching Out to the Youth, Young Adults, and the Brokenhearted

It's Never Too Late to Get Help!

Storm M. Rubin

To: Mr. Martin and Nina

God bless!
In Jesus Name. Amen.

5-30/2015

ISBN: 1508922853
ISBN 13:9781508922858

This book is inspired by God for you, the reader.

I dedicate this book to God the Father, God the Son, and God the Holy Spirit.

I also dedicate this book to my mom (Bridgett); dad (Lee); brothers (Jeremy, Joe, and Andrew); grandmas (Eve Thomas and Beverly Jenkins); the rest of my family; my pastor (Terry L. Harris), his wife (Mrs. Georgina Harris), and their family; my friends; the youth; young adults; the brokenhearted; and everyone who reads it.

May God bless you all!

In Jesus name,

amen.

My pastor, Terry L. Harris, is the senior pastor of Tacoma Christian Center in Tacoma, Washington.

Throughout this book, I was inspired by my pastor's teachings.

Table of Contents

The Purpose

The Purpose of *The Word* is:

- ❖ To help begin or deepen your relationship with God

- ❖ To equip you with the word of God that you can use in your everyday life

- ❖ To strengthen your walk with God

- ❖ To motivate you for the things of God

- ❖ To help build your faith

- ❖ To inspire you to grow and change

- ❖ To help you be an overcomer

- ❖ To aid you with your relationships (family, friends, and so on)

- ❖ To bring healing and deliverance to your life

- ❖ To teach you spiritual warfare, prayer, discernment, worship, wisdom, and so on

- ❖ To help make your walk with God fun

For I know the plans I have for you, says the Lord, plans to prosper you and not to harm you, plans to give you a future and a hope, [Jer. 29:11].

Healing
and
Deliverance

His Stripes; His Wounds

James Goll, who guest-starred on Sid Roth's *It's Supernatural*, shared this:

Jesus told him, "For every wound I received I obtained a special level of healing for My people."

In a vision Goll saw **Jesus**, and on **Jesus**'s back were thirty-nine stripes. Goll saw the names of every sickness and disease written within each stripe, because each stripe was peeled back for him so that he could see each name written on it.

Goll said that in a vision, he saw **Jesus**'s back laid open, and within every one of **His wounds** was written the name of every sickness and disease.

Jesus obtained healing for every mental disease through the crown of thorns.

Most diseases are transferred by touch (the hands). Through the piercing of His hands, **Jesus** obtained healing for every contagious disease.

His feet were nailed for paralysis.

Jesus has received healing for every heart condition (such as a hole in the heart, heart disease, and so on) through the piercing of His side.

That is what James Goll shared with Sid Roth on *It's Supernatural*.

There's healing for your body in the stripes and through the wounds of Jesus! You just have to believe and receive it. (The Lord revealed.) Amen.

As they were eating, Jesus took bread, and blessed it, and broke it, and gave it to the disciples, saying, Take, eat, this is my body, broken for you, [Matt. 26:26; 1 Cor. 11:24].

Violations to the Body (Rape, Incest, Molestation, Abuse)

'I've been bruised, beaten, raped, molested, abused…I've been hurt. What can I do? What can Jesus do for me?'

Jesus carried your griefs and bore your sorrows (all your emotional wounds). Yet we esteemed Him stricken, smitten by God, and afflicted. But He was wounded for our transgressions; He was bruised for our iniquities, the chastisement of our peace was upon Him. And by His Stripes we are Healed! [Isa. 53:4–5].

You learned from James Goll that "for every wound Jesus received, He obtained a special level of healing for His people."

Jesus bore thirty-nine stripes, and each one represented healing somewhere in or on your body. Each stripe represents an area of healing. (The Lord revealed.) Amen.

One stripe is for any violation done to the body.

Jesus bore your sorrows. (This represents any emotional wounds you may have suffered.)

He also carried your fears, worries, thoughts, mental torment, pain and suffering, grief, and any agony you may have suffered, by carrying your griefs. Amen.

This is what Jesus did for you.

What can you do?

Believe, receive, pray with faith, and lay everything at His feet.

First, believe His word [Isa. 53:4–5]. Believe Jesus carried your griefs and bore your sorrows. Believe His stripes represent healing. Believe He was wounded for your sake. Believe He bore any emotional wounds you may have suffered. Believe

He carried your griefs, mental torment, pain, and agony any violation may have caused. *Believe.*

Once you believe, receive your healing in Jesus's name.

Once you receive, pray with faith. Faith is the key to answered prayer [Heb. 11:6].

Faith is the belief that God is going to do what you're asking Him to do. Amen.

Pray in this manner:

"Heavenly Father, I believe your stripes represent healing. I believe one of your stripes represents any violation done to my body. I believe you bore my emotional wounds, and I believe you carried all my sorrows, pain, mental torment, grief, and any agony I have suffered. I believe you did all this for me, I receive what you've done for me, and by Your stripes I am healed. In Jesus name, amen."

Once you've prayed with faith, lay everything at His feet and pour out your heart to God, [Ps. 62:8].

Jesus says, Come to Me, all who are weary and heavy laden and I will give you rest, [Matt. 11:28].

Rest from your worries, your fears, insecurities, emotional wounds and scars, griefs, pain, doubts, anxieties, brokenness, pain, bitterness toward God or man, resentment, unworthiness, stress, unforgiveness, strife, blame, shame, hatred, guilt, condemnation, toil, tiredness, fatigue, and burdens.

Rest in Him... and lay it all at His feet. Amen.

Pray with faith:

"Heavenly Father, I come to you wearied and heavy laden with fear, worry, anxiety, insecurity, emotional wounds and scars, grief, pain, doubt, brokenness, bitterness, resentment, hatred, stress, unforgiveness, unworthiness, guilt, shame, blame, condemnation, fatigue, strife, and toil; I lay it all at your feet and receive your rest. In Jesus name, amen."

It's hard, I know it's hard, to let go of the pain, the hurt, the feelings of guilt, shame, or unforgiveness, but lay it all at His feet anyway. Amen.

Don't take back any of those feelings, wounds, pain, suffering, negative emotions, mental torment, and so on, once you've given it all to the Lord. **Leave it in His hands**, and trust and believe that **God is in control** and will take care of you. Amen.

Believe and receive His word.

Walk by faith and not by sight, [2 Cor. 5:7].

And Jesus answered them, "**Have faith in God**." [Mark 11:22 ESV]. Amen.

It may take some time to heal, but you will see the results of God healing you of your wounds, scars, negative emotions, mental scars, pain, torment, and more. Amen.

Put your faith in God and receive that He will come through for you. Amen.

Believe the word, speak the word, receive the word, think on His word, and apply the word of God to your life and you will see results. (The Lord revealed.) Amen.

To discover how much you are **loved by God** please read Sarah Young's devotional *Jesus Lives*. (The Lord revealed.) Amen.

To Those Who Have Been Violated, Speak Up and Speak Out!

Let your voice be heard!

If you or someone you know has been or is being raped, molested, or abused, or if there is incest, **do not** keep silent about it.

Open up your mouth and speak. Speak the truth without fear. Let your voice be heard, (The Lord revealed). Amen.

Do not be silent by allowing the enemy to whisper his lies to you, in your mind or through someone else. **These are some of the lies the enemy tells you and some of their effects:**

- It's your fault.
- No one will believe you.
- You'll get in trouble if you tell.
- Your family will get hurt if you tell.
- If you tell, it could ruin your family.
- Don't tell anybody.
- Just live with it.
- It's normal.
- You're to blame.
- No one will like you if you tell.
- What would everyone think?
- You'll get over it.
- Keep it a secret.
- You deserve it.
- Pretend like it never happened.
- You're a bad boy or you're a bad girl who needs to be punished.
- Thoughts of blame
- Thoughts of feeling disgusting, dirty, filthy, or unloved
- Thoughts of having no value or importance in someone else's eyes
- Thoughts of suicide
- The person cries and tells you not to tell, promising you, they won't do it again.

- The person who harmed you pleads with you not to tell.
- The person who harmed you tries to bribe you with gifts or money not to tell.

Do not believe the lies or tricks of the enemy!

Do not let the enemy silence you by using these tactics!

<u>Fight back</u> by cancelling out the enemy's lies and ***telling an adult*** about what's going on.

- You are **not** to blame.
- It's **not** your fault.
- You're **not** a bad boy or girl who needs to be punished.
- Do **not** keep it a secret.
- Someone **will** believe you.
- You **won't** get in trouble if you tell.
- Your family **will** not get hurt if you tell.
- You're **not** filthy, you're **not** disgusting, you're **not** worthless. You're priceless. Amen.
- It's **not** normal.
- You **don't** have to live with it.
- **Tell** somebody.
- It will **not** ruin your family.
- **Don't** worry about what others think.
- We **will** like you, even if you tell.
- You **won't** just get over it. (It takes time, Jesus, prayer, and faith.)
- You're **not** unloved. (**Jesus loves you!** You **are** loved!)
- You're **not** dirty.
- You **are** valued. You **are** important.
- **Cast down** thoughts of suicide and live!
- Do **not** believe those who do harm to you. **Tell** anyway!
- Do **not** accept the bribes or gifts of money, and so on that those who do harm to you offer. **Tell** anyway!
- Do **not** believe the pleas of those who've done harm to you. Tell anyway!
- You **don't** deserve it.

- Do **not** pretend like it never happened. **Tell** anyway!
- You **are** beautiful, you **are** handsome, **you are loved**!

Do not internalize your problems or struggles. Do not hold everything in. Open up your mouth and speak! **Tell** an adult, parent, teacher, youth pastor, police officer—anyone who can help you—and receive the help you need.

God Promises:

I will turn your mourning into dancing, I will turn your sorrow into joy, [Ps. 30:11].

Come to Me all who are worried and heavily laden and I will give you rest, [Matt. 28:11].

"Let not your heart be troubled, neither let it be afraid." [John 14:27 NKJV].

Hope in God, [Ps. 42:11].

Jesus loves you! His unfailing love surrounds you (*daily*), [see Ps. 33:22 NLT]. Amen.

Turn to the word of God. Begin to develop a habit of reading the word of God daily. His word provides peace, stillness, hope, strength, deliverance, healing, and love, and reveals more of the promises of God. Amen.

Jesus is the Word, and the Word is life. Amen.

Also, to transform and renew your mind, wiping it clean from all the lies of the enemy, refer to the **Battle of the Mind** strategy. You'll learn how to renew your thinking, and meditate on scriptures on page 58.

Ask the Holy Spirit to replace your thoughts with His.

Pray with faith: "Holy Spirit, think through me. In Jesus's name, amen."

The Holy Spirit needs your cooperation in this massive effort to renew your mind, so do your part by renewing your mind with the word of God and He will do His. Amen.

Breach of Trust

A breach of trust reveals someone who is no longer worthy of your trust.

According to www.thefreedictionary.com, "A breach of trust is any act in violation of the duties of a trustee or violating the terms of trust. A breach means enmity or the state of being hostile to someone or something, hatred, or violence. A violation is an act done unlawfully and with force." (This includes abuse, repeated cruel treatment, rape, molestation, and so on.)

If any person commits a violation to you or to someone you know, such as rape, molestation, abuse, incest, and so on, they are <u>no longer</u> worthy of your trust. Regardless if it's a parent, sibling, teacher, youth counselor, grandparent, uncle, aunt, cousin, any other relative, friend, adult, peer, or stranger, they have crossed the line and are <u>no longer</u> worthy of your trust. For your own safety and for the safety of others you *must* tell on them.

Report them to the police, another teacher, another parent, another relative, or an adult you trust, and keep telling on them until the problem gets resolved.

Do not allow any abuse, molestation, incest, or rape to continue.

Speak up and speak out!

Neglect and Abandonment; Runaway

'I've been neglected, abandoned, forgotten. I ran away to escape my problems, my parents, my situation.'

"Can a mother forget the baby at her breast and have no compassion on the child she has borne? Though she may forget, I will not forget you!" [Isa. 49:15 NIV].

"Before I formed you in the womb I knew you;" [Jer. 1:5 NKJV].

Even if my father and mother abandon me, **the Lord** will hold me close, [Ps. 27:10]. (The Lord Jesus personally revealed this verse above for you. Amen.)

Lord, when I felt or feel…

Used   Abused   Abandoned   Unsafe   Neglected   Discouraged

Depressed (without hope) Unforgiving Hatred   Afraid   Lonely

Grieved   Mad   Angry   Like no one understands me or how I feel

Doubtful   Vengeful   Hurt   In pain   Lost   Helpless

Hopeless   Sorrowful   Sad Insecure   Worthless   Worried

Low self-esteem   Low self-worth   Self-pity   To blame   Shame

Broken   Brokenhearted   Guilt   Forsaken   Shattered   Unnerved

Like no one cares   Unaccepted   Like no one listens   Like I don't matter

Unloved   Trapped   Gloom   Like no one supports me   Ill

Like no one believes me   Rejected   Vulnerable   Weak   Aggravated

Bitter or resentful toward God and others   Subdued   Disappointed

Empty   Disturbed   Frustrated   Irritable   Peeved   Pessimistic

Miserable   Misled   Confused   Defeated   Detached   Unwanted

Unnoticed   Intimidated Furious   Frightened Betrayed Misunderstood

Lack of confidence   Afraid   Distressed   Anxious   Stressed out

Scared   In disbelief Wounded   Fearful   Like I have unmet needs

Unable to Trust   Devastated Terrified   Uneasy   Troubled

Withdrawn   Introverted (keep feelings in)   Aggravated   Paranoid

Where were you, Lord, when I felt this way?

Are you My child? If so, I **have** been with you; have I not promised that "I will never leave you nor forsake you." [Heb. 13:5 NKJV]. **I love you! says the Lord.**

I will never leave you, but you can leave me by forgetting that I am with you.

Return to Me by taking My hand, Believing My word, and trusting in Me, **says the Lord.**

"For the LORD will not cast off His people, Nor will He forsake His inheritance." [Ps. 94:14 NKJV].

You are a chosen people, a royal priesthood, a holy nation, His own special people, [1 Pet. 2:9].

Affirm your trust in the Lord, by saying, **"The Lord is with me."** Repeat this as many times as it takes for you to believe it and receive it as the truth, because it is true. Amen.

If you are not My child, receive Me, says the Lord.

Pray this prayer with faith:

"Lord, I come before you today at the cross to confess to You that I'm a sinner in need of a Savior. Lord, please forgive me of all my sins, and cleanse me of all unrighteousness, wash me with Your blood that I may be forgiven, cleanse me so that I may be whiter than snow. Come into my heart today, as I acknowledge You as my Lord and Savior. I thank You for all that You have done for me on the cross. I thank You for receiving me. I'm now Your child, a new creation. In Jesus holy name, amen."

His Suffering

I bore your griefs and suffered your sorrows [Isa. 53:4].

I have suffered your abandonment, your rejection, your loneliness, your troubles, your emotional suffering, your mental torment… On the cross I was forsaken by God and man for you, **says the Lord.**

"He is despised and rejected by men, A Man of sorrows and acquainted with grief." [Isa. 53:3 NKJV].

On the cross Jesus cried out, "My God, My God, why have You forsaken Me?" [Matt. 27:46 NKJV].

"Yet it pleased the LORD to bruise Him; He has put *Him* to grief. When You make His soul an offering for sin, He shall see *His* seed, He shall prolong *His* days, And the pleasure of the LORD shall prosper in His hand." [Isa. 53:10 NKJV].

"But He *was* wounded for our transgressions, He *was* bruised for our iniquities; The chastisement for our peace *was* upon Him, And by His stripes we are healed." [Isa. 53:5 NKJV].

I was wounded for you, beaten for you, tried for you, forsaken for you. And by My stripes, you are healed, says the Lord.

Each of My stripes represents an area of healing for your life.

One stripe represents suffering.

Suffering from neglect, abandonment, emotional suffering, mental suffering, or torment; I bore it all for you, says the Lord.

Where have I been? My child, I **have** been with you.

Come to Me, all who are weary and heavy laden and I will give you rest, [Matt. 11:28].

Rest from your troubles, your hurt, your pain, your suffering, your sorrow…

Pray this prayer with faith:

"Heavenly Father, I lay all my feelings of neglect and abandonment, and all of my guilt, pain, my rejection, turmoil, loneliness, emotional suffering, and mental torment at your feet. I receive your rest and Your healing by Your stripes for my suffering. In Jesus name, amen."

Keep it all at His feet, believe, and receive your healing. Amen.

It may take some time to heal, but you will see the results of God healing you of your wounds, scars, negative emotions, feelings, mental scars, suffering, pain, torment, and more.

Put your faith in God and believe that He will come through for you. Always remember **Jesus loves you**! Amen. ☺

Refer to the **Battle of the Mind** strategy to learn how to renew your thinking, and to learn how to meditate on Scriptures, on page 58.

Turn to the word of God. Begin to develop a habit of reading the word of God daily. His word provides peace, stillness, hope, strength, deliverance, healing, and love, and reveals the promises of God. Amen.

Jesus is the Word, and the Word is life. Amen.

Believe His word, speak His word, receive His word, think on His word, and apply the word of God to your life, and you will see a change and results. (The Lord revealed.) Amen.

If possible, purchase the teaching on *The 40 Day Soul Fast* by Dr. Trimm. This is not about fasting from food or drink; it is an eight-week study on the soul to help you grow in your relationship with God. This teaching can further help you heal from feelings of neglect or abandonment. You can purchase it on Amazon.com, sidroth.com, or soulfast.com.

Feeling Neglected or Abandoned? Are You a Runaway? Speak Up and Speak Out!

Do not remain silent. Do not hold your peace; **speak the truth without fear**, [Ps. 35; 2 Tim. 1:7].

If you are being neglected or abandoned, or you are a runaway, or someone you know is, **tell** an adult, police officer, youth pastor, counselor, or relative **immediately**. To relieve your suffering and the suffering of others, let an adult know about your situation, and they will be able to offer you the help and assistance you need.

"Let not your heart be troubled, neither let it be afraid." [John 14:27 NKJV].

Let your voice be heard! Amen.

Drugs

'I've tried drugs… What's the big deal?'

The big deal is that as a **child of God**, you are not your own.

"Or do you not know that your body is a temple of the Holy Spirit within you, whom you have from God? You are not your own," [1 Cor. 6:19 ESV].

"Be sober-minded; be watchful. Your adversary the devil prowls around like a roaring lion, seeking someone to devour." [1 Pet. 5:8 ESV].

"No temptation has overtaken you that is not common to man. God is faithful, and He will not let you be tempted beyond your ability," [1 Cor. 10:13 ESV].

Remember, **"I will never leave you nor forsake you,"** says the Lord.

Do not be conformed (following the same pattern), to this world, but be transformed (changed), by the renewing (cleansing) of your mind, that by testing, you might discern (know), what is the good, acceptable, and perfect will of God, [Rom. 12:2].

What are the main drugs often tried by young people?

1. Marijuana
2. Tobacco
3. Ecstasy
4. Inhalants (such as glue and markers)
5. Prescription drugs (whether their own or someone else's)
6. Cocaine
7. Heroin
8. Date rape drugs (for example, rohypnol, which is often used at parties and clubs)

Why do young people try drugs?	What God has to say: (Please look up each scripture)
1. Boredom	1 Pet. 5:8; Rom. 12:1; 1 Cor. 9:27
2. Peer pressure (wanting to fit in or belong)	1 Cor. 15:33; 1 Cor. 10:13 Matt. 6:13; 1 Tim. 4:12; Ps. 25:21
3. Curiosity	1 Cor. 6:19–20; 1 Cor. 3:16 Prov. 22:3; Rom. 13:12–14
4. To escape life, or to escape physical, emotional, or mental pain	Come to Me all who are weary… [Matt. 11:28] [read also Isa. 53:4–5; John 10:10]
5. Thinking they will help them relax or be fun to do	Eph. 5:15–18; Ps. 16:11; Rom. 6:12–14
6. To be social with friends (trying to fit in)	Rom. 12:2; Eph. 5:11; 2 Cor. 5:17
7. Thinking they will help them feel better	Gal. 5:19–21 (drugs are sorceries, according to evangelist Perry Stone; you will see why later); 1 Cor. 9:27; Luke 21:34; Isa. 53

Information on why teens (young people) try drugs and the names of the drugs they often try was retrieved from www.betterhealth.vic.gov.

Are drugs sorceries?

According to Evangelist Perry Stone, (after he looked up the Greek definition of *sorceries*), anything that takes your mind or alters your personality to the point where it's no longer the real you **is** sorcery. Drugs take your mind and alters your personality to the point where it's no longer the real you. That **is** sorcery. <u>Keep away</u> from such things. Amen.

What are the effects of drug use?

To discover some of the devastating effects of drug use, please view Evangelist Perry Stone's DVD teaching *Overcoming Addiction*. This DVD teaching can be purchased at www.voe.org or www.perrystone.org. If it's still available online, this teaching can be viewed on YouTube® by searching for Perry Stone's "How

Addictions Affect the Brain, Part 1 and Part 2," "The Invisible Side of Addiction," and "The Principles for Freedom from Bondage."

The Truth About Drugs

Drugs, (often tried by young people), are **not** fun, nor are they an escape from life. They aren't an answer to physical problems or ailments, and they are **not** a feel-good, feel-better, now-you-can-relax substance. **Drugs kill, steal, and destroy**. (The Lord revealed.) Amen.

Who is the one who comes to steal, kill, and destroy?

It's satan; "The thief comes only to steal and kill and destroy." [John 10:10 ESV]. Amen.

"If you do well, will you not be accepted? And if you do not do well, sin lies at the door. And its desire *is* for you, but you should rule over it." [Gen. 4:7 NKJV].

Drugs' desire is for you, but **you** should rule over it.

If you are a child of God, you have dominion. God has given you authority over serpents and scorpions and nothing will by no means harm you, [Luke 10:19].

This means you have the power to say **no** to drugs.

Will you?

Keep in mind that when you no longer have control over your desire for drugs and drugs hold power or control over you, you are lost. Not only are you lost physically, mentally, and emotionally, but you are lost spiritually when you begin to desire something <u>more</u> than you desire God. This is idolatry, because you have allowed a substance to take the place of God.

If this has happened to you, what can you do?

Repent.

"If we confess our sins, He is faithful and just to forgive us *our* sins and to cleanse us from all unrighteousness." [1 John 1:9 NKJV].

How? **With faith, pray this prayer:**

"Lord, I confess to You that I'm a sinner in need of a Savior. I confess I've allowed drugs to take Your place and I have allowed them to rule over me. Forgive me, Lord, for doing so, and set me free. Cleanse me of all my sins and cleanse me of all unrighteousness. I repent and return to You today, receiving You as my Lord and Savior. In Jesus name, amen."

If you have prayed this prayer, and believe what you have prayed, you have been forgiven and set free.

Now that you have been set free:

Transform your thinking by renewing your mind. Turn to the **Battle of the Mind** strategy on page 58.

Turn to the word of God. Begin to develop a habit of reading the word of God daily. His word provides peace, stillness, hope, strength, deliverance, healing, and love, and reveals the promises of God. Amen.

Jesus is the Word, and the Word is life. Amen.

Believe His word, speak His word, receive His word, think on His word, and apply the word of God to your life, and you will see change in your life and results. (The Lord revealed.) Amen.

Begin to **praise and worship** God daily [Heb. 13:15]. Praise lifts your focus off of the problem and onto the presence of God.

Overcome and Stand

Take a stand, even when you see those around you participating in sinful behavior (such as trying drugs). Regardless of whether they are your family members, friends, peers, and so on, it doesn't have to be you!

Take a stand [Gal. 5:1], and overcome [Rom. 12:21].

Overcome by doing right, being an example for others to follow.

- Live in such a way that many will see and know that you are a follower of Christ [1 Pet. 2:12, 15; 3:15–16]. Let your light shine before men in such a way they see your good works and in doing so, glorify the Father in Heaven [Matt. 5:16].

Overcome by speaking positively:

- "Death and life *are* in the power of the tongue," [Prov. 18:21 NKJV]. Speak life, speak positively; even when loved ones, friends, or peers speak against you, talk bad about you, and speak down or negatively toward you. Continue to speak life, cast down word curses, bless those who curse you, do good to those who wrong or hate you and pray for those who mistreat you [Luke 6:27–28, 35–36; Rom. 12:14–21]. Amen.

Remember this:

- All things will work out for the good, to those who love God and are called according to His purpose [Rom. 8:28].
- Have faith in God; trusting and believing that He will come through for you. Amen.
- **Jesus loves you!**

Use these strategies to overcome and stand. Use them as often as you need to, never give up, and you will receive the victory. Amen.

If you need more help, use the strategies outlined in the section on spiritual warfare on pages 340-410.

If you still need help or suspect there's demonic activity involved in your situation, please **talk** to your pastor, youth pastor, or someone who specializes in deliverance and spiritual warfare, and follow their instructions.

Never give up. Stand, and overcome! Amen.

"having done all, to stand." [Eph. 6:13 NKJV].

Struggling with Drugs? Speak Up and Speak Out!

Do <u>not</u> remain silent. Do not hold your peace; speak the truth without fear [Ps. 35; 2 Tim. 1:7].

If you are currently fighting an addiction with drugs, or someone you know is, **tell** a youth pastor, counselor, relative, or other trusted adult immediately. To relieve your suffering and the suffering of others, let an adult know about your situation, and they will be able to offer you all the help and assistance you need.

"Let not your heart be troubled, neither let it be afraid." [John 14:27 NKJV].

Let your voice be heard! Amen.

A Place to Write Notes after watching the Perry Stone DVD Teaching on Addiction

_____

_____

_____

_____

_____

_____

_____

_____

_____

_____

_____

_____

_____

_____

_____

_____

_____

_____

_____

_____

_____

_____

_____

_____

34

Alcohol

'I drink... So what? What's the big deal?'

Alcoholic Beverages

You see alcohol on TV (commercials, electronic billboards, billboards, TV shows, movies, music videos, and so on.)

You see alcohol at parties, games, gatherings, get-togethers, reunions, and so on.

You see alcohol at dinnertime, at a restaurant, at your grandparents' house, in bars, and more.

You see alcohol at a friend's house, in a friend's car, or in their possession.

You see alcohol all the time, everywhere, and repeatedly. So what's the big deal?

Here's the big deal...

"And do not get drunk with wine, for that is debauchery, but be filled with the Spirit," [Eph. 5:18 ESV].

"Those who linger long at the wine, Those who go in search for mixed wine. Do not look on the wine when it is red, When it sparkles in the cup, *When* it swirls around smoothly;" [Prov. 23:30–31 NKJV].

Be sober (abstaining from drink) minded (uninfluenced by alcohol), be watchful, your adversary the devil, walks about as a roaring lion, seeking whom he may devour (destroy). [1 Pet. 5:8]. (Definition inspired/acquired from biblehub.com.)

Nor thieves...nor drunkards...nor...will inherit the Kingdom of God [1 Cor. 6:10].

"Wine is a mocker, strong drink a brawler, and whoever is led astray by it is not wise." [Prov. 20:1 ESV].

"For you are all children of light, children of the day. We are not of the night or of the darkness. So then let us not sleep, as others do, but let us keep awake and be sober. For those who sleep, sleep at night, and those who get drunk, are drunk at night. But since we belong to the day, let us be sober, having put on the breastplate of faith and love, and for a helmet the hope of salvation." [1 Thess. 5:5–8 ESV].

Do you not know that your bodies are the temples (dwelling place) of the Holy Spirit, Who is in you, whom you have received from God? You are not your own; you were bought at a price (bought with the **Blood of Jesus**). Therefore glorify God in your body and in your spirit, which are God's. [1 Cor. 6:19–20].

"Do not be conformed to this world, but be transformed by the renewal of your mind," [Rom. 12:2 ESV].

If you are a **child of God**, you are not your own. **You belong to God**, and His word is your guide. (The Lord revealed.) Amen.

Reasons why young people try alcohol	**What God says** (Please look up each scripture.)
1. To relieve stress or relax	Matt. 11:28–30; John 7:37–39; John 4:14; Phil. 4:6–7; 1 Pet. 5:7; Matt. 6:25–34; John 14:27; Prov. 3:5–6; Rom. 8:28.
2. Peer pressure	Rom. 12:2; 1 Cor. 10:13; 1 Cor. 15:33–34; Gal. 1:10; Prov. 1:10; Acts 5:29; James 1:12–15; Prov. 4:14–15, 29:25; Heb. 2:18.
3. Trying to copy or mimic adult or parent behavior	Rom. 12:1–2; Gal. 6:9; Eph. 4:27; 1 Cor. 15:33; 1 John 2:1.
4. Trying to be cool, fit in, be liked or accepted	John 15:16, 19; 1 Pet. 2:9; John 17:15–18; Rom. 12:1–2; 1 Cor. 6:19–20; Gal. 2:20; Rom. 13:14; 2 Cor. 5:17; 2 Cor. 6:14–18, 9–11.
5. Curiosity	1 Pet. 5:8; Gal. 5:21; Hosea 4:11; Prov. 23:31–32.
6. To feel good, from need or dependency	Turn to Me, **says the Lord** [Zech. 1:3].

7. It's easy to get	Be wise, [Prov. 20:1; 1 Thess. 5:5–8; Prov. 3:13–18; Prov. 3:5–6; Eph. 5:18].
8. Advertising, media, commercials	Be not conformed to this world, [1 Cor. 6:19–20]; [also see 1 Pet. 2:9; 1 John 2:16; 1 Thess. 5:22; John 14:26].

Information on why teens shouldn't drink was retrieved from www.kidshealth.org and www.pamf.org.

Alcohol, like drugs, **is** sorcery. How? Sorcery is anything that takes your mind or alters your personality to the point where it's no longer the real you. Alcohol takes your mind and alters your personality to the point where it's no longer the real you. <u>Refrain</u> from such things. Amen.

What are the effects of alcohol use?

To discover some of the devastating effects of alcohol use, please view Evangelist Perry Stone's DVD teaching *Overcoming Addiction*. This DVD teaching can be purchased at www.voe.org or www.perrystone.org. If it's still available online, it can be viewed on YouTube® by searching for Perry Stone's "A Little Toddy for the Body, Part 1 and Part 2," and "The Principles for Freedom from Bondages."

What is an addiction, how does alcohol become one, and how can I overcome it?

According to www.merriam-webster.com, an ***addiction*** is a "strong and harmful need to regularly have something or do something."

Alcohol becomes an addiction when it becomes a need. (The Lord revealed.) Don't let that happen to you! Amen.

Overcome in Christ Jesus. (The Lord revealed.) Amen.

He who the Son sets free, is free indeed [John 8:36].

If alcohol has become an addiction, **repent**.

"If we confess our sins, He is faithful and just to forgive us *our* sins and to cleanse us from all unrighteousness." [1 John 1:9 NKJV].

How? **With faith, pray this prayer:**

"Lord, I confess to You I'm a sinner in need of a Savior. I confess I've allowed alcohol to take Your place and I have allowed it to rule over me. Forgive me, Lord, for doing so, and set me free. Cleanse me of all my sins and cleanse me of all unrighteousness. I repent and return to You today, receiving You as my Lord and Savior. In Jesus name, amen."

If you have prayed this prayer, and believe what you have prayed, you have been forgiven and set free.

Now that you have been set free:

Transform your thinking by renewing your mind. Turn to the **Battle of the Mind** strategy, on page 58.

Turn to the word of God. Begin to develop a habit of reading the word of God daily. His word provides peace, stillness, hope, strength, deliverance, healing, and love, and reveals the promises of God. Amen.

Jesus is the Word, and the Word is life. Amen.

Believe His word, speak His word, receive His word, think on His word, and apply the word of God to your life and you will see a change in your life and results. (The Lord revealed.) Amen.

Begin to **praise and worship** God daily [Heb. 13:15]. Praise lifts your focus off the problem and onto the presence of God.

Overcome and Stand

Take a stand. Even when you see those around you participating in sinful behavior (such as getting drunk), and even if they are your family members, friends, or peers, it doesn't have to be you!

Take a stand [Gal. 5:1], and overcome [Rom. 12:21].

Overcome by doing right and being an example for others to follow.

- Live in such a way that many will see and know that you are a follower of Christ [1 Pet. 2:12, 15; 3:15–16]. Let your light shine before men in such a way they see your good works and in doing so, glorify the Father in Heaven [Matt. 5:16].

Overcome by speaking positively:

- "Death and life *are* in the power of the tongue," [Prov. 18:21]. Speak life, speak positively, even when loved ones, friends, or peers speak against you, talk bad about you, and speak down or negatively toward you. Continue to speak life, cast down word curses, bless those who curse you, do good to those who wrong or hate you, and pray for those who mistreat you [Luke 6:27–28, 35–36; Rom. 12:14–21]. Amen.

Remember this:

- All things will work out for the good, to those who love God and are called according to His purpose [Rom. 8:28].
- Have faith in God; trusting and believing that He will come through for you. Amen.
- **Jesus loves you!**

Use these strategies to overcome and stand. Use them as often as you need to, never give up, and you will receive the victory. Amen.

If you need more help, use the strategies outlined in the section on spiritual warfare on pages 340-410.

If you still need help or suspect there's demonic activity involved in your situation, please **talk** to your pastor, youth pastor, or someone who specializes in deliverance and spiritual warfare, and follow their instructions.

Never give up. Stand and overcome! Amen.

"having done all, to stand." [Eph. 6:13 NKJV].

Are You Fighting an Alcohol Addiction? Speak Up and Speak Out!

Do not remain silent. Do not hold your peace; speak the truth without fear [Ps. 35; 2 Tim. 1:7].

If you or someone you know are currently fighting an addiction with alcohol **tell** a youth pastor, counselor, relative, or other trusted adult immediately. To relieve your suffering and the suffering of others, let an adult know about your situation, and they will be able to offer you all the help and assistance you need.

"Let not your heart be troubled, neither let it be afraid." [John 14:27 NKJV].

Let your voice be heard! Amen.

A Place to Write Notes after watching the Perry Stone DVD Teaching on Addiction

The Anointing Breaks the Yoke

Do not be ashamed if you have received treatment from an addiction center for a drug or alcohol addiction. My pastor, Pastor Terry L. Harris, taught his congregation that God has two healing hands; one is physical (for medicine, surgery, and so on), and the other is supernatural. This section will explain God's supernatural healing hand and one of the methods He uses to heal in this way. (The Lord revealed.) Amen.

According to www.biblehub.com a **yoke** is "a heavy burden or hardship." A yoke is also a weight, (The Lord revealed.) Amen.

A weight, burden, or hardship can be any addiction, including drugs and alcohol.

God says, Come to Me all who are heavy laden or burdened and I will give you rest [Matt. 11:28].

Rest from your fears, troubles, and addictions. Rest (and peace) for your soul. Amen.

How? One way is through the **anointing**.

The **anointing** (the Lord revealed) is "a release of who God is; it flows from Him, it issues out of Him, it flows from the presence of God." Amen.

It shall come to pass in that day, That his burden will be taken off your shoulder, and his yoke from your neck, and the yoke will be destroyed because of the anointing [Isa. 10:27].

Believe this word, receive this word, stand on this word, speak this word, meditate on this word, and apply this word of God to your life.

There is power in the spoken word of God! Amen.

You can receive freedom by the anointing. How? **Have faith in God,** [Mark 11:22] and receive His word. Amen.

How can you usher in the anointing of God and receive your healing and freedom by faith?

1. **Worship**

   God inhabits the praises of His people [Ps. 22:3]. **Worship ushers in the presence of God,** and the presence of God ushers in the anointing.

To God give all the honor, all the glory, all the credit, and all the praise for this new revelation that He has given me. Bless and praise His holy, mighty, and righteous name. Amen.

"The Art of Worship" was given to the author on June 28, 2013.

The Art of Worship

In the book of Psalm, King David writes, **As the deer pants for the water, so thirsts my soul after You O God** [Ps. 42:1].

When you read this verse, you think nothing of it at first, but as you dig deeper into the heart of this true worshipper [see King David, in Acts 13:22], you find the art of worship written within these two lines.

When you look at the first line and the second line of verse 1 in Psalm 42, you see the words *pants* and *thirsts*. Pants and thirsts? What do these two words mean?

As the Lord led me to dwell on the word ***thirst*** (which is the same word for panting), He revealed that *to thirst* or *a **soul thirsts*** means "a longing, to search after, to think on, to dwell on, to look for, to yearn for, to desire, to run after, to want, to have a passion for (and more)." (This is worship.) Amen.

What are you longing for, desiring, dwelling on, yearning for, or running after? Is it God?

Begin to **search after God**, not man.

How? **Where do I start?** How can I become thirsty after God? (You might be thinking these three questions.)

It's simple. It all begins **in the heart**. The **heart** has to <u>want</u> to seek after God, to search for Him, to yearn for Him, to desire Him. **True worship** begins within the heart. Amen.

How is this done or where do I begin?

Through your thoughts. It is written, "For as he thinketh in his heart, so is he:" [Prov. 23:7 NKJV]. A thought begins in one's heart. (The Lord revealed.) Amen.

Where do your inward thoughts lie?

What do you think about the most? Are you thinking about God or something/someone else more?

When you come into the presence of God to worship or pray, are your thoughts on Him? Are you thinking about Him, His goodness, His mercy, His love, or who He is? Are you picturing God? Or are you allowing your thoughts to wander?

Are you more focused on what others might think, who's watching you, or what your friends might think?

Then your heart is not on God. It's too busy worrying about everyone and everything else.

How can I stay focused on God?

It's simple: by casting down thoughts and imaginations not of God and replacing them with thoughts of God and His word [2 Cor. 10:5].

Casting down thoughts or imaginations not of God, and replacing them with thoughts of God and His word, meditating on God's word, whispering His name, or worship can shift your focus off of those around you and onto the **One** it should be on.

When you shift your focus onto God, this quiets the mind and silences the enemy, who uses worrying about what others might think against you, to get your mind off of worshipping God. (The Lord revealed.) Amen.

Is all this possible?

Nothing is impossible with God! [Matt. 19:26]. Amen. ☺

Where do I begin?

You can begin now, with...a breath of praise (hallelujah), a word of thanksgiving, a voice of singing, a groan of the Spirit (the use of tongues), a move of dancing, a thought toward God, on His name, and on His word, and a heart of worship—longing for God.

This is the **art of worship**. (The Lord revealed.) Amen.

True worship (as defined by the author) is **an intense focus on God (with a mind and heart longing for Him), coupled with praises, thanksgiving, singing, and dancing—movement (arms extended/raised), and the use of tongues.**

(The Lord revealed this definition of true worship to the author on June 25, 2013.)

Is it that simple? Yes, it's that simple. ☺ God never intended for worship to be complicated. Amen.

2. Prayer

The power of praying in agreement with two or three people can break any yoke [Matt. 18:19–20]. Amen.

If you need healing, deliverance, or freedom, or you have a special need that you would like to have your pastor pray for, ask your pastor if he or she can lay hands on you and pray over you. You must **have faith** to receive your healing, freedom, or deliverance, or to have your special need met. Follow the directions of your pastor if he or she gives you instructions on how to build your faith. Amen.

3. Fasting

Fasting breaks the yoke [Matt. 6:16–18]. To find out the details of fasting, how long you should fast, the types of fasting, what you should fast for, and so on, please talk to your youth pastor or counselor and come up with a plan together.

Each of these strategies has the power to usher in the presence of God.

The presence of God ushers in the anointing of God, and the anointing of God breaks the yoke. You can receive your healing and freedom, that is available in the anointing, by your faith. Amen.

It takes faith to receive your healing and freedom from God. The anointing is there; you just have to tap into it and receive your blessing of healing and freedom by faith. Amen.

In the end, the anointing breaks the yoke [Isa. 10:27]. Amen.

Eating Disorders

'I've been struggling with an eating disorder...Is that bad?'

Yes, it is bad, but you can **overcome** it. Always remember **Jesus loves you**. ☺

"Or do you not know that your body is a temple of the Holy Spirit within you, whom you have from God? You are not your own, for you were bought with a price. (the **blood of Jesus**) So glorify God in your body." [1 Cor. 6:19–20 ESV].

You do not glorify God in your body when you are bound to an eating disorder. Amen.

"I praise you, for I am fearfully and wonderfully made." [Ps. 139:14 ESV].

"The thief comes only to steal and kill and destroy. I (Jesus) came that they may have life and have it abundantly." [John 10:10 ESV].

"For freedom Christ has set us free; stand firm therefore, and do not submit again to a yoke of slavery." [Gal. 5:1 ESV].

Yoke, slavery, imprisonment, bondage. Each of these words describes what an eating disorder truly is.

To be *bound,* according to www.dictionary.refrence.com, refers to "the state of being bound by or subjected to some external power or control. The state of being physically restrained, tied up, chained, or put in handcuffs (this includes imprisonment and slavery)."

A *yoke* (as we already defined) means "a weight or to be heavily oppressed."

Eating disorders are a state of being bound by an external force, a state of being physically restrained, tied up or chained, imprisoned and enslaved; and a yoke of oppression.

This is one true definition of an eating disorder. Amen.

Eating Disorders

The world's definition of eating disorders, according to Google.com, is "any range of psychological disorders characterized by abnormal or disturbed eating habits."

Eating Disorders	How They Harm the Body
Anorexia Nervosa—"not eating, fearful of gaining weight, self-esteem and body issues, binge eating or purging."	**Anorexia Nervosa** "causes slow heart rate, risk of heart failure, low blood pressure, excess dehydration, osteoporosis, hair loss, fainting, weakness, and more."
Bulimia Nervosa—"consuming large amounts of food and then vomiting, binge eating, low self-esteem, and being wrapped up in body image."	**Bulimia Nervosa** "causes heart failure, tooth decay because of stomach acid from frequent vomiting, rupture in the esophagus caused by constant vomiting, constipation, irregular bowel movements caused by laxative abuse, possible gastric rupture, and more."
Purging—"consuming large amounts of food and then vomiting it all up."	**Purging** "causes the same health risks as Bulimia Nervosa."
Rumination Disorder—"regurgitating food that has been swallowed and then spitting it out or re-swallowing it."	**Rumination Disorder** "causes deficiencies in vitamin and minerals, and dental problems."
Restrictive Food Intake—"avoiding certain types of food and not consuming enough food."	**Restrictive Food Intake** "has nutritional consequences and more."
Binge Eating Disorder—"consuming large amounts of food, forced vomiting, out-of-control binge eating, and guilt and shame over behavior."	**Binge Eating Disorder** "causes high blood pressure, high cholesterol, type 2 diabetes, heart disease, and gallbladder disease."
Anorexia Athletica—"compulsive and obsessive exercise to control weight; poor self-image."	**Anorexia Athletica** "causes protein and iron deficiencies, hair loss, infertility, irregular menstrual cycles for women, and low oxygen levels to the heart, leading to a heart attack."
Female Athlete Triad Syndrome—"a combination of three conditions: eating disorder, amenorrhea	**Female Athlete Triad Syndrome** "causes low energy, bone fragileness and low bone density (caused by

(menstrual cycle doesn't occur between the ages of fourteen and sixteen, and sex characteristics don't develop), and osteoporosis (loss of bone density). This is often seen in those who participate in sports such as gymnastics, figure skating, and ballet."	osteoporosis) leading to bone fractures and fractures to the hips and vertebral column; menstrual irregularities, anemia (not enough iron); and the health risks of the eating disorder."
Body Dysmorphic Disorder— "Comparing one's appearance to another's frequently, checking oneself in the mirror repeatedly, wearing excessive makeup and clothing, to hide an imagined flaw. Causes a person to avoid contact with the outside world, feeling anxious or self-conscious that their imagined flaw might be noticed; they may seek surgery despite recommendations against it."	**Body Dysmorphic Disorder** "causes eating disorders, anxiety, depression, low self-esteem, poor self-image, and more."
Muscle Dysmorphia—"Affects men more than women and is when men view themselves as being too small, when in reality they look normal. They go on diets or work out excessively to reach a certain image, need constant affirmation of their physical appearance, and engage in excessive bodybuilding routines; some even turn to drugs to make them look bigger."	**Muscle Dysmorphia** "causes eating disorders, poor self-image, low self-worth, low self-esteem, turning to steroids causing further health risks, infertility in men, high blood pressure, abnormalities with the liver, masculinization of women, causing absent periods, deeper voices, and so on."

Information acquired from the following sources: www.nationaleatingdisorders.org/general-information, www.aboutkidsgi.org/site/upper-gi-disorders/rumination-syndrome, www.eatingdisordersonline.com/explain/anorathletica.php, www.futuresofpalmbeach.com/anorexia-athletica/health-concerns/, www.futuresofpalmbeach.com/anorexia-athletica/health-concernswww.mayoclinic.org/diseases-conditions/body-dysmorphic-disorder/basics/risk-factors, www.futuresofpalmbeach.com/male-eating-disorders/effects-muscular-dysmorphia-steroid-abuse, and *Christian Paths to Health and Wellness* by Peter Walters and John Byl.

In the end, eating disorders wreak havoc on the body. (The Lord revealed.) Amen.

What causes an eating disorder?

Choice   Peers   Bullying or cyberbullying   Poor self-image

Low self-esteem Low self-worth   Peer pressure   Influenced by family

Media   Puberty   Cultural ideas   Dissatisfaction with body image

Models in magazines   Mimicking actors, actresses, and singers

Reasons behind eating disorders were retrieved and inspired by *Christian Paths to Health and Wellness* by Peter Walters and John Byl.

Overcome these **lies** of the enemy! It is the thief that comes to steal, kill, and destroy, Jesus came to give life and life abundantly [John 10:10]. Amen.

The enemy destroys your self-image, your self-worth, and your self-esteem; he **lies** by using your peers, magazines, models, actors/actresses, singers, or family members against you, to influence you negatively. He **lies** through the media and culture to get you to become dissatisfied with your body image. He uses bullying, cyberbullying, and peer pressure to insult you, control you, and steal your joy. This is the **work of the enemy**. He desires for you to be bound, not free.

The truth is, **eating disorders keep you in bondage.**

If that's true, how can I be set free?

Christ has come to set you free! Amen.

"For freedom Christ has set us free; stand firm therefore, and do not submit again to a yoke of slavery." [Gal. 5:1 ESV].

"Therefore if the Son makes you free, you shall be free indeed." [John 8:36 NKJV].

How? Surely **Jesus** has borne your griefs and carried your sorrows, your low self-esteem, your poor self-image, your lack of self-confidence, your low self-worth, your pressure, your fears, your worries, your anxieties, your troubles, your turmoil, your teasing, your suffering, and your grief, all on the cross. It is here (at the Cross), that you find freedom. (The Lord revealed.) Amen.

Come to Me, all who are weary and heavy laden and I will give you rest [Matt. 11:28].

Pray this prayer with faith:

"Heavenly Father, I come to you beaten, oppressed, enslaved and bound by an eating disorder. [Tell God which eating disorder(s) you suffer from.] I confess I suffer from low self-esteem, low self-worth, poor self-image, lack of self-confidence, fear over how I look, and fear of what others think of me. [You can tell God what else you suffer from.] I confess I have allowed the enemy to keep me in bondage, but I come to You today to be set free. I believe You bore my griefs, sorrows, sufferings, worries, pain, everything. I believe You bore it all for me on the cross, and I receive Your freedom now. In Jesus name, amen."

If you have prayed this prayer, and believe what you have prayed, you will be set free. Amen.

If you have not yet received Jesus Christ as Your Lord and Savior, pray this prayer with faith:

"Lord, I come before you today at the cross, to confess to You that I'm a sinner in need of a Savior. Lord, please forgive me of all my sins, and cleanse me of all unrighteousness, wash me with Your blood that I may be forgiven, cleanse me so that I may be whiter than snow. Come into my heart today, as I acknowledge You as my Lord and Savior. I thank You for all that You have done for me on the cross. I thank You for receiving me. I'm now Your child, a new creation. In Jesus holy name, amen."

Congratulations! You are now a child of God!

If you confess with your mouth the Lord Jesus Christ and believe in your heart that God raised Him from the dead, you shall be saved [Rom. 10:9]. Amen.

Now that you have been set free:

Don't take back any of those feelings, wounds, pain, suffering, negative emotions, mental torment, and so on, once you've already given everything to the Lord. Leave it all in His hands, and believe that He already bore it all on the cross. You are free. Amen.

Always remember **Jesus loves you!** ☺

Battle of the Mind Strategy

The Battle of the Mind strategy was inspired by my pastor, Terry L. Harris.

Transform your thinking by renewing your mind. Below are strategies outlined to help you:

Renew Your Mind, Change Your Thinking, Meditate on Scriptures, and Sing Scripture

Be not conformed to this world, but be transformed by the renewing of your mind [Rom. 12:2].

Transform means "to renew or change."

To transform your thinking, you have to <u>change</u> the way you think and what you're thinking about, and let go of any negative thought patterns.

If you constantly think *Woe is me,* and you constantly have negative thoughts full of lust, self-pity, low self-esteem, poor self-image, worry, and pessimism, your outlook on life will be negative.

As a man thinketh in his heart, so is he [Prov. 23:7].

Pastor Creflo Dollar said, **"Changing the way you think, will change the way you live."** Amen.

If you can just grasp hold of your thinking and renew your mind, you can **overcome** any negative, harmful, or sinful thoughts that come against you.

How? By <u>replacing your negative thoughts with the word of God</u>. (The Lord revealed.) Amen.

Instead of thinking, *Why can't I look like her or him?* start thinking, "I will praise you, for I am fearfully and wonderfully made." [Ps. 139:14 NKJV].

Instead of thinking, *Woe is me, I can't do anything right,* start thinking, "I can do all things through Christ who strengthens me." [Phil. 4:13 NKJV].

Instead of thinking, *Life is so boring—day after day, it's the same thing,* start thinking, "This is the day the LORD has made; We will rejoice and be glad in it." [Ps. 118:24 NKJV].

Replacing each negative thought with the word of God, can transform your thinking and change your outlook on life from negative to positive. Amen.

You can also change your thinking by **meditating** on the word of God.

To meditate means: to ponder, to dwell on, or to speak repeatedly aloud. (You can also sing scriptures). Amen.

If you know how to worry, you know how to meditate, because worrying is just meditating on something negative or what-ifs.

You can change your thinking from the negative to the positive by meditating on the word of God.

"But his delight *is* in the law of the LORD, And in His law (word) he meditates day and night." [Ps. 1:2 NKJV].

Here is a list of scriptures you can **meditate** on:

Philippians 4:13	Jeremiah 29:11	Psalm 1:3	Psalm 23
Ephesians 2:10	Philippians 4:19	John 3:16	Romans 8:28
John 8:36	Psalm 118:24	Isaiah 53	Psalm 122:1
2 Timothy 2:15	Ephesians 6:1	John 8:32	Galatians 5:22–25
Proverbs 3:5–6	Psalm 91:1–4	Romans 10:9	Matthew 11:28
Galatians 2:20	John 14:6	Romans 5:8	Matthew 28:20
Romans 12:1	Psalm 150	Ephesians 3:20	Psalm 139:14

The Benefits of Meditating on the Word of God

"But his delight *is* in the law (word) of the LORD, And in His law (word) he meditates day and night. He shall be like a tree Planted by the rivers of water, That brings forth its fruit in its season, Whose leaf also shall not wither; And whatever he does shall prosper." [Ps. 1:2–3 NKJV]

Psalm 1:3 reveals some of the many benefits of meditating on the word of God.

Allow the Holy Spirit to reveal the meaning of this verse [Psalm 1:3] to you. Amen.

Ask the Holy Spirit to replace your thoughts with His.

Pray with faith: "Holy Spirit, think through me. In Jesus name, amen."

The Holy Spirit needs your cooperation in this massive effort to renew your mind, so do your part by renewing your mind with the word of God and He will do His. Amen.

Torment of the Mind

To **torment,** according to www.thefreedictionary.com, is "to inflict with great pain, suffering or anguish; physical or mental pain; to undergo mental anguish; to inflict with great usually incessant or repeatedly bodily or mental suffering."

The torment of the mind is repetitive, evil, sinful, dark, sinister, harmful, (and constant evil thoughts) sent by the enemy against your mind.

Strategies to Overcome the Torment of the Mind:

1. **Plead** the **blood of Jesus** over your mind daily by speaking aloud, **Heavenly Father, I plead <u>the blood of Jesus</u> over my mind. In Jesus name. amen.** (Believe in the power of **the blood of Jesus** and receive by faith that there is a spiritual protective hedge in the **blood of Jesus** to protect your mind. Amen.)

2. **Cast down** repetitive, evil, sinful, dark, sinister, or harmful thoughts (sent by the enemy against your mind), and <u>replace</u> them with the word of God.

3. With faith, **ask** the Holy Spirit to replace your thoughts with His.

   Pray with faith: "Holy Spirit, think through me. In Jesus name, amen."

   The Holy Spirit needs your cooperation in this massive effort to renew your mind, so do your part by renewing your mind with the word of God and He will do His. Amen.

4. If you need healing, deliverance, or freedom from the torment of the mind that you would like to have **your pastor pray** for, ask your pastor if he or she can lay hands on you and pray over you. You must have faith to receive your healing, freedom, or deliverance. Amen. Follow the directions of your pastor if he or she gives you instructions on how to build your faith.

"You will keep *him* in perfect peace, *Whose* mind *is* stayed *on You*, Because he trusts in You." [Isa. 26:3 NKJV].

("Torment of the Mind" was inspired by Pastor Terry L. Harris's teaching *A Night of Healing*, on February 27, 2015. Amen.)

Keep in mind that renewing the mind is a <u>lifetime process</u>.

Changing the way you think doesn't happen overnight; it takes time.

Time is a good thing, because allowing your mind to daily be renewed by the Word of God can change your life! Amen.

"Therefore, if anyone *is* in Christ, *he is* a new creation; old things have passed away; behold, all things have become new." [2 Cor. 5:17 NKJV]. Amen.

When Battling an Eating Disorder

Turn to the word of God. Begin to develop a habit of reading the word of God daily. His word provides peace, stillness, hope, strength, deliverance, healing, and love, and reveals the promises of God. Amen.

Jesus is the Word, and the Word is life. Amen.

Believe His word, speak His word, receive His word, think on His word, and apply the word of God to your life and you will see change in your life and results. (The Lord revealed.) Amen.

Begin to **praise and worship** God daily [Heb. 13:15]. Praise lifts your focus off the problem and onto the presence of God.

If you need more help, use the strategies outlined in the section on spiritual warfare on pages 340–410.

If you still need help or suspect there's demonic activity involved in your situation, **contact** your pastor, youth pastor, or someone who specializes in deliverance and spiritual warfare, and follow their instructions.

"Now the Lord is the Spirit, and where the Spirit of the Lord is, there is freedom." [2 Cor. 3:17 ESV].

Fighting an Eating Disorder? Speak Up and Speak Out!

Let your voice be heard!

Speak the truth; speak the truth without fear [2 Tim. 1:7].

Pour out your heart and speak [Ps. 62:8].

Let the truth be made known. (The Lord revealed.) Amen.

If you or someone you know is battling an eating disorder **tell** a parent, teacher, counselor, youth pastor, relative, or other trusted adult. Let someone know, so that you can receive treatment, freedom, and healing, and be provided with all the help you need. **You are not alone in this fight**; let us help you receive the victory! Amen.

"Let not your heart be troubled, neither let it be afraid." [John 14:27 NKJV].

Please, open up your mouth and speak. Amen.

Remember you are not alone. **"I am with you always,"** says the Lord. Amen.

Jesus loves you!

Brokenness; the Broken Heart

'I am broken, wounded, deeply disappointed, hurt, and devastated... How could they leave me?'

"**The LORD is near to the brokenhearted and saves the crushed in spirit**." [Ps. 34:18 ESV].

"He **heals** the brokenhearted and binds up their wounds." [Ps. 147:3 ESV].

"My flesh and my heart may fail, but God is the strength of my heart and my portion forever." [Ps. 73:26 ESV].

"fear not, for I am with you; be not dismayed, for I am your God; I will strengthen you, I will help you, I will uphold you with my righteous right hand." [Isa. 41:10 ESV].

"Cast your burden on the LORD, and he will sustain you; he will never permit the righteous to be moved." [Ps. 55:22 ESV].

"And He said to me, "My grace is sufficient for you, for My strength is made perfect in weakness." Therefore most gladly I will rather boast in my infirmities, that the power of Christ may rest upon me. Therefore I take pleasure in infirmities, in reproaches, in needs, in persecutions, in distresses, for Christ's sake. For when I am weak, then I am strong." [2 Cor. 12:9–10 NKJV].

"**Come to me**, all who labor and are heavy laden, and I will give you rest. Take my yoke upon you, and learn from me, for I am gentle and lowly in heart, and you will find rest for your souls. For my yoke is easy, and my burden is light." [Matt. 11:28–30 ESV].

"who Himself bore our sins in His own body on the tree, that we, having died to sins, might live for righteousness—by whose stripes you were healed." [1 Pet. 2:24 NKJV].

"The *righteous* cry out, and the LORD hears, And delivers them out of all their troubles." [Ps. 34:17 NKJV].

"You number my wanderings; Put my tears into Your bottle; Are *they* not in Your book?" [Ps. 56:8 NKJV].

"No weapon formed against you shall prosper, And every tongue *which* rises against you in judgment You shall condemn. This *is* the heritage (inheritance) of the servants of the LORD, And their righteousness *is* from Me," Says the LORD." [Isa. 54:17 NKJV].

"**Trust in the LORD** with all your heart, and do not lean on your own understanding. In all your ways acknowledge him, and he will make straight your paths." [Prov. 3:5–6 ESV].

Please read all of Psalm 31. ☺

"The Spirit of the LORD is upon Me, Because He has anointed Me To preach the gospel to the poor; He has sent Me to heal the brokenhearted, To proclaim liberty to *the* captives, And recovery of sight to *the* blind, *To* set at liberty those who are oppressed;" [Luke 4:18 NKJV] [also see Isa. 61:1].

Brokenness, according to www.thefreedictionary.com, means "Forcibly separated in two or more pieces, fractured, crushed by grief, weakened, humbled, subdued." Brokenness includes being disappointed. (The Lord revealed.) Amen.

A *broken heart*, according to www.merriam-webster.com, means "a state of extreme grief and depression," and according to www.dictionary.refrence.com, it means "devastating sorrow and despair, (especially disappointment in love)."

Causes of a Broken Heart	Causes of Brokenness
Loss (such as the death of a loved one, friend, or pet)	Loss (of any kind)
Loss (such as a home, possessions, job, bankruptcy)	Change
Terminated friendships or relationships	Separation, divorce, grief, suffering, pain, depression
Abuse, neglect, abandonment, suffered violation of some sort, forced to be on the streets (from homeless, prostitution, sex trafficking, and more)	Abandoned, neglected, violated

Divorce, separation, separated from parents or loved ones (taken out of the home)	Wondering about the cause of something, worry
Health issues, health scares, wounds, sickness, disease (of oneself and others)	Stress-related issues or problems
Tragedies, stress-related issues or problems, stressful situations, depression, disorders, anxieties, and so on	Subdued, tied down
Grief, sadness, sorrow, worry, fear, suffering, broken promises, disappointments	Disappointment, broken promises, loss of friendships, relationships, and so on

(Information on causes of brokenness and a broken heart inspired by: mayoclinic.com/broken-heart-syndrome)

Brokenness is similar to having a broken heart. (The Lord revealed.) Amen.

I have **not** left you, I have **not** abandoned you. **I have carried you, says the Lord.**

I have suffered your griefs, I have borne your sorrows, I have carried your brokenness and your broken heart. **Turn to Me**, says the Lord.

I am **near** to the brokenhearted, and save the crushed in spirit. **Turn to Me**, says the Lord.

How? Pour out your heart to Me, says the Lord. I will **mend** your brokenness, and I will **heal** your broken and troubled heart.

In this manner, pray with faith:

"Heavenly Father, I suffer from brokenness, and I suffer from a broken heart. I believe you carried my griefs, I believe you bore my sorrows. Mend my brokenness, and heal my broken heart. I receive what You have done for me. In Jesus name, amen."

"He heals the brokenhearted and binds up their wounds." [Ps. 147:3 ESV]. Amen.

It may take some time to heal, but you will see the results of God healing you of your brokenness and your broken (wounded) heart.

In the meantime, renew your thinking; use the **Battle of the Mind** strategy on page 58.

When battling brokenness or a broken heart, **turn to the word of God.** Begin to develop a habit of reading the word of God daily. His word provides peace, stillness, hope, strength, deliverance, healing, and love, and reveals the promises of God. Amen.

Jesus is the Word, and the Word is life. Amen.

Believe His word, speak His word, receive His word, think on His word, and apply the word of God to your life and you will see a change in your life and results. (The Lord revealed.) Amen.

Begin to **praise and worship** God daily [Heb. 13:15]. Praise lifts your focus off the problem and onto the presence of God.

"Cast your burden on the LORD, and he will sustain you; he will never permit the righteous to be moved." [Ps. 55:22 ESV]. Amen.

A Heavy Heart

A heavy heart is a heart that yearns to be loved.

Often this aching heart turns to something or someone to fill the void of their emptiness. Instead, **turn to Me**, says the Lord. The only way that this heart can be filled is by crying out to God and receiving His love. Amen.

Pray this prayer, with faith:

"Heavenly Father, I suffer from a heavy heart. Fill me with your love. In Jesus name, amen."

God will never deny your request! [John 14:14] Amen.

During the calm of prayer, this is what the Lord also revealed to me (the author) concerning a heavy heart:

To those who have struggled with a **heavy heart** and dealt with a deficit of love (*deficit* means a loss, someone has fallen short, inadequate—not enough) from others (such as a loved one, friends, or parents), there is a **love** that is unfailing, unending, overflowing, never disappoints, and does no harm. It is a secure, protective love—**His love**. Amen.

His love is a love you can depend on, count on, fall back on, dwell in, cling to, and find rest in, a faithful, trusting, true love: **this is the love of God the Father, God the Son, and God the Holy Spirit.** This is the love you will receive when you ask God to fill your heavy (aching) heart. Amen.

A Hardened Heart

Inspired by Pastor Guillermo Maldonado

Having their understanding darkened, being alienated from the life of God…because of their blindness of heart [Eph. 4:18].

"And in them the prophecy of Isaiah is fulfilled, which says: 'Hearing you will hear and shall not understand, And seeing you will see and not perceive; For the hearts of this people have grown dull. *Their* ears are hard of hearing, And their eyes they have closed, Lest they should see with *their* eyes and hear with *their* ears, Lest they should understand with *their* hearts and turn, So that I should heal them.'" [Matt. 13:14–15 NKJV].

"Happy *is* the man who is always reverent, But he who **hardens his heart** will fall into calamity." [Prov. 28:14 NKJV].

"Do not **harden your hearts** as in the rebellion, In the day of trial in the wilderness," [Heb. 3:8 NKJV].

"The heart *is* deceitful above all *things*, And desperately wicked; Who can know it?" [Jer. 17:9 NKJV].

"For the word of God *is* living and powerful, and sharper than any two-edged sword, piercing even to the division of soul and spirit, and of joints and marrow, and is a discerner of the thoughts and **intents of the heart**." [Heb. 4:12 NKJV].

According to www.merriam-webster.com, a ***hardened heart*** means "lacking in sympathetic understanding and feeling."

Signs of a Hardened Heart
(Inspired by Pastor Guillermo Maldonado)

Unresponsive to the things of God	Unfeeling	Bitter (toward God and man; because of unanswered prayer, broken promises, and so on)
Cold	Cruel	Icy
Mean	Negative	Vindictive
Argumentative	Jealous	Envious
Judgmental	Angry	Resentful
Unkind	Unforgiving	Bears or holds grudges
Broken	Prideful	Boastful
Fearful	Blind	

Overcome a hardened heart by asking God to heal, soften, and clean out the one within you.

Remove the calluses from your heart. How?

In this manner, pray with faith:

"Heavenly Father, I confess that I suffer from a hardened heart. Create in me a clean heart, O God, renew a steadfast spirit within me, and heal me from my brokenness, my pain, my resentment, my bitterness, my pride, my jealousy. Soften my heart toward [place name(s) here]. Help me to forgive them, O God, and remove any calluses from my heart. I receive your healing, I receive your cleansing, and I forgive [place name(s) here]. In Jesus name, amen."

"Create in me a clean heart, O God, And renew a steadfast spirit within me." [Ps. 51:10 NKJV].

Keep your heart from being re-hardened.

Continue to **praise, thank, and give God glory** for delivering you from a hardened heart. Praise lifts your focus from the problem onto the presence of God. Amen.

Turn to the word of God. Begin to develop a habit of reading the word of God daily. His word provides peace, stillness, hope, strength, deliverance, healing, and love, and reveals the promises of God. Amen.

Jesus is the Word, and the Word is life. Amen.

Believe His word, speak His word, receive His word, think on His word, and apply the word of God to your life and you will see a change in your life and results. (The Lord revealed.) Amen.

Renew your thinking; use the **Battle of the Mind** strategy on page 58.

"Do not harden your hearts as in the rebellion, In the day of trial in the wilderness," [Heb. 3:8 NKJV].

Dealing with Brokenness or a Broken Heart?
Speak Up and Speak Out!

Do not internalize your struggles or hardships; instead **confess** your heart to God and receive His love and healing. Amen.

Pour out your troubles to a friend, parent, teacher, youth counselor, youth pastor, or other trusted adult, who in turn can provide you with help, advice, support, encouragement, and assistance.

Open up your heart and speak.

When you are vulnerable, do not allow anyone to take advantage of you in any way. If anyone attempts to do so, **report** them immediately to the police or another adult. Do not be afraid to tell on them.

Depression

'I feel hopeless...down...discouraged...worn...defeated...in despair...Will I ever recover?'

Yes: **hope in God.** (The Lord revealed.) Amen.

"Hope deferred makes the heart sick," [Prov. 13:12 NKJV].

"Why are you cast down, O my soul? And why are you disquieted within me? Hope in God; For I shall yet praise Him, The help of my countenance and my God." [Ps. 43:5 NKJV].

"**Uphold** me according to Your word, that I may live; And do not let me be ashamed of my hope." [Ps. 119:116 NKJV].

"Fear not, for I am with you; Be not dismayed, for I am your God. **I will strengthen you**, Yes, I will help you, I will uphold you with My righteous right hand.'" [Isa. 41:10 NKJV].

"Cast your burden on the LORD, And He shall sustain you; He shall never permit the righteous to be moved." [Ps. 55:22 NKJV].

"And He said to me, "My grace is sufficient for you, for My strength is made perfect in weakness." Therefore most gladly I will rather boast in my infirmities, that the power of Christ may rest upon me. Therefore I take pleasure in infirmities, in reproaches, in needs, in persecutions, in distresses, for Christ's sake. For when I am weak, then I am strong." [2 Cor. 12:9–10 NKJV].

Come to Me, all who are weary and heavy laden and I will give you rest. Take My yoke upon you and learn from Me, for I am gentle and lowly in heart, and you will find rest for your souls. For My yoke is easy and My burden is light. [Matt. 11:28–30].

"Rejoice in hope, be patient in tribulation, be constant in prayer." [Rom. 12:12 ESV].

For I know the plans I have for you, declares the Lord, plans to prosper you, and not to harm you, plans to give you a future and a hope [Jer. 29:11].

Hope in God!

Depression, according to www.merriam-webster.com, means "a state of feeling sad; a serious medical condition in which a person feels very sad, hopeless, unimportant, and often is unable to live a normal way. This includes inactivity, increase or decrease in appetite, feeling dejected, hopeless, and sometimes having suicidal tendencies."

Causes of Depression		
Sense of hopelessness	High levels of stress	Trauma in childhood or adulthood
Loss of loved one; grief	Finances (such as debt, bankruptcy)	Inherited (runs in the family)
Not enough sleep	Broken relationships; broken friendships	Discouragement
Broken promises; someone being deceitful or constantly lying	Divorce; separation	

(Causes of depression information acquired from: mayoclinic.com; webmd.com and merriam-webster.com)

Come to Me, all who are weary and heavy laden and I will give you rest [Matt. 11:28].

Hope

Pastor Dutch Sheets, whose mission is to restore hope in America, appeared on the Christian television show *It's Supernatural*, hosted by Mr. Sid Roth (around June 18, 2014). Pastor Dutch Sheets spoke a few words on depression:

"Hope deferred makes the heart sick," [Prov. 13:12 NKJV] Pastor Sheets said. He also revealed that there are **six stages to hope deferred**:

1. The first stage is ***discouragement,*** (this is a loss of confidence, according to www.Google.com.)
2. The second stage is ***confusion,*** (this refers to being unclear about something, according to www.merriam-webster.com.)
3. The third stage is ***unbelief,*** (an absence of faith, according to www.google.com).
4. The fourth stage is ***disillusionment,*** (this is being bummed out because you no longer believe in something, according to www.vocabulary.com.)
5. The fifth stage is *bitterness* (hatred or ill will toward something, according to www.merriam-webster.com).
6. The last and worst stage of all is ***cynicism,*** (this is when you no longer believe anything.) You don't ever want to get to this stage. Amen.

Then Pastor Dutch Sheets talked about the **power of choice**. He said that God revealed this to him: "It is your decision to remain depressed, because God is willing and ready to heal you. You have to choose to activate your will and receive His help. Make the choice, and His power will come along and help you defeat depression."

Make the choice now and **receive** God's healing power today **by faith**! Amen.

This information was revealed by Pastor Dutch Sheets on *It's Supernatural*. Learn more about hope by reading Pastor Dutch Sheets's book *The Power of Hope*.

Receive your freedom and get healed from depression by allowing God to heal you. Amen.

His Suffering

I bore your griefs and suffered your sorrows [Isa. 53:4].

I have suffered your grief, your brokenness, your discouragement, your weakness, your loneliness, your troubles, your emotional suffering, your mental torment... <u>On the cross</u>, I bore it all for you, **says the Lord**.

"He is despised and rejected by men, A Man of sorrows and acquainted with grief." [Isa. 53:3 NKJV].

"Yet it pleased the LORD to bruise Him; He has put *Him* to grief. When You make His soul an offering for sin, He shall see *His* seed, He shall prolong *His* days, And the pleasure of the LORD shall prosper in His hand." [Isa. 53:10 NKJV].

"But He *was* wounded for our transgressions, *He* was bruised for our iniquities; The chastisement for our peace *was* upon Him, And by His stripes we are healed." [Isa. 53:5 NKJV].

I was wounded for you, beaten for you, tried for you, forsaken for you. And by My stripes, you are healed, **says the Lord**.

Each of My stripes represents an area of healing for your life. One stripe represents suffering. If you are suffering from depression, worry, emotional suffering, mental suffering or torment; I already bore it all for you. My child, My power is made available for you, **says the Lord**. Amen.

Come to Me, all who are weary and heavy laden and I will give you rest [Matt. 11:28].

Rest from your troubles, your hurt, your pain, your suffering, your sorrow.

Pray this prayer with faith:

"Heavenly Father, I lay all my feelings of depression at your feet and I receive my healing by Your stripes. I receive your rest from my pain and suffering. In Jesus name, amen."

Keep everything at His feet, believe, and receive your healing. Amen.

It may take some time to heal, but you will see the results of God healing you of your depression, wounds, scars, hurts, negative emotions, feelings, mental scars, suffering, pain, torment, and more.

Put your faith in God and receive that He will come through for you. Always remember **Jesus loves you**! Amen. ☺

When and if depression tries to return to your heart, don't let it in. Cast it down and renew your mind using the **Battle of the Mind** strategy on page 58 and by asking the Holy Spirit to replace your thoughts with His.

Pray with faith: "Holy Spirit, think through me. In Jesus name, amen."

The Holy Spirit needs your cooperation in this massive effort to renew your mind, so do your part by renewing your mind with the word of God, and He will do His. Amen.

Turn to the word of God. Begin to develop a habit of reading the word of God daily. His word provides peace, stillness, hope, strength, deliverance, healing, and love, and reveals the promises of God. Amen.

Jesus is the Word, and the Word is life. Amen.

Believe His word, speak His word, receive His word, think on His word, and apply the word of God to your life and you will see a change in your life and results. (The Lord revealed.) Amen.

Meditate on scripture

Here is a list of scriptures you can meditate on to overcome depression:

Psalm 42	Psalm 43	Psalm 34:17	Romans 8:38–39
John 14:1–2	Isaiah 41:13	Isaiah 41:10	Philippians 4:13
Psalm 118	Romans 5:3–5	Proverbs 3:5–6	Philippians 4:4
Psalm 37:25	Romans 8:26	James 1:2–4	2 Timothy 1:7
Psalm 91	Matthew 11:28–30	Romans 8:28	Jeremiah 29:11
Romans 10:17	Psalm 40:1–3	Psalm 9:9	Deuteronomy 31:8
Psalm 46:10	Matthew 28:20	Deuteronomy 33:27	

Overcome depression with **praise and worship**. Praise lifts your focus off the problem and onto the presence of God. Learn more about worship and what true worship is by reading "**The Art of Worship**" on page 48. Amen.

Overcome depression by **speaking** in your prayer language (tongues). Speaking in tongues builds you up [1 Cor. 14:4]. Amen.

To further overcome depression, please read Sarah Young's devotional book *Jesus Today.*

Hope in God!

"I wait for the LORD, my soul waits, And in His word I do hope." [Ps. 130:5 NKJV].

Dealing with Depression? Speak Up and Speak Out!

Let your voice be heard!

Do not internalize your struggles or hardships. Instead confess your heart to God and receive His love and healing. **Pour out** your troubles to a friend, parent, teacher, youth counselor, youth pastor, or other trusted adult who in turn can provide you with help, advice, support, encouragement, and assistance.

Open up your heart and speak. Amen.

When you are vulnerable, do not allow anyone to take advantage of you in any way. If anyone attempts to do so, **report** them immediately to the police or another adult. Do not be afraid to tell on them. Amen.

Stress, Worry, and Anxiety

'I can't take it anymore…What if…What if there's danger…What should I do…What if…What if…'

Stress, according to www.google.com, means "a state of anxiety and uncertainty over actual or potential problems. Allow one's mind to dwell on difficulty or troubles, give way to anxiety or unease."	**Worry**, according to www.merriam-webster.com/dictionary/anxiety, means "fear or nervousness about what might happen. Fearful concern or interest." According to www.dictionary.refernce.com it means "distress or uneasiness of mind caused by fear of danger or misfortune."	**Anxiety**, according to www.merriam-webster.com/dictionary/stress, means "A state of mental tension and worry caused by problems in your life, work, etc. Something that causes strong feelings of worry and anxiety. Physical force or pressure; strain."

Worry for nothing. (The Lord revealed.) Amen.

"Therefore I say to you, do not worry about your life, what you will eat or what you will drink; nor about your body, what you will put on. Is not life more than food and the body more than clothing? Look at the birds of the air, for they neither sow nor reap nor gather into barns; yet our Heavenly Father feeds them. Are you not more of value then they? Which of you by worrying can add one cubit to his stature?

"So why do you worry about clothing? Consider the lilies of the field, how they grow; they neither toil nor spin; and yet I say to you that even Solomon in all his glory was arrayed like one of these. Now if God so clothes the grass of the field, which today is, and tomorrow is thrown in the oven, *will He* not much more *clothe* you, O you of little faith?

"Therefore do not worry saying, 'what shall we eat?' or 'what shall we drink?' or 'what shall we wear?' For after all these things the Gentiles seek. For your Heavenly Father knows that you need all these things. But seek thee first the kingdom of God and His righteousness, and all these things shall be added unto you. Therefore **do not worry** about tomorrow, for tomorrow will worry about its own things. Sufficient for the day *is* its own trouble." [Matt. 6:25–34 NKJV].

Be anxious for nothing, but in everything by prayer and supplication, with thanksgiving, present your requests to God, and the peace of God which surpasses all understanding, will guard your hearts and minds in Christ Jesus [Phil. 4:6–7].

"casting all your care upon Him, for He cares for you." [1 Pet. 5:7 NKJV].

"And my God shall supply all your need according to His riches in glory by Christ Jesus." [Phil. 4:19 NKJV].

"What then shall we say to these things? If God *is* for us, who *can be* against us?" [Rom. 8:31 NKJV].

Come to Me, all who are weary and heavy laden and I will give you rest. Take My yoke upon you and learn from Me, for I am gentle and lowly in heart, and you will find rest for your souls. For My yoke is easy and My burden is light [Matt. 11:28–30].

"There is no fear in love; but perfect love casts out fear, because fear involves torment. But he who fears has not been made perfect in love." [1 John 4:18 NKJV].

"And we know that all things **work together for good** to those who love God, to those who are called according to *His* purpose." [Rom. 8:28 NKJV].

"Peace I leave with you, My peace I give to you; not as the world gives do I give to you. Let not your heart be troubled, neither let it be afraid." [John 14:27 NKJV].

"**Let not** your heart be troubled; you **believe** in God, **believe** also in Me." [John 14:1 NKJV].

"**Be still**, and know that I *am* God;" [Ps. 46:10 NKJV].

"I can do all things **through Christ** who strengthens me." [Phil. 4:13 NKJV].

"Yet in all these things we are more than conquerors through Him who loved us." [Rom. 8:37 NKJV].

"Be strong and of good courage, **do not fear** nor be afraid of them; for the LORD your God, He *is* the One who goes with you. He will not leave you nor forsake you."

"And the LORD, He *is* the One who goes before you. He will be with you, He will not leave you nor forsake you; **do not fear nor be dismayed.**" [Deut. 31:6, 8 NKJV].

Please read all of Psalm 56.

"And **let the peace of God rule in your hearts**, to which also you were called in one body; and be thankful." [Col. 3:15 NKJV].

"**Cast your burden on the LORD**, And He shall sustain you; He shall never permit the righteous to be moved." [Ps. 55:22 NKJV].

Worry for nothing. Amen.

Overcome Stress, Worry, and Anxiety

How?

Cast your burden on the Lord, and He will sustain you. **Give** all your worry, stress, and anxiety over to God; and lay it at His feet. Amen. It takes faith: "So then faith *comes* by hearing, and hearing by the word of God." [Rom. 10:17 NKJV]. Have faith when you pray and you will see results. Amen.

In this manner pray, with faith:

"Heavenly Father, I give all my worries, all my anxiety, and all my stress over to You; I lay it all your feet. Casting all my burdens on thee O Lord, I believe You will sustain me. I receive Your peace and I receive Your rest for my life. In Jesus name, amen."

"**Peace** I leave with you, My peace I give to you; not as the world gives do I give to you. Let not your heart be troubled, neither let it be afraid." [John 14:27 NKJV]. Amen.

When and if stress, worry, or anxiety tries to distress your thoughts again, don't let it. Cast down stress, worry, or anxiety, and renew your mind using, the **Battle of the Mind** strategy on page 58 and by asking the Holy Spirit to replace your thoughts with His.

Pray with faith: "Holy Spirit, think through me. In Jesus name, amen."

The Holy Spirit needs your cooperation in this massive effort to renew your mind, so do your part by renewing your mind with the word of God and He will do His. Amen.

Turn to the word of God. Begin to develop a habit of reading the word of God daily. His word provides peace, stillness, hope, strength, deliverance, healing, and love, and reveals the promises of God. Amen.

Jesus is the Word, and the Word is life. Amen.

Believe His word, speak His word, receive His word, think on His word, and apply the word of God to your life and you will see a change in your life and results. (The Lord revealed.) Amen.

Meditate on scripture

Here is a list of scriptures you can meditate on to overcome stress, worry, and anxiety:

Psalm 16:8	Psalm 56	Philippians 4:13	Deuteronomy 31:6, 8
John 16:33	John 4:27	Romans 8:37	Philippians 4:6–7
Psalm 32	Psalm 34	Romans 8:6	Matthew 6:25–34
Psalm 55:22	Colossians 3:15	2 Corinthians 11:27–28	Romans 8:31

The word of God in your mouth is mightier than anything that comes at you, because the word of God will not return void, but it will accomplish what it has been set at to do [Isa. 55:11]. Amen.

There is power in the spoken word of God! (The Lord revealed.) Amen.

Overcome stress, worry, and anxiety by **pouring out your heart to God and man.** Pouring out your heart can help relieve your suffering. Amen. When pouring out your troubles to a friend, parent, teacher, youth counselor, youth pastor, or other trusted adult, listen to them, and they can provide you with help, advice, support, encouragement, and assistance.

Spend time alone in the presence of God

In his sermon on stress, Dr. Charles Stanley lists the benefits of solitude with God, some of which are the following:

- Repairs the damage of stress
- Equips a person to face tough or hard days
- Develops and deepens one's relationship with God
- Protects one's health
- Makes one's busy days more fruitful
- Answers are given
- Strength from God
- Deeper trust in God
- Gives one a sense of peace, joy, and confidence
- It lets one know that God hears and understands

These are some of the benefits of spending quiet time alone in the presence of God. These benefits will help you overcome stress, worry, and anxiety. Amen.

Overcome stress, worry, and anxiety with **praise and worship**. Praise lifts your focus off the problem and onto the presence of God.

Overcome stress, worry, and anxiety by **speaking** in your prayer language (tongues). Speaking in tongues builds you up [1 Cor. 14:4]. Amen.

Overcome stress, worry, and anxiety by **being confident** that God has equipped you to handle the task at hand [Phil. 2:13–16; Rom. 8:28], and God will carry you through [Jer. 29:11]. Always remember **Jesus loves you!** Amen.

Pastor Joyce Meyer said, **"You can't control when emotions, stress, worry, or anxiety will come, but <u>don't</u> let them control you."** Amen.

Peer Pressure

'You should try this…Come with us tonight…You should come over…No one will know… This is peer pressure.'

"My son, if sinners entice you, **Do not consent**." [Prov. 1:10 NKJV].

"No temptation has overtaken you that is not common to man. **God is faithful**, and he will not let you be tempted beyond your ability, but with the temptation he will also provide the way of escape, that you may be able to endure it." [1 Cor. 10:13 ESV].

"Do not be conformed to this world, but be transformed by the renewal of your mind, that by testing you may discern what is the will of God, what is good and acceptable and perfect." [Rom. 12:2 ESV].

"Whoever walks with the wise becomes wise, but the companion of fools will suffer harm." [Prov. 13:20 ESV].

"**Do not be deceived**: "Bad company ruins good morals." [1 Cor. 15:33 ESV].

"But Peter and the apostles answered, "We must obey God rather than men." [Acts 5:29 ESV].

"The fear of man brings a snare, But whoever trusts in the LORD shall be safe." [Prov. 29:25 NKJV].

"For in that He Himself has suffered, being tempted, He is able to aid those who are tempted." [Heb. 2:18 NKJV].

"Blessed *is* the man Who walks not in the counsel of the ungodly, Nor stands in the path of sinners, Nor sits in the seat of the scornful;" [Ps. 1:1 NKJV].

"delivering you from the way of evil, from men of perverted speech." [Prov. 2:12 ESV].

"Therefore go out from their midst, and be separate from them, says the Lord," [2 Cor. 6:17 ESV].

In the midst of (and before and after) a peer pressure situation, **remember** the word of God. The **word of God** is a lamp to your feet and a light to your path [Ps. 119:105]. The word points you in the right direction. The word gives you discretion in your decision making. The word is a stepping-stone on your journey through life. The word provides correction, discipline, and answers in the midst of a tight spot. **God's Word** is living, powerful, sharper than any two edged sword, piercing even to the division of soul and spirit, and of joints and marrow, and is a discerner of the thoughts and the intents of the heart, [Heb. 4:12].

(The Lord revealed the verse [Heb. 4:12], written above for you.) Amen.

Read God's word, believe His word, receive His word, stand on His word, memorize His word, meditate on His word, quote His word, research His Word, and speak His word, and you will prevail in the midst of any peer pressure situation. Amen.

"Do not be deceived: "Bad company ruins good morals." [1 Cor. 15:33 ESV]. Amen.

Overcome Peer Pressure

Overcome peer pressure with the word of God! Begin to learn and memorize scriptures. Amen.

If your church has decided to come up with a youth crisis hotline, use it in the midst of or after a peer pressure situation. Please see your youth pastor for details.

Renew your thinking; use the **Battle of the Mind** strategy on page 58 and ask the Holy Spirit to replace your thoughts with His.

Pray with faith: "Holy Spirit, think through me. In Jesus name, amen."

The Holy Spirit needs your cooperation in this massive effort to renew your mind, so do your part by renewing your mind with the word of God and He will do His. Amen.

Use the **Overcome and Stand** strategy on page 29 to overcome peer pressure.

Pray with faith, asking God (daily) to equip you for the day ahead, in Jesus name. Amen.

Overcome peer pressure by **speaking** in your prayer language (tongues) in the morning, before you head off to school and during the day (when no one notices). Do not speak in tongues to draw attention to yourself. Amen.

Speaking in tongues builds you up [1 Cor. 14:4]. Amen.

"No temptation has overtaken you that is not common to man. **God is faithful**, and he will not let you be tempted beyond your ability, but with the temptation he will also provide the way of escape, that you may be able to endure it." [1 Cor. 10:13 ESV].

Struggling with Peer Pressure? Speak Up and Speak Out!

Peer pressure, according to www.dictionary.refernce.com, means "social pressure by members of one's peer group to take a certain action, adopt certain values, or otherwise conform in order to be accepted."

Do not be conformed (similar, following the same pattern) to this world, but be transformed (changed) by the renewing (complete change for the better) of your mind, that by testing (proving), you might discern (know) what is the will of God, which is good, acceptable (pleasing), perfect (complete) [Rom. 12:2].

(Hebrew definition of words were acquired from www.biblehub.com.)

If caught in the midst of peer pressure (other than reading or meditating on the word of God or calling/texting a youth hotline center that your church sets up), you can **walk away** and **tell** the nearest teacher, counselor, youth pastor, or other trusted adult what happened, what took place, and how it affected you.

It's important not to internalize your struggles or hardships. Instead confess your heart to God and receive His wisdom and guidance. Also when pouring out your troubles to a friend, parent, teacher, youth counselor, youth pastor, or other trusted adult, listen to them. They can provide you with help, advice, support, encouragement, and assistance.

Open up your mouth and speak. Amen.

Reasons why someone might not tell an adult about their peer pressure experience	What God says
1. Fear	God has not given you a spirit of fear, but of power, love, and a sound mind [2 Tim. 1:7]. "In God I have put my trust; I will not be afraid. What can man do to me?" [Ps. 56:11 NKJV]; [also see 1 Cor. 10:13].
2. I'll be labeled a tattletale or a snitch. (Be not afraid. The Lord revealed. Amen.)	"Be not deceived: "Bad company ruins good morals." [1 Cor. 15:33 ESV]. "For am I now seeking the approval of man, or of God? Or am I trying to please man?" [Gal. 1:10 ESV]. We must obey God rather than man, [Acts 5:29]. Be not afraid, [Ps. 56:11; Isa. 41:10; Isa. 35:4; 1 Pet. 5:7; Prov. 24:25].
3. I want to fit in.	"Do not be conformed to this world," [Rom. 12:2 ESV] [also see Ps. 1:1–2; 2 Cor. 6:17; 1 Pet. 2:9; Prov. 2:12; 1 Cor. 15:33; Prov. 4:14–15; Prov. 1:10; Gal. 1:10].
4. No one will listen to me. (Rest assured, I will listen to you, says the Lord.)	Then you will call upon Me, and pray to me, and I will listen to you [Jer. 29:12]; [also see John 10:27; Prov. 2:1–5]. "Listen to advice and accept instruction, that you may gain wisdom in the future." [Prov. 19:20 ESV].

Open up your mouth and speak. Speak the truth without fear.

Jesus is with you and Jesus loves you! Amen. ☺

Bullying/Cyberbullying

'I've been bullied…pushed aside…shoved. Or I was the bully and hurt people…'

Bullying, according to www.google.com, means "using superior strength or influence to intimidate someone, typically by forcing him or her to what one wants; to oppress; harass." According to www.thefreedictionary.com *bully* means "to treat in an overbearing or intimidating manner; a person who is habitually cruel or overbearing."

Cyberbullying, according to www.desc.sa.gov.au, means "bullying which uses e-technology to victimize others. It is in the use of Internet services or mobile tech; such as emails, chat rooms, discussion groups, instant messaging, SMS, text messaging, social media, websites, etc." According to www.stopbullying.com, "examples of cyberbullying are the following, 'posting mean messages or sending mean text messages about someone, spreading around embarrassing photos of someone. Spreading vicious and malicious rumors through social media, etc. and creating fake profiles of someone, sharing embarrassing videos of someone, etc.'"

Treat others how you would want to be treated [Luke 6:31]. (**Yes, the Golden Rule originated from the Bible**.) God desires for us to do as He commands, and to live according to His word. (The Lord revealed.) Amen.

"**Love one another**. As I have loved you, so you must love one another." [John 13:34 NIV].

"And you shall **love the LORD your God** will all your heart, with all your soul, with all your mind, and with all your strength.' This *is* the first commandment. And the second, like *it*, *is* this: 'You shall **love your neighbor as yourself**.' There is no other commandment greater than these." [Mark 12:30–31 NKJV].

Neighbor, in the Greek (the original language the New Testament was written in), means "anyone you meet."

"Love does **no harm** to a neighbor;" [Rom. 13:10 NKJV].

Harm, in Greek (according to www.biblehub.com), means "inwardly foul, rotten, inner malice, wickedness, inner evil. Bad things, evil morally of a mode of thinking, feeling, acting, wrong, wicked of persons, injurious, ill, work ill to one."

Bullying and cyberbullying are inwardly foul, rotten, bad, wrong, and injurious, resulting in harm to one's neighbor (who is anyone you meet). Amen.

If you love God, you would love your neighbor. (The Lord revealed.) Amen.

Love your neighbor as yourself.

Loving your neighbor as yourself does not include bullying, slandering, spreading vicious or malicious rumors about someone, cyberbullying, causing harm, treating cruelly, and so on.

"Do not let any unwholesome talk come out your mouths, but only what is helpful for building others up according to their needs, that it may benefit those who listen." [Eph. 4:29 NIV].

Unwholesome, according to www.biblehub.com, means "worthless, corrupt, bad, and rotten."

Love is **not** cruel, vicious, unkind, hateful, bitter, resentful, evil, rotten, foul, without mercy, quick-tempered, harmful, or unruly.

"Love does no harm to a neighbor;" [Rom. 13:10 NKJV]. Amen.

Love is patient, love is kind; loves does not envy; love does not parade itself, is not puffed up, does not behave rudely, does not seek its own, is not provoked, thinks no evil, does not rejoice in iniquity, but rejoices in the truth…love never fails [1 Cor. 13:4–6, 8].

This love is accomplished through you, with the help of the Holy Spirit.

Ask the Holy Spirit to love through you daily, in Jesus name; ask the Holy Spirit with faith, so you can learn to love your neighbor as yourself. Amen.

Love **overcomes** the wickedness of bullying/cyberbullying. Amen.

Forgive

Forgive those who have wronged you and caused you harm. Forgiving is hard, but the benefits outweigh the process. You will be blessed for doing so. Amen.

To the Bully	To the Victim
Stop bullying or cyberbullying! Treat others how you would want to be treated [Luke 6:31]. "And you shall love the LORD your God will all your heart, with all your soul, with all your mind, and with all your strength.' This *is* the first commandment. And the second, like *it, is* this: 'You shall love your neighbor as yourself.' There is no other commandment greater than these." [Mark 12:30–31 NKJV]. *Neighbor*, in Greek (the original language the New Testament was written in), means "anyone you meet." "Do not let any unwholesome talk come out your mouths, but only what is helpful for	<u>Do not</u> internalize your struggles, troubles, or hardships. When somebody bullies you, **tell** a parent, teacher, youth counselor, youth pastor, or other trusted adult <u>immediately</u>. They can provide you with the help and assistance you need. Also, confess your heart to God and receive His love and healing. Amen. **Open up your heart and speak.** Do not be silent! Do not be afraid to speak [2 Tim. 1:7]. Amen. "Let not your heart be troubled, neither let it be afraid." [John 14:27 NKJV]. You need not fear man, nor what other people think or say. Save yourself or others who are being bullied, by **speaking up** immediately to put a stop to the bullying/cyberbullying. You can **save** a life. (The Lord

building others up according to their needs, that it may benefit those who listen." [Eph. 4:29 NIV].

Unwholesome, according to www.biblehub.com, means "worthless, corrupt, bad, and rotten."

"Love does **no harm** to a neighbor;" [Rom. 13:10 NKJV].

Bullying/cyberbullying is **wrong**, resulting in harm to one's neighbor (who is anyone you meet). Amen.

If you love God, you would love your neighbor. (The Lord revealed.) Amen.

Love is patient, love is kind; loves does not envy; love does not parade itself, is not puffed up, does not behave rudely, does not seek its own, is not provoked, thinks no evil, does not rejoice in iniquity, but rejoices in the truth...love never fails [1 Cor.

revealed.) Amen.

After you **tell** an adult:

Forgive those who've wronged you.
This may be the hardest thing you have to do, but you must forgive those who have done you wrong (bullied you). Amen.

"For if you forgive men their trespasses, your heavenly Father will also forgive you." [Matt. 6:14 NKJV].

"And whenever you stand praying, if you have anything against anyone, forgive him, that your Father in heaven may also forgive your trespasses." [Mark 11:25 NKJV].

"And be kind to one another, tenderhearted, forgiving one another, even as God in Christ forgave you." [Eph. 4:32 NKJV].

13:4–6, 8].

This love is accomplished through you, with the help of the Holy Spirit.

Ask the Holy Spirit to love through you daily, in Jesus name; ask the Holy Spirit with faith, so you can learn to love your neighbor as yourself. Amen.

To receive the Holy Spirit's help, first you need to receive Jesus Christ as your Lord and Savior (if you haven't already).

Receive Me, says the Lord.

Pray this prayer with faith:

"Lord, I come before you today at the cross, to confess to You that I'm a sinner in need of a Savior. Lord, please forgive me of all my sins, and cleanse me of all unrighteousness. Wash me with Your blood that I may be forgiven; cleanse me so that I may be whiter than snow. Come into my

You may be thinking, *Why? Why should I forgive when they harmed me and harassed me? They bullied me. Why should I forgive those who trespassed against me? Why?* Simple. Because while you were still a sinner, Christ forgave you, and demonstrated His love for you by dying for you [Rom. 5:8], that you might be forgiven, and so that you might be saved [John 3:16].

When we were still in darkness (and sinners), Jesus died for us and forgave us of our sins; how much more should we forgive someone who has wronged us, when Christ forgave us when we were still considered the enemies of God [Rom. 5:10]. Amen.

We must **forgive** our enemies. Amen.

This doesn't mean you are okaying the bullies behavior. You forgive them, so that you

heart today, as I acknowledge You as my Lord and Savior. I thank You for all that You have done for me on the cross. I thank You for receiving me. I'm now Your child, a new creation. In Jesus holy name, amen."

After you have prayed this prayer with faith, continue reading.

Although there are no excuses for being a bully, ask yourself what caused you to be a bully?

1. Unmet needs or desires at home? God promises in His word to supply all your needs [Phil. 4:19; Eph. 3:20; Ps. 62:8].

2. Abuse (of any kind), violence at home, neglect, or abandonment? If so, tell an adult who can help provide you with assistance right away.

3. Not receiving enough

may be forgiven [Matt. 6:14]; forgiving someone releases their control over you. Not forgiving someone allows a person to keep their control over you, by keeping you angry and bitter at them. Forgiving someone helps you receive forgiveness and the blessings of God. Amen.

Forgive those who have trespassed against, wronged, and bullied you. Amen.

In this manner, pray with faith:

"Heavenly Father, I forgive [name(s)] for trespassing against me, wronging me, and bullying me. In Jesus name, amen."

Truly mean it in your heart, when you seek to forgive someone. Amen.

If you **need help** forgiving someone, pray the following prayer with faith:

attention at home? Find a listening ear. God promises to listen to you [Ps. 34:17]; many adults such as counselors or youth pastors will listen to you too.

4. You want to fit in or be a part of a clique or group, so you join in when others are bullying someone? **Dare to be different!** <u>Stand up</u> for what is **right**; stand in the gap for someone who needs help, stand apart from the crowd, and speak up for someone who is being bullied (because it could be you). Put yourself in somebody else's shoes for a day and feel someone else's pain. This is mercy—showing compassion for someone. Amen.

5. Is it jealousy, rage, anger, envy, hatred, or malice toward someone?

"Heavenly Father, help me forgive [name(s)]. In Jesus name, amen."

In the end, forgiving those who have wronged you and caused you harm makes you more like Christ, who forgave those who wronged Him [Luke 23:34]. Amen. Forgiving is hard, but the benefits outweigh the process. You will be blessed for doing so. Amen.

Forgiveness is one key to living an abundant life, [John 10:10] Amen.

"But I say to you who hear: Love your enemies, do good to those who hate you, bless those who curse you, and pray for those who spitefully use you." [Luke 6:27–28 NKJV].

I have forgiven them. Now what?

Repent. In your heart, you never want to get to the point where you feel so strongly against someone that you are willing to hurt them. This is wrong, wickedness, and sin. **Repent**. *Repent* means to change your thinking, turning your heart back to God (confessing your wrong), and seek to do good instead of evil. Amen.

No matter the excuse. Bullying/cyberbullying is never the answer!

These are some of **the harmful effects** a victim suffers from being bullied or cyberbullied:

Harm, fear, depression,

worry, anxiety, Low self-

esteem, low self-worth,

When and if the person you've forgiven seeks your forgiveness:

1. **Listen** (Listen to what they have to say.)
2. **Speak** (Tell them how you feel; speak from your heart. Amen.)
3. **Forgive** (Forgive them face-to-face, just as you have forgiven them before God. Amen.)

Now, come to Me, when you are hurting, says the Lord.

Are you Suffering

I bore your griefs and suffered your sorrows [Isa. 53:4].
I have suffered your grief, your brokenness, your discouragement, your weakness, your loneliness, your troubles, your

injury, Suicide, avoiding

school (cutting class),Turning

to drugs or alcohol, loss of

friends, Turning to gangs,

turning to violence, Eating

disorders, isolation, rejection,

Physiological torment, stress,

nightmares, Humiliation,

embarrassment, cutting,

Insecurities, change in moods

(mood swings), and more

(The list of the effects of bullying was provided by "The Science of Bullying" at www.scienceofpeople.com. You can learn more about the effects of bullying on this website.)

If you are a bully, turn yourself in. Seek to **change** with the help of an adult, youth counselor, or pastor to

emotional suffering, your mental torment... <u>On the cross</u>, I bore it all for you, **says the Lord.**

"He is despised and rejected by men, A Man of sorrows and acquainted with grief." [Isa. 53:3 NKJV].

"Yet it pleased the LORD to bruise Him; He has put *Him* to grief. When You make His soul an offering for sin, He shall see *His* seed, He shall prolong *His* days, And the pleasure of the LORD shall prosper in His hand." [Isa. 53:10 NKJV].

"But He was wounded for our transgressions, *He was* bruised for our iniquities; The chastisement for our peace was upon Him, And by His stripes we are healed." [Isa. 53:5 NKJV].

I was wounded for you, beaten for you, tried for you, forsaken for you. And by My

right the wrong you have done.

Seek Forgiveness

From God [1 John 1:9]

In this manner, pray with faith:

"Heavenly Father, forgive me for being a bully. Forgive me for causing harm to my neighbor. Forgive me for all the pain I have caused them. I now know I have no excuse for being a bully. To be honest, I was a bully because [tell God why you were a bully]. I have no excuse for my behavior. I've done wrong and acknowledge my wrong before you. Help me to do right and to love my neighbor as myself. In Jesus name, amen."

From the victim(s): [Col. 3:15; James 5:16]

Seeking forgiveness from those you have bullied may

stripes, you are healed, **says the Lord**.

Each of My stripes represents an area of healing for your life.
One stripe represents suffering.

If you are suffering from depression, worry, emotional suffering, mental suffering or torment; hurt and pain from being bullied; I already bore it all for you, **says the Lord**.

My child, My power is made available for you. (The Lord revealed.) Amen.

Come to Me, all who are weary and heavy laden and I will give you rest [Matt. 11:28].

Rest from your troubles, your hurt, your pain, your suffering, your sorrow…

require an adult's help. If so, request help from an adult who can help provide supervision and further guidance, and keep things from escalating any further.

Step 1: **Before** approaching the victim(s):

Pray
- Pray that God prepares your heart with grace and love.

- Pray and ask God to prepare the victim(s) heart to receive.

Prepare
- Research what you should say.

- Write down what you should say. Plan your words carefully.

- Rehearse what you've written down.

- Seek guidance from a teacher, youth

Pray this prayer with faith:

"Heavenly Father, I lay all my hurt and pain from being bullied at your feet and I receive your healing. I receive your rest for my suffering. In Jesus name, amen."

Keep everything at His feet, believe, and receive your healing. Amen.

It may take some time to heal, but you will see the results of God healing you of your wounds, pain, and suffering from bullying, scars, hurts, negative emotions, feelings, mental scars, suffering, torment, and more.

Put your faith in God and believe that **He will** come through for you. Always remember **Jesus loves you!** Amen.

I **will** heal your wounds and relieve you of your sufferings, counselor, youth pastor, parent, or mature Christian friend.

- Plan when you should talk to them and where.

- Come sincerely, assuming all will work out for the good [Rom. 8:28].

Step 2: **When** you go (to talk to the victim(s):

- Go with sincerity, seeking forgiveness.

- Find the victim and ask to talk with them. This may require an adult's help. Keep in mind when you go to talk to the victim(s) that you should not seek to gang up on them in any way. You're coming to apologize, not to make matters worse.

Step 3: In **your confession** to the victim:

says the Lord. "He heals the brokenhearted And binds up their wounds." [Ps. 147:3 NKJV]. Amen.

Love yourself
(The Lord revealed.) Amen.

God commands you to love your neighbor as yourself [Mark 12:31]. Before you can love your neighbor, you first have to love yourself.

Do you love yourself? If not, ask God to help you. Amen.

Pray this prayer with faith:

"Heavenly Father, help me love myself. In Jesus name, amen."

You are fearfully and wonderfully made [Ps. 139:14]. Amen.

Do you know Me? Have you received Me (Jesus) as your Lord and Savior?

- Do not say things like *if* or *but*; using these words cancels out your entire apology.

- Be specific; identify exactly what you did wrong. Acknowledge your wrong. Amen.

- Identify with the victim(s) by confessing how sorry you are for hurting them and causing them pain.

- Listen to the victim(s) speak. Listen intently, seeking to understand them and to understand how much you have caused them pain and suffering.

- Accept any consequences for your actions.

- **Listen** to what the victim(s) has to say. Always keep an open ear [James 1:19]. Amen.

Have you received Me? Says the Lord Jesus.

If not, receive Me now:

"Lord, I come before you today at the cross, to confess to You that I'm a sinner in need of a Savior. Lord, please forgive me of all my sins, and cleanse me of all unrighteousness. Wash me with Your blood that I may be forgiven; cleanse me so that I may be whiter than snow. Come into my heart today as I acknowledge You as my Lord and Savior. I thank You for all that You have done for me on the cross. I thank You for receiving me. I'm now Your child, a new creation. In Jesus holy name, amen."

Congratulations. You are now a child of God!

After you pray this prayer with faith, continue reading.

Love

"'You shall love your neighbor as yourself.'" [Mark 12:31 NKJV].
Love is patient, love is kind;

- Seek to change your ways, your heart, and so on, and refuse to participate in bullying or cyberbullying again. Amen.

Step 4: **Ask** for forgiveness:

- Ask the victim(s) for forgiveness.

- Seek their response.

- Keep in mind it might take time for the victim(s) to forgive you. (This is understandable.)

- Do not get offended if the victim(s) do not forgive you right away.

- Give them time and space to think.

- After one week or so, approach the victim(s) again, seeking forgiveness if they did

loves does not envy; love does not parade itself, is not puffed up, does not behave rudely, does not seek its own, is not provoked, thinks no evil, does not rejoice in iniquity, but rejoices in the truth...love never fails [1 Cor. 13:4–6, 8].

This love is accomplished through you, with the help of the Holy Spirit.

Ask the Holy Spirit to love through you daily, in Jesus name; ask Him with faith, so you can learn to love your neighbor as yourself. Amen.

This will help you; "Love your enemies, do good to those who hate you, bless those who curse you, and pray for those who spitefully use you." [Luke 6:27–28 NKJV].

It may take some time to heal, but you will see the results of God healing you of your wounds from bullying.

not forgive you on your first attempt. Do not get mad if they still don't forgive you, and if you sincerely apologized, I commend you for your effort. You have done your part; God will work on their heart(s). Go forward. Do not grow bitter or angry and do not harass the victim. Move forward. Amen.

Step 5: **Be reconciled** one to another [Eph. 4:32].

Reconciled, according to www.google.com, means "cause to coexist in harmony."

Step 6: You must be able to **accept** the victim's feedback, advice, or (brainstormed) solutions:

- Learn from this experience.

- Keep any advice, feedback, or

Amen.

Overcome

In the meantime, renew your thinking; use the **Battle of the Mind** strategy on page 58.

Ask the Holy Spirit to replace your thoughts with His.

Pray with faith: "Holy Spirit, think through me. In Jesus name, amen."

The Holy Spirit needs your cooperation in this massive effort to renew your mind, so do your part by renewing your mind with the word of God and He will do His. Amen.

Begin to develop a habit of **reading the word of God** daily. His word provides peace, stillness, hope, strength, peace, deliverance, healing, and love, and reveals the promises of God. Amen.

brainstormed answer the victim(s) gave you.

- Seek to change (your thinking, your ways, your words—no more bullying or cyberbullying).

- Start reading the word, praying, going to a Christ-filled church, seeking to become more like Christ daily [2 Cor. 5:17]. Amen.

Overcome

Overcome bullying and cyberbullying and keep it from reentering your life:

Renew your mind using the **Battle of the Mind** strategy on page 58 and asking the Holy Spirit to replace your thoughts with His.

Pray with faith: "Holy Spirit, think through me. In Jesus name, amen."

Jesus is the Word and the Word is life. Amen.

Believe His word, speak His word, receive His word, think on His word, and apply the word of God to your life, and you will see change in your life and results. (The Lord revealed.) Amen.

Begin to **praise and worship** God daily [Heb. 13:15]. Praise lifts your focus off the problem and onto the presence of God. (Please see **"The Art of Worship"** on page 48.)

Once again, it may take time, but rest assured, you will recover. Amen.

Jesus says, **Come to Me**, all who are weary and heavy laden and I will give you rest [Matt. 11:28]. Amen.

The Holy Spirit needs your cooperation in this massive effort to renew your mind, so do your part by renewing your mind with the word of God and He will do His. Amen.

Turn to the word of God. Begin to develop a habit of reading the word of God daily. His word provides peace, stillness, hope, strength, deliverance, healing, and love, and reveals the promises of God. Amen.

Jesus is the Word, and the Word is life. Amen.

Believe His word, speak His word, receive His word, think on His word, and apply the word of God to your life and you will see a change in your life and results. (The Lord revealed.) Amen.

Love covers a multitude of sins [1 Pet. 4:8]. Amen.

Cease bullying/cyberbullying, seeking to love your neighbor as yourself. Amen. **Jesus loves you.**	

Conflict Management

The outline in the bullying/cyberbullying above can be used to overcome any conflict; the outline below was inspired by Kevin Sande's student edition of *The Peacemaker*.

Use the strategy below to manage conflicts

Step 1: **Before** approaching the person with whom you are in conflict, do the following:

Pray

- Pray that God prepares your heart with grace and love.
- Pray and ask God to prepare the hearts of the person(s) involved to receive.

Prepare

- Research what you should say.
- Write down what you should say (plan your words carefully).
- Rehearse (what you've written down).
- Seek guidance from a teacher, peer, youth counselor, youth pastor, parent, or a mature Christian friend.
- Plan when you should talk to them and where.
- Come sincerely, assuming all will work out for the good [Rom. 8:28].

Step 2: **When you go** (to talk to the person(s) involved in the conflict):

- Go with sincerity, seeking forgiveness.
- Find the person(s) involved and ask to talk with them (this may require an adult's help). Keep in mind when you go to talk to those involved that you should not seek to gang up on them in any way. You're going to apologize, not to make matters worse.

Step 3: **In your confession** (to the persons(s) involved in the conflict):

- Do not say things like *if* or *but*; using these words cancels out your entire apology.
- Be specific; identify exactly what you did wrong. (Acknowledge your wrong. Amen.)
- Identify with the person(s) involved by confessing how sorry you are for hurting them and causing them pain.
- Listen to them speak. Listen intently, seeking to understand them and to understand how much you have caused them pain and suffering.
- Accept any consequences for your actions.
- Listen to what everyone has to say. Always keep an open ear [James 1:19]. Amen.
- Seek to change your ways, your heart, and so on. Amen.

Step 4: **Ask for forgiveness:**

- Ask the people involved for forgiveness.
- Seek their response.
- Keep in mind that it might take time for the each person to forgive you. (This is understandable.)
- Do not get offended if they don't forgive you right away. (Do not get bitter or resentful.)
- Give them time and space to think.
- After a week or so, approach the people involved again, seeking forgiveness if they did not forgive you on your first attempt. Do not get mad if they still don't forgive you, and if you sincerely apologized, I commend you for your effort. You have done your part; God will work on their heart(s). Go forward. Do not grow bitter or angry and do not harass the victim. Move forward. Amen.

Step 5: **Be reconciled** one to another [Eph. 4:32].

Reconciled, according to www.google.com, means "cause to coexist in harmony."

Step 6: You must be able to **accept** everyone's feedback, advice, or (brainstormed) solutions:

- Learn from this experience.
- Keep any advice, feedback, or brainstormed answer each person gave you.
- Seek to change your thinking, your ways, your words, and so on.
- Start reading the word, praying, going to a Christ-filled church, seeking to become more like Christ daily [2 Cor. 5:17]. Amen.

Doing all this will help you **overcome** conflict. Amen.

"Keep your conduct among the Gentiles **honorable**, so that when they speak against you as evildoers, they may see your good deeds and glorify God on that day of visitation." "For this is the will of God, that by doing good you should put to silence the ignorance of foolish people." [1 Pet. 2:12, 15 ESV].

"but in your hearts **honor Christ** the Lord as holy, always being prepared to make a defense to anyone who asks you for a reason for the hope that is in you; yet do it with gentleness and respect, having a good conscience, so that, when you are slandered, those who revile your good behavior in Christ may be put to shame." [1 Pet. 3:15–16 ESV].

Overcome a conflict and become an example of Christ daily. Amen.

Suicide and Self-Harm

'I'm at the end of my rope...'

Give Me the rope, says the Lord.

Suicide is "the murder of self; self-hatred."

Suicide, according to www.google.com, means "the intentional taking of one's life."

Self-Harm, according to www.mayoclinic.com, means "deliberately harming your body such as cutting or burning yourself, etc. Usually it is not a suicide attempt." (Harming yourself includes cutting).

"Do you not know that **you are God's temple** and that **God's Spirit dwells in you**? If anyone destroys God's temple, God will destroy him. For God's temple is holy, and you are that temple." [1 Cor. 3:16–17 ESV].

"Or do you not know that your body is a temple of the Holy Spirit within you, whom you have from God? You are not your own, for you were bought with a price. (the **blood of Jesus**) So glorify God in your body." [1 Cor. 6:19–20 ESV].

"Be not overly wicked, neither be a fool. Why should you die before your time?" [Eccles. 7:17 ESV].

Do not be conformed (following the same pattern) to the world, but be transformed (changed) by the renewing (cleansing) of your mind, that by testing, you might discern (know) what is the good, acceptable, and perfect will of God [Rom. 12:2].

"You shall not murder." [Exod. 20:13 NKJV].

"The thief comes only to steal and kill and destroy." [John 10:10 ESV].

The day you take your own life, is the day you will be separated from God for all eternity.

Reasons for Suicide or Self-Harm

Rejection	Loss (of loved ones, property, job, business, etc.)	Sense of hopelessness or despair	Depression or grief	Lack of support
Mental torment	Terminated friendships or relationships	Separation or divorce	Bullying or cyberbullying	Illnesses (mental, emotional, terminal, physical)
Violations done to the body (abuse, rape, incest, molestation)	Feeling trapped (no way out)	Disappointment or broken promises	Bankruptcies or loss of fortune	Teasing, feeling left out, or not fitting in
Loneliness	Sense of failure	Physical pain	School, failing tests, failing grades, failing to make it into college, family pressure, etc.	Finances or debt

Allow <u>nothing</u> to drive you to the point where you are willing to take your own life or harm yourself. (The Lord revealed.) Amen.

Live.

Life is worth living. (The Lord revealed). Amen.

If you have not already received Me, receive Me, says the Lord, I have promised to give life and life more abundantly [John 10:10]. Amen.

Pray this prayer with faith:

"Lord, I come before you today at the cross, to confess to You that I'm a sinner in need of a Savior. Lord, please forgive me of all my sins, and cleanse me of all unrighteousness. Wash me with Your blood that I may be forgiven; cleanse me so that I may be whiter than snow. Come into my heart today, as I acknowledge You as my Lord and Savior. I thank You for all that You have done for me on the cross. I thank You for receiving me. I'm now Your child, a new creation. In Jesus holy name, amen."

Congratulations you are now a Child of God! Amen.

Love

When battling with suicide or self-harm... **love yourself**.

God commands you to love your neighbor as yourself [Mark 12:31]. Before you can love your neighbor, you first have to **love yourself**.

Do you love yourself? If not, ask God to help you. Amen.

Pray this prayer with faith:

"Heavenly Father, help me to love myself. In Jesus name, amen."

You are fearfully and wonderfully made [Ps. 139:14].Amen.

Always remember **Jesus loves you!**

What Is Love?

Love is patient, love is kind; loves does not envy; love does not parade itself, is not puffed up, does not behave rudely, does not seek its own, is not provoked, thinks no evil, does not rejoice in iniquity, but rejoices in the truth...love never fails [1 Cor. 13:4–6, 8].

This love is accomplished through you, with the help of the Holy Spirit.

If you already received Jesus Christ as your Lord and Savior, the Holy Spirit now dwells inside you. **Ask the Holy Spirit to love through you daily, in Jesus name**; ask the Holy Spirit with faith, so you can learn to love God, yourself, and others. Amen.

Love does no harm [Rom. 13:10].

Harm, in Greek, according to www.biblehub.com, means "inwardly foul, rotten, inner malice, wickedness, inner evil. Bad things, evil morally of a mode of thinking, feeling, acting, wrong, wicked of persons, injurious, ill, work ill to one."

When you love, you will seek to do no harm to others or to yourself, because you love yourself and others. Amen.

Walk in God's love. (The Lord revealed.) Amen.

The Reality of God's Love

God loves you!

Below is a list of scriptures detailing **God's love** for you:

[Please note: Scriptures are not word for word, please look up each Scripture in the Bible.]

Romans 8:35–39, Nothing will be able to separate us from the love of God.

Romans 5:8, God showed His love for us, that while we were still sinners, Christ died for us.

1 John 4:16, So we have come to know and believe the love that God has for us. God is love, and whoever in love abides in God, and God abides in Him.

John 15:8–12, As the Father has loved me, so I have I loved you. Abide in my Love.

John 3:16, For God so loved the world that He gave His only Begotten Son…

Isaiah 41:10, Fear not, for I am with you, be not dismayed for I am your God, I will strengthen you, yes I will help you, I will uphold you with My righteous Right Hand.

1 John 4:10, In this is love, not that we have loved God, but He loved us and sent His Son to be the propitiation for our sins.

1 John 3:1, See what kind of love the Father has given to us, that we should be called the children of God, so we are.

Psalm 103:8, The Lord is slow and gracious; slow to anger and abounding in steadfast love.

Jeremiah 31:3, The Lord appeared to him from far away. I have loved you with an everlasting love; therefore I have continued my faithfulness to you.

Lamentations 3:22–23, The steadfast love of the Lord never ceases; his mercies never come to an end; they are new every morning, great is thy faithfulness.

Romans 5:5, And hope does not put us to shame, because God's love has been poured in our hearts through the Holy Spirit who has been given to us.

Galatians 5:22–23, But the fruit of the Spirit is love, joy, peace, patience…

This is the **love** of the Father, the Son, and the Holy Spirit **for you**. Amen.

Have you received Jesus Christ as your Lord and Savior? If not, pray this prayer with faith:

"Lord, I come before you today at the cross, to confess to You that I'm a sinner in need of a Savior. Lord, please forgive me of all my sins, and cleanse me of all unrighteousness. Wash me with Your blood that I may be forgiven; cleanse me so that I may be whiter than snow. Come into my heart today, as I acknowledge You as my Lord and Savior. I thank You for all that You have done for me on the cross. I thank You for receiving me. I'm now Your child, a new creation. In Jesus holy name, amen."

God loves you! Love yourself and love others. Amen.

His Suffering

I bore your griefs and suffered your sorrows [Isa. 53:4].

I have suffered your grief, your brokenness, your discouragement, your weakness, your loneliness, your troubles, your rejection, your disappointment, your teasing, your pain, your emotional suffering, your mental torment... On the Cross, I bore it all for you, **says the Lord.**

"He is despised and rejected by men, A Man of sorrows and acquainted with grief." [Isa. 53:3 NKJV].

"Yet it pleased the LORD to bruise Him; He has put *Him* to grief. When You make His soul an offering for sin, He shall see *His* seed, He shall prolong *His* days, And the pleasure of the LORD shall prosper in His hand." [Isa. 53:10 NKJV].

"But He *was* wounded for our transgressions, *He was* bruised for our iniquities; The chastisement for our peace was upon Him, And by His stripes we are healed." [Isa. 53:5 NKJV].

I was wounded for you, beaten for you, tried for you, forsaken for you. And by My stripes, you are healed, **says the Lord.**

Each of My stripes represents an area of healing for your life. One stripe represents suffering. If you are suffering from a sense of failure, worry, emotional suffering, mental suffering or torment; I already bore it all for you, says the Lord.

Struggling with thoughts of suicide or trying to harm yourself? **Turn to Me** instead, **says the Lord.**

My child, My power is made available for you, (The Lord revealed). Amen.

Come to Me, all who are weary and heavy laden and I will give you rest [Matt. 11:28].

Rest from your troubles, your hurt, your pain, your suffering, your sorrow...

Pray this prayer with faith:

"Heavenly Father, I lay all my worries, my pain, my sense of failure and hopelessness, and suicidal thinking at your feet and I receive your healing, I receive your rest from my suffering, and I receive Your love. In Jesus name, amen."

Keep everything at His feet, believe, and receive your healing. Amen.

Do not take back anything you have already laid at His feet. Amen.

It may take some time to heal, but you will see the results of God healing you of your wounds, scars, hurts, negative emotions, feelings, mental scars, suffering, pain, mental torment, and more.

Put your faith in God and believe that He will come through for you. Always remember **Jesus loves you!** Amen.

When and if suicidal thoughts or thoughts of harming yourself try to return to your mind, don't let them in. Cast it down immediately and renew your mind using, the **Battle of the Mind** strategy on page 58 and by asking the Holy Spirit to replace your thoughts with His.

Pray with faith: "Holy Spirit, think through me. In Jesus name." Amen.

The Holy Spirit needs your cooperation in this massive effort to renew your mind, so do your part by renewing your mind with the word of God and He will do His. Amen.

Overcome suicide and self-harm with the word of God

Turn to the word of God. Begin to develop a habit of reading the word of God daily. His word provides peace, stillness, hope, strength, deliverance, healing, and love, and reveals the promises of God. Amen.

Jesus is the Word, and the Word is life. Amen.

Believe His word, speak His word, receive His word, think on His word, and apply the word of God to your life and you will see a change in your life and results. (The Lord revealed.) Amen.

Meditate on scripture

Here is a list of scriptures you can meditate on:

Psalm 42	Psalm 43	Psalm 34:17	Romans 8:38–39
John 14:1–2	Isaiah 41:13	Isaiah 41:10	Philippians 4:13
Psalm 118	Romans 5:3–5	Proverbs 3:5–6	Philippians 4:4
Psalm 37:25	Romans 8:26	James 1:2–4	2 Timothy 1:7
Psalm 91	Matthew 11:28–30	Romans 8:28	Jeremiah 29:11
Romans 10:17	Psalm 40:1–3	Psalm 9:9	Deuteronomy 31:8
Psalm 46:10	Matthew 28:20	Deuteronomy 33:27	

Overcome suicide and self-harm with praise and worship

Praise lifts your focus off the problem and onto the presence of God. Learn more about worship and what true worship is by reading **"The Art of Worship"** on page 48. Amen.

Overcome suicide and self-harm by speaking in your prayer language (tongues).

Speaking in tongues builds you up [1 Cor. 14:4]. Amen.

To further overcome suicide or self-harm, please **read** Sarah Young's devotional book *Jesus Today.*

Hope in God!

"I wait for the LORD, my soul waits, And in His word I do hope." [Ps. 130:5 NKJV]

Do not internalize your struggles, troubles, or hardships when you are struggling with suicide or self-harm. <u>Seek help immediately</u> and tell a parent, teacher, youth counselor, youth pastor, or other trusted adult that you are struggling with suicide or self-harm. They can provide you with the help and assistance you need. Also, confess your heart to God and receive His love and healing. Amen.

Open up your heart and speak. Amen.

The Spiritual Side of Suicide and Self-Harm

Suicidal thinking and self-harm are both demonic oppressions (heavy weights), sent by the enemy.

"The thief comes only to steal and kill and destroy." [John 10:10 ESV].

Suicide kills the body, and self-harm destroys the body. Both are strategies sent by the enemy for your demise. Amen.

The **Truth** About Suicide and Self-Harm

Evangelist Perry Stone reveals these truths about suicide and self-harm found within the word of God.

In Matthew 8:28–34, two demon-possessed men in the country of Gergesenes dwelt among the tombs (the dead). These men could not be constrained and literally had the strength to break any chain used to hold them down. (It was the people who placed the chains on these men to keep them from harming themselves and others.)

The demons caused the men to hurt themselves (self-harm).

When Jesus came before the men, the demons cried out to Jesus, asking Him if He was there to torment them before their time of judgement. After seeing a herd of swine afar off, the legion begged Jesus not to be cast into the abyss or utter darkness, but instead to be cast into the herd of swine (the swine were grazing near a cliff.) So Jesus said, "Go." Then the demons came out of the two men and went into the herd of swine. (Swine have no free will like man does.) When the demons went into the swine, the swine had no choice but to obey the demons' commands and run violently off the cliff and into the sea, where they died.

It is here that Evangelist Perry Stone reveals that the demons' intent was to get the two men to kill themselves (commit suicide), but every man has the freedom of choice or free will, so the two men could choose not to obey the demons and **live** instead of taking their own lives. Amen. Animals do not have free will or the freedom of choice and had no choice but to obey the demons, killing themselves.

In the end the same demonic spirit that causes suicide causes self-harm. (The Lord revealed.) Amen.

The truth (revealed above), about suicide and self-harm may come across as scary, but both suicide and self-harm are serious matters.

There is a difference between demonic oppression and demonic possession.

Demonic Oppression	Demonic Possession
A demonic oppression is a heavy weight or burden. Use this definition to discover if you are demonically oppressed or possessed. If you believe you are experiencing demonic oppression, speak out and use the strategies outlined in the "**His Suffering**" section. Amen. "Or do you not know that your body is a temple of the Holy Spirit within you, whom you have from God? You are not your own, for you were bought with a price (the **blood of Jesus**). So glorify God in your body." [1 Cor. 6:19–20 ESV].	Demonic possession, according to www.dictionary.refrence.com, means "to be controlled or dominated by evil spirits, having ownership." According to www.merriam-webster.com it means "the act of having or taking into control, control or occupancy of property without regard to ownership, domination by something (evil spirit)." Use this definition to discover if you are demonically oppressed or possessed. If you suspect you may be possessed, immediately **seek help** from a pastor, youth pastor, or a deliverance ministry who specializes in deliverance and spiritual warfare, and follow their instructions. Remembering this: after the demons were cast into the swine, the men were set free [Matt. 8:16–17, 32–24]. **He who the Son sets free is free indeed** [John 8:36]. (The Lord revealed.) Amen.

Overcome in Christ Jesus! Amen.

Struggling with Thoughts of Suicide or are you trying to Harm Yourself? Speak Up and Speak Out!

"Let not your heart be troubled, neither let it be afraid." [John 14:27 NKJV].

Hope in God (the Father), hope also in Me (Jesus) [John 14:1]. Amen.

Pour out your heart and speak [Ps. 62:8].

Speak the truth without fear [2 Tim. 1:7].

If you are contemplating suicide, having suicidal thoughts, or trying to harm yourself, or if someone you know is, **tell** a parent, youth counselor, pastor, youth pastor, or guardian <u>immediately</u>. They will be able to provide the help you need right away.

Do not be silent; seek to be set free [John 8:36]. **Live.** Amen.

Disobedience, Rebellion, and Witchcraft

'I don't want to listen to my parents…Why should I do anything anyone tells me to do? I practice witchcraft.'

"Children, obey your parents in the Lord, for this is right." Children, <u>obey</u> your parents so your life will be long. [Eph. 6:1 NKJV; Exod. 20:12].

"The coming of the *lawless one* is according to the working of Satan, with all power, signs, and lying wonders," [2 Thess. 2:9 NKJV]. This verse reveals the origins of witchcraft.

Disobedience, according to www.google.com and www.wikipedia.com, means **"a failure or refusal to obey rules or someone in authority; refusal to obey certain laws."**	*Rebellion,* according to Pastor Guillermo Maldonado, means **"to undermine set authority placed by God and seeking to overthrow it."**	*Witchcraft,* according to www.merriam-webster.com and www.dictionary.refrence.com, means **"the use of sorcery or magic; communication with the devil or with a familiar spirit; an irresistible influence or fascination; magical powers obtained from evil spirits."**

Scriptures On		
Disobedience	**Rebellion**	**Witchcraft/Divination**
Ephesians 6:1–3	1 Samuel 15:23	Acts 16:16
Proverbs 13:24	Joshua 5:6	1 John 4:1–3
Proverbs 23:13–14	Deuteronomy 1	Micah 5:2
James 4:17	Psalm 68:6	Leviticus 20:27
Proverbs 5:15	John 14:15	Deuteronomy 18:10
	2 Corinthians 5:17	Galatians 5:20–21
	Proverbs 17:11	Isaiah 8:17, 19
		Psalm 1:1–3
		1 Chronicles 10:13–14
		Deuteronomy 18:14
		2 Thessalonians 2:9

Disobedience leads to rebellion, and rebellion leads to witchcraft. Amen.

Please read **"The Story of Saul"** to see how disobedience leads to rebellion, and how rebellion leads to witchcraft. Amen.

The Story of Saul

A Tale of Disobedience, Leading to Rebellion, to Ruin, to Tragedy

This is the **story of Saul**. It was the will of the people to desire a king, like other nations. Samuel the prophet was grieved, but God heeded the people's request, warning them first about the behaviors of a king, who would rule over them [see 1 Sam. 8].

Israel refused to heed God's warning through Samuel, and demanded a king be set over them, so God chose their king [see 1 Sam. 9–10].

He chose a king out of the tribe of Benjamin, a small tribe, few in number. His family was the least in Benjamin, but his father was Kish, a Benjamite, a mighty man of power. This was the man God chose for Israel.

Saul was anointed king [see 1 Sam. 9; 1 Sam. 10:1–4].

The people cheered, but not all were convinced [see 1 Sam. 10:17–27].

Saul proved himself, with the Lord's help, leading his men to battle against the Ammonites and coming out victorious [see 1 Sam. 11].

The people no longer doubted him as king, and the prophet Samuel took the people to Gilgal, where Saul was made king before the Lord. Offerings were made, and the men of Israel rejoice [see 1 Sam. 11:14–15].

The will of the people prevailed, but would Saul prove himself to be a worthy king? [1 Sam. 12].

It was in the second year of his reign that Saul chose mighty men to fight on his behalf for Israel. The Philistines had begun to attack Israel, and Saul and his son Jonathan fought back against them. The Philistines, with their chariots, came in great multitudes against the children of Israel, causing them to run and hide within caves, rocks, and mountains while Samuel the prophet remained in Gilgal.

The prophet Samuel had charged King Saul to wait for him seven days, but when Samuel did not show in time and the people were all in a panic, Saul became desperate.

Saul decided to take matters into his own hands [see 1 Sam. 13:1–9].

That was the beginning of Saul's downfall... How?

1. Saul let fear trump his faith, causing him to grow impatient.

2. Saul stepped out of the will of God by leaning to his own understanding, incurring the consequences.

3. Saul took matters into his own hands instead of trusting God.

4. Saul disobeyed and Saul lost faith.

Saul took matters into his own hands and took it upon himself to make both peace offerings and burnt offerings to God [see 1 Sam. 13:9].

As soon as Saul finished presenting the burnt offering to God, the prophet Samuel came, and Saul went to meet him [see 1 Sam. 13:10].

"What have you done?" Samuel asked.

King Saul responds to his question with excuses:

Excuse one: The people were scattered from him.

Excuse two: Samuel didn't come at the time appointed.

Excuse three: The Philistines had gathered at Micmash.

Excuse four: He thought the Philistines would come where he was at Gilgal, and he had not made supplication to the Lord.

Excuse five: Therefore he felt compelled to offer a burnt offering.

The prophet Samuel answered him and said he had done foolishly by not keeping the commandments of the Lord when the Lord would have established his kingdom forever [see 1 Sam. 13:13].

The kingdom would go to another, for God had sought for Himself a man after His own heart [1 Sam. 13:14].

Saul had let fear trump his faith and incurred the consequences; his kingdom would not continue, but would be given to another more worthy than he. How sad.

Disobedience incurs consequences. Amen.

The prophet Samuel arose and headed to Gibeah and Saul numbered his mighty men [see 1 Sam. 13:15].

The wars of Saul continued [1 Sam. 13–14].

Saul spoke a rash oath in 1 Samuel 14; his son Jonathan did not hear the oath and defeated the Philistines in a battle, causing him to grow hungry. His men told Jonathan about the oath, but he dismissed it as his father troubling the land, and ate anyway. Saul tried to punish his own son Jonathan for disobeying the oath, but he did not heed. The people rose and spoke on Jonathan's behalf, sparing his life. Afterward, the war with the Philistines continued [1 Sam. 14].

Saul was given a second chance.

The prophet Samuel reminded Saul of how the Lord sent him to anoint Saul king over Israel, and now Saul was supposed to heed (obey) the voice of the Lord.

Samuel gave instructions:

The Lord desired to punish the Amalekites for how they ambushed Israel on their way out of Egypt. He commanded Saul to go and attack Amalek, destroying all that they had and sparing no one or anything [see 1 Sam. 15:3].

Saul gathered the people together, numbering them in Telaim. He went to the city of Amalek and waited in the valley [1 Sam. 15:4–5].

It is here, in Amalek, that Saul's disobedience turned to rebellion (remember, according to Pastor Guillermo Maldonado, *rebellion* means "to undermine set authority placed by God and seeking to overthrow it").

First, Saul let the Kenites, who had showed kindness to Israel, depart from the Amalekites so they would not get caught in the slaughter, so they did. Second, he rebelled against God, by sparing King Agag of the Amalekites and having everyone else slaughtered. He also took the best of the sheep, oxen, lambs, and so on and destroyed what he deemed worthless [see 1 Sam. 15:6–9].

What were Samuel's instructions?

To punish the Amalekites for how they ambushed Israel on their way out of Egypt. God commanded Saul to go and attack Amalek, destroying all that they had and sparing no one and nothing [1 Sam. 15:3].

Did Saul listen? According to 1 Samuel 15:6–9, he didn't listen to or heed God's instructions.

Read 1 Samuel 15:10–12 to see how God reacts to Saul's deliberate disobedience and rebellion against Him.

To disobey is to not heed instructions, commands, rules, and so on that are given. To rebel is not to obey someone who is in authority or to disobey the rules.

Saul was guilty of both.

God was grieved that He had ever made Saul king over Israel and sent the prophet Samuel to Saul.

What was Saul's first reaction upon seeing the prophet Samuel? Did he lie? Did he repent? Did he hurry and do what God had commanded him before he came?

If you chose that he lied, you're right: Saul lied [see 1 Sam. 15:13], but that wasn't the first time. Saul had lied before when his uncle asked him what the prophet Samuel told him and he concealed the truth from him [see 1 Sam. 10:14–16].

Samuel asked King Saul, then why did his ears hear the bleating of sheep and the lowing of oxen?

King Saul not only came up with an excuse, but lied again, by blaming the people for what he had done. He showed neither leadership nor accountability.

Here is how King Saul responds:

Excuse one: they (the people) brought them (the animals) from the Amalekites.

Blame one: The people spared the best of the animals.

Lie three: He wanted to use the animals to sacrifice to God.

Saul lied. Not only did he blame the people, but he used God as an "out" for deliberately disobeying His instructions [see 1 Sam. 15:14–15].

The prophet Samuel told Saul to be quiet and then reminded him of what the Lord did for him and how the Lord sent him on a mission to utterly destroy all the Amalekites and all of their spoil, but instead he took the spoil and did evil in the sight of God.

Still King Saul gave excuses (like Adam did when he blamed Eve for his demise and fall); Saul refused to repent and own up to his responsibilities, blaming the people for his disobedience and open rebellion [1 Sam. 15:20–21].

Then Samuel spoke and said one of the Bible's famous verses: "Behold, to obey is better than sacrifice," [1 Sam. 15:22 NKJV]. Amen.

He also said **rebellion is the sin of witchcraft and stubbornness is like iniquity and idolatry [1 Sam. 15:23].**

Samuel continued and said that because Saul rejected the word of God, God had rejected him as king.

It is here that King Saul cried out and repented, pleading with the prophet Samuel, but it was too late.

Saul seized the edge of Samuel's robe and it tore, and Samuel said that like the robe had been torn, so God tore the kingdom away from him and gave it to his neighbor, who was better than him [see 1 Sam. 15:27–28].

Saul admitted again that he had sinned, but he still wanted Samuel to come with him before the people to worship the Lord, so Saul did, and then the prophet Samuel made a quick end to King Agag. Afterward Samuel returned to Ramah and would never go to see Saul again. He mourned for Saul, and God regretted ever making Saul king [1 Sam. 15:30–35].

God anointed another as king: David, the last of Jesse's sons, and a shepherd boy over a flock of sheep [1 Sam. 16].

Soon after David was anointed, the Spirit of the Lord departed from Saul and a distressing spirit from the Lord troubled him and would trouble him all his days [1 Sam. 16:14].

Rebellion became a snare to King Saul, costing him his kingdom and his peace. Amen.

Saul was ruined.

Saul's jealousy of David would lead to his downfall [see 1 Sam. 18].

God's departure from Saul would lead Saul to consult a medium in 1 Samuel 28, although it was forbidden by God and carried the death penalty. **(Consulting a medium is witchcraft, and mediums operate in witchcraft).**

Saul's demise would be in war against the Philistines in 1 Samuel 31, where he and his sons would each die in battle. It was a tragedy.

In the end, Saul's one act of disobedience led to rebellion, which led to ruin and finally to tragedy.

That is the sad story of Saul. (The Lord revealed.) Amen.

Disobedience, rebellion, and witchcraft: these three things spell disaster for the human soul.

Don't let this happen to you. Choose light rather than darkness and right instead of wrong.

Choose whom you will serve this day: God or Satan [1 Kings 18:20–39].

Choose God [Josh. 24:15]. Amen.

To see further consequences of disobedience or rebellion, please read Deuteronomy 9 and Deuteronomy 28.

In the end, **disobedience breeds consequences and obedience incurs blessings.** Amen.

Overcome Disobedience and Rebellion

Children obey your parents, so your life will be long [Eph. 6:1].

Obedience **overcomes** disobedience and rebellion. Amen.

Overcome with confession and prayer. Pray this prayer with faith:

"Heavenly Father, I confess I have been disobedient or I confess I have been rebellious; I have learned these are two things that displease you. Forgive me for my disobedience; forgive me for my rebellion. Help me to overcome it, help me to obey my parents, and help me to be obedient toward You and others too. Make me a new creation in Christ Jesus. In Jesus name, amen."

Overcome with the word of God

Turn to the word of God. Begin to develop a habit of reading the word of God daily. His word provides peace, stillness, hope, strength, deliverance, healing, and love, and reveals the promises of God. Amen.

Jesus is the Word, and the Word is life. Amen.

Believe His word, speak His word, receive His word, think on His word, and apply the word of God to your life and you will see a change in your life and results. (The Lord revealed.) Amen.

Renew your mind using the **Battle of the Mind** strategy on page 58 and by asking the Holy Spirit to replace your thoughts with His.

Pray with faith: "Holy Spirit, think through me. In Jesus name, amen."

The Holy Spirit needs your cooperation in this massive effort to renew your mind, so do your part by renewing your mind with the word of God and He will do His. Amen.

Meditate on scripture

Here is a list of scriptures you can meditate on:

Psalm 42	Psalm 43	Psalm 34:17	Romans 8:38–39
John 14:1–2	Isaiah 41:13	Isaiah 41:10	Philippians 4:13
Psalm 118	Romans 5:3–5	Proverbs 3:5–6	Philippians 4:4
Psalm 37:25	Romans 8:26	James 1:2–4	2 Timothy 1:7
Psalm 91	Matthew 11:28–30	Romans 8:28	Jeremiah 29:11
Romans 10:17	Psalm 40:1–3	Psalm 9:9	Deuteronomy 31:8
Psalm 46:10	Matthew 28:20	Deuteronomy 33:27	

Overcome with praise and worship

Praise lifts your focus off the problem and onto the presence of God. Learn more about worship and what true worship is by reading **"The Art of Worship"** on page 48. Amen.

Overcome by pouring out your heart

Tell a counselor, teacher, or other trusted adult and let them know how you feel. Listen to their response, and see what you can do to make a change in your situation(s) and overcome disobedience and rebellion. (Do not react violently, but in love. Amen.)

If you need more help, use the strategies outlined in the section on spiritual warfare on pages 340–410.

Examples of Witchcraft:

Books (which talk about witchcraft), other books or magazines talking about or promoting witchcraft, movies pertaining to witchcraft or sorcery, games geared toward witchcraft, such as séances, conjuring, reciting spells or casting spells, talking to the dead, fortune-telling, soothsaying, and so on are all considered witchcraft.

Witchcraft is a **sin** and an abomination to the Lord [Deut. 18:9–14]. Amen.

Overcome

If you are involved in witchcraft, **contact** your pastor, youth pastor, or a ministry that specializes in deliverance and spiritual warfare immediately, and follow their instructions.

He who the Son sets free, is free indeed [John 8:36]. Amen.

Always remember Jesus loves you!

Idolatry

'I love God but…I love this…'

Do you love someone or something more than you love God?

God is a jealous God. (The Lord revealed.) Amen. He will **<u>not</u>** share His place with anyone or anything.

> "And God spoke all these words, saying: "I am the LORD your God, who brought you out of the land of Egypt, out of the house of bondage. "You shall have no other gods before Me. "You shall not make yourself a carved image—any likeness of *anything* that *is* in heaven above, or that *is* in the earth beneath, or that i*s* in the water under the earth; you shall not bow down to them nor serve them. For I, the LORD your God, *am* a jealous God, visiting the iniquity of the fathers upon the children to the third and fourth *generations* of those who hate Me, but showing mercy to thousands, to those who love Me and keep My commandments." [Exod. 20:1–6 NKJV].

Please read Numbers 25, because it also reveals how **God is a jealous God**.

"And you shall love the LORD your God with all your heart, with all your soul, with all your mind, and all your strength.' This is the first commandment. And the second, like *it, is* this: 'You shall love your neighbor as yourself.' There is no other commandment greater than these." [Mark 12:30–31 NKJV].

Idolatry is not just bowing down to a molded or carved image; *idolatry*, according to www.google.com/idolatry, means "the extreme admiration, love, or reverence for something or someone."

Scriptures on Idolatry			
Jonah 2:8 Isaiah 44:9–20 Psalm 135	Galatians 5:19–21 1 Corinthians 10:20–22	1 Corinthians 10:14 Jeremiah 10:3–16	Deuteronomy 18:9-14 Isaiah 45:20

1 Corinthians 10:20–22 reveals that behind every idol (carved or molded image) is a demon. Amen.

Flee from idolatry! Amen.

Whom Do You Love More?

Remember, *idolatry* means having an extreme love or reverence from someone or something.	
Do you love... Nature? Famous People? Hollywood stars? An actor? An actress? A singer or songwriter; a producer? An athlete (such as a basketball player, baseball player, boxer, weight lifter, etc.)? A friend? A politician? A boyfriend or girlfriend? A parent or guardian? A very rich person? A pet or animal? A spouse? A car? Trading cards? A cartoon character? Anime? A TV show? A movie? A video game? Characters in a game, TV show, movie, etc.? Exercise (working out all the time, until it becomes a need)? Yourself? Your goals? Your ambitions? Your success? Money? Sex? Something else? A carved image? Someone else? Yourself? Beauty? More?	Or, do you love... # God more?

God says you shall have <u>no</u> other god before Him. Have you made someone or something else your god?

The Lord your God is a jealous God and **will not** share His place with another person or thing.

If you suspect you have made something or someone else your god, and you have made them a need you can't live without, repent. You have lost your **first love** [Rev. 2:4–5], and what can they (the thing you have made your idol) do for you?

I, **God the Father, God the Son, and God the Holy Spirit created you** [Gen. 1:27].

I, **God the Father, God the Son, and God the Holy Spirit delivered you** [Gen. 3:15 – in this verse Jesus is revealed; Psalm 91:3].

I, **God the Father, God the Son, and God the Holy Spirit saved you** [John 3:16].

I, **God the Father, God the Son, and God the Holy Spirit carried you** [Ps. 62:8; Deut. 1:31].

I, **God the Father, God the Son, and God the Holy Spirit love you**. (I betrothed you to Myself) [Rom. 8:37–39; John 3:16; Rom. 5:8; 2 Cor. 11:2].

I, **God the Father, God the Son, and God the Holy Spirit will take care of you** [Phil. 4:19; Matt. 6:25–34].

I, **God the Father, God the Son, and God the Holy Spirit listen to you** [1 John 5:15].

I, **God the Father, God the Son, and God the Holy Spirit treasure you** [Mal. 3:17].

I, **God the Father, God the Son, and God the Holy Spirit shepherd you** [John 10; Psalm 23].

I, **God the Father, God the Son, and God the Holy Spirit provide for you** [Phil. 4:19].

I, **God the Father, God the Son, and God the Holy Spirit protect you** [Ps. 121:7; Luke 10:19; Isa. 54:17; Eph. 6:10–18; Rom. 8:28].

I, **God the Father, God the Son, and God the Holy Spirit give you strength** [Phil. 4:13; Isa. 40:31].

I, **God the Father, God the Son, and God the Holy Spirit give you peace** [John 14:27; Phil. 4:6–7].

I, **God the Father, God the Son, and God the Holy Spirit give you rest** [Matt. 11:28].

I, **God the Father, God the Son, and God the Holy Spirit give you the victory** [Isa. 54:17; 1 Cor. 15:57; 2 Cor. 2:14].

I, **God the Father, God the Son, and God the Holy Spirit give you hope** [Jer. 29:11; Ps. 43:5; Luke 1:37; Romans 15:13].

I, **God the Father, God the Son, and God the Holy Spirit give you joy** [Rom. 15:13; Ps. 16:11].

I, **God the Father, God the Son, and God the Holy Spirit give you purpose** [Jer. 29:11].

I, **God the Father, God the Son, and God the Holy Spirit love you always** [Jer. 31:3].

I, **God the Father, God the Son, and God the Holy Spirit fill your emptiness.**

I, **God the Father, God the Son, and God the Holy Spirit give you everything you need.**

Everything you need is found in **Me**. I am everything you need. (The Lord revealed.) Amen.

Turn to Me, says the **Lord**. Nothing/No one else can do for you what I have already done. Amen.

Do **not** turn to the mother of Jesus, the different saints, carved images, or anyone or anything else. They are not God. Turn to Me, I am the Lord your God, the **One** who gives life and life abundantly, the **One** who gives strength and answers prayer. **No one** else can. Amen.

Do **not** compromise. Please read Judges 17-18, which reveals compromise. Amen.

Choose whom you will serve this day [1 Kings 18:21].

If **God the Father, God the Son, and God the Holy Spirit are God**, <u>serve Him</u>. Amen.

Receive Me, says the Lord, "All that the Father gives Me will come to Me, and the one who comes to Me I will by no means cast out." [John 6:37 NKJV].

Receive Jesus by praying this prayer with faith:

"Lord, I come before you today at the cross to confess to You that I'm a sinner in need of a Savior. Lord, please forgive me of all my sins, and cleanse me of all unrighteousness, wash me with Your blood that I may be forgiven, cleanse me so that I may be whiter than snow. Come into my heart today, as I acknowledge You as my Lord and Savior. I thank You for all that You have done for me on the cross. I thank You for receiving me, I'm now Your child, a new creation. In Jesus holy name, amen."

If you would like to rededicate your life to God (return to Him), please pray this prayer with faith:

"Lord Jesus, I recommit my life to you. Forgive Me for falling away, forgive me for creating an idol of [tell God who or what you made an idol]. I repent of my sin and I return to you today. In Jesus name, amen."

You belong to **Me**! You are **Mine** [Isa. 43:1], says the **Lord**.

Keep **Me** the center of your heart. (The Lord revealed.) Amen.

Whenever someone or something tries to take the place of God, <u>don't</u> let it. Start putting God first. Amen.

Renew your mind, using the **Battle of the Mind** strategy on page 58 and by asking the Holy Spirit to replace your thoughts with His.

Pray with faith: "Holy Spirit, think through me. In Jesus name, amen."

The Holy Spirit needs your cooperation in this massive effort to renew your mind, so do your part by renewing your mind with the word of God and He will do His. Amen.

Turn to the word of God. Begin to develop a habit of reading the word of God daily. His word provides peace, stillness, hope, strength, deliverance, healing, and love, and reveals the promises of God. Amen.

Jesus is the Word, and the Word is life. Amen.

Believe His word, speak His word, receive His word, think on His word, and apply the word of God to your life and you will see a change in your life and results. (The Lord revealed.) Amen.

Overcome idolatry with praise and worship

Praise lifts your focus off the problem and onto the presence of God.

Learn more about worship and what true worship is by reading **"The Art of Worship"** on page 48. Amen.

Overcome idolatry by pouring out your heart

Tell a counselor, teacher, or other trusted adult and let them know how you feel. Listen to their response, and see what you can do to make a change in your situation(s) and overcome.

Pour out your heart to God, who can help you overcome any idol. Amen.

If you need more help, use the strategies outlined in the section on spiritual warfare on pages 340–410.

Do <u>**not**</u> allow anyone or anything to take the place of God. Amen.

Remember: He is the Lord Your God, and you shall have no other god but Him [Deut. 4:35–39]. Amen.

Violence

'I hit them…I pushed someone down…I shoved him…Is that bad?'

Yes, that is bad. **Cease** violence and seek peace.

Please read Proverbs 1.

Do not be given to wine, <u>not violent</u> but gentle, not quarrelsome, nor a lover of money [1 Tim. 3:3].

"Do **not** envy a man of violence and do not choose any of his ways," [Prov. 3:31 ESV].

"You have heard that it was said, 'An eye for an eye and a tooth for a tooth.' But I tell you not to resist an evil person. But whoever slaps you on the right cheek, turn the other to him also." "But I say to you, love your enemies, bless those who curse you, do good to those who hate you, and pray for those who spitefully use you and persecute you, that you may be sons of your Father in heaven; for He makes the sun rise on the evil and on the good, and sends rain on the just and on the unjust." [Matt. 5:38–39, 44–45 NKJV].

Violence: we witness it (*daily*) on TV, in movies, in video games, in the media, at home, at work, at school, on the streets in gangs, and more.

Violence, according to www.merriam-webster.com, means "the use of physical force to harm someone; to damage property, etc. an instant of violent treatment or procedure, or abuse; physical force to cause injury."

Causes of Violence

Learned behavior	Believing people come across as threatening, when they don't	Too much stress, anxiety, resentment, or bitterness
Anger; frustration; rage	Feeling threatened or boxed into a corner	Emotional neglect or abandonment; past hurts
Exposed to violent media or video games	Feeling offended or rejected	Being beaten, hit; abused
Violence in the home; abuse (of any kind)	Isolation; feeling blacklisted	Violent culture
Violence in one's neighborhood (including gangs or shootings)	Bullying/cyberbullying; teasing	Not releasing pent-up feelings

Cease violence and seek to do no harm to thy neighbor. *Neighbor*, in Greek, means "anyone you meet." (The Lord revealed.) Amen.

Turn from violence and <u>seek peace</u>. Lay each cause of violence at God's feet and receive His peace.

Come to Me, all who are weary and heavy laden and I will give you rest [Matt. 11:28].

Rest from your troubles, your worries, your emotions, your anger, your frustration, your stress and anxiety, your emotional neglect, and more. Come to Me and I will relieve you of all these things, **says the Lord**. Amen.

How? Lay them all at God's feet with this prayer prayed in faith:

"Heavenly Father, I come before You laying all my [tell God what you desire to lay at His feet] at Your feet. I confess I have been violent toward [tell God who you've been violent to]. Forgive me for causing them harm. Help me to love my neighbor as myself and relieve me of all my troubles. In Jesus name, amen."

Change (The Lord revealed.) Amen.

Treat others how you would want to be treated [Luke 6:31]. (Yes, the Golden Rule originated from the Bible.) God desires for us to do as He commands, and to live according to His word. (The Lord revealed.) Amen.

"Love one another. **As I have loved you**, so you must love one another." [John 13:34 NIV].

"And you shall love the LORD your God will all your heart, with all your soul, with all your mind, and with all your strength.' This *is* the first commandment. And the second, like *it, is* this: 'You shall love your neighbor as yourself. There is no other commandment greater than these." [Mark 12:30–31 NKJV].

Neighbor, in Greek (the original language the New Testament was written in), means "anyone you meet."

"Love does **no harm** to a neighbor;" [Rom. 13:10 NKJV].

Harm, in Greek, according to www.biblehub.com, means "inwardly foul, rotten, inner malice, wickedness, inner evil. Bad things, evil morally of a mode of thinking, feeling, acting, wrong, wicked of persons, injurious, ill, work ill to one."

Violence is wrong, resulting in harm to one's neighbor (who is anyone you meet). Amen.

If you love God, you would love your neighbor. (The Lord revealed.) Amen.

Love your neighbor as yourself.

Loving your neighbor as yourself does not include violence, bullying, slandering, spreading vicious or malicious rumors about someone, cyberbullying, causing harm, treating cruelly, and so on.

"Do not let any unwholesome talk come out your mouths, but only what is helpful for building others up according to their needs, that it may benefit those who listen." [Eph. 4:29 NIV].

Unwholesome, according to www.biblehub.com, means "worthless, corrupt, bad, and rotten."

Love is **not** cruel, vicious, unkind, hateful, bitter, resentful, evil, rotten, foul, without mercy, quick-tempered, harmful, or unruly.

Love does no harm to anyone you meet [Rom. 13:10]. Amen.

Love is patient, love is kind; loves does not envy; love does not parade itself, is not puffed up, does not behave rudely, does not seek its own, is not provoked, thinks no evil, does not rejoice in iniquity, but rejoices in the truth...love never fails [1 Cor. 13:4–6, 8].

This love is accomplished through you, with the help of the Holy Spirit.

Ask the Holy Spirit to love through you daily, in Jesus name; ask Him with faith, so you can learn to love your neighbor as yourself. Amen.

If you desire to reconcile with someone you have harmed, use the strategy outlined in **"Conflict Management"** on page 113.

To continue to cease being violent, use the **Overcome and Stand** strategy on page 29.

Renew your mind using the **Battle of the Mind** strategy on page 58 and by asking the Holy Spirit to replace your thoughts with His.

Pray with faith: "Holy Spirit, think through me. In Jesus name, amen."

The Holy Spirit needs your cooperation in this massive effort to renew your mind, so do your part by renewing your mind with the word of God and He will do His. Amen.

Turn to the word of God. Begin to develop a habit of reading the word of God daily. His word provides peace, stillness, hope, strength, deliverance, healing, and love, and reveals the promises of God. Amen.

Jesus is the Word, and the Word is life. Amen.

Believe His word, speak His word, receive His word, think on His word, and apply the word of God to your life and you will see a change in your life and results. (The Lord revealed.) Amen.

Overcome with praise and worship

Praise lifts your focus off the problem and onto the presence of God. Learn more about worship and what true worship is by reading **"The Art of Worship"** on page 48. Amen.

Overcome by pouring out your heart

Tell a counselor, teacher, or other trusted adult, and let them know how you feel. Listen to their response, and see what you can do to make a change in your situation(s) and overcome. Pour out your heart to God, who can help you overcome any idol. Amen.

If you need more help, use the strategies outlined in the section on spiritual warfare on pages 340–410.

If you or someone you know are being abused in any away, or are being neglected at home, please <u>seek help immediately</u>.

Stealing

'I took this, without asking…I swiped it when no one was looking…No one caught me, so…'

Stop! Stealing will ruin your life. You can be deemed untrustworthy and dishonest, and you can go to jail or juvenile detention.

Thus says the Lord, "You shall **not** steal." [Exod. 20:15 NKJV].

To steal is to take something that <u>doesn't</u> belong to you. Do **not** steal. Amen.

"And my God shall supply all your need according to His riches in glory by Christ Jesus." [Phil. 4:19 NKJV].

Worry for nothing,

"Therefore I say to you, do not worry about your life, what you will eat or what you will drink; nor about your body, what you will put on. Is not life more than food and the body more than clothing? Look at the birds of the air, for they neither sow nor reap nor gather into barns; yet our Heavenly Father feeds them. Are you not more of value than they? Which of you by worrying can add one cubit to his stature?

"So why do you worry about clothing? Consider the lilies of the field, how they grow; they neither toil nor spin; and yet I say to you that even Solomon in all his glory was arrayed like one of these. Now if God so clothes the grass of the field, which today is, and tomorrow is thrown in the oven, will He not much more clothe you, O you of little faith?

"Therefore do not worry saying, 'what shall we eat?' or 'what shall we drink?' or 'what shall we wear?' For after all these things the Gentiles seek. For your Heavenly Father knows that you need all these things. But seek thee first the kingdom of God and His righteousness, and all these things shall be added unto you. Therefore do not worry about tomorrow, for tomorrow will worry about its own things. Sufficient for the day is its own trouble." [Matt. 6:25–34 NKJV].

This is one reason why you should <u>not</u> steal. God already knows what you are in need of; just ask Him. **Always remember <u>God loves you</u>**! Amen.

If God promises to supply all your needs, and He already knows what you are in need of, why steal? Instead seek to love your neighbor as yourself. Love does no harm to their neighbor, and stealing is doing harm to someone. Amen.

"Love one another. As I have loved you, so you must love one another." [John 13:34 NIV].

"And you shall love the LORD your God will all your heart, with all your soul, with all your mind, and with all your strength.' This *is* the first commandment. And the second, like *it*, *is* this: 'You shall love your neighbor as yourself.' There is no other commandment greater than these." [Mark 12:30–31 NKJV].

Neighbor, in Greek (the original language the New Testament was written in), means "anyone you meet."

"Love does **no harm** to a neighbor;" [Rom. 13:10 NKJV].

Harm, in Greek, according to www.biblehub.com, means "inwardly foul, rotten, inner malice, wickedness, inner evil. Bad things, evil morally of a mode of thinking, feeling, acting, wrong, wicked of persons, injurious, ill, work ill to one."

Stealing is wrong, resulting in harm to one's neighbor (who is anyone you meet). Amen.

If you love God, you would love your neighbor. (The Lord revealed.) Amen.

Love your neighbor as yourself.

Loving your neighbor as yourself does not include violence, bullying, stealing, slandering, causing harm, treating cruelly, and so on.

"Do not let any unwholesome talk come out your mouths, but only what is helpful for building others up according to their needs, that it may benefit those who listen." [Eph. 4:29 NIV].

Unwholesome, according to www.biblehub.com, means "worthless, corrupt, bad, and rotten."

Love is **not** cruel, vicious, unkind, hateful, bitter, resentful, evil, rotten, foul, without mercy, quick-tempered, harmful, or unruly.

Love does no harm to anyone [Rom. 13:10]. Amen.

Love is patient, love is kind; loves does not envy; love does not parade itself, is not puffed up, does not behave rudely, does not seek its own, is not provoked, thinks no evil, does not rejoice in iniquity, but rejoices in the truth…love never fails [1 Cor. 13:4–6, 8].

This love is accomplished through you, with the help of the Holy Spirit.

Ask the Holy Spirit to love through you daily, in Jesus name; ask Him with faith so you can learn to love your neighbor as yourself. Amen.

In this manner pray with faith:

"Holy Spirit, love through me, so I can love my neighbor as myself. In Jesus name, amen."

In this manner pray with faith:

"Heavenly Father, forgive me for taking things that don't belong to me. I believe You will supply all my needs and that You know already what I need. Help me to be honest and trustworthy, and to do my part to make an honest living. In Jesus name, amen."

Turn to the word of God. Begin to develop a habit of reading the word of God daily. His word provides peace, stillness, hope, strength, deliverance, healing, and love, and reveals the promises of God. Amen.

Jesus is the Word, and the Word is life. Amen.

Believe His word, speak His word, receive His word, think on His word, and apply the word of God to your life and you will see change in your life and results. (The Lord revealed.) Amen.

Renew your mind using the **Battle of the Mind** strategy on page 58 and by asking the Holy Spirit to replace your thoughts with His.

Pray with faith: "Holy Spirit, think through me. In Jesus name, amen."

The Holy Spirit needs your cooperation in this massive effort to renew your mind, so do your part by renewing your mind with the word of God and He will do His. Amen.

God says, I will provide everything for you, everything you need; you need not worry, you need not steal, **trust Me**. I am everything you need. (The Lord revealed.) Amen.

"Let the thief no longer steal, but rather let him labor, doing honest work with his own hands, so that he may have something to share with anyone in need." [Eph. 4:28 ESV].

(This verse includes everyone, both men and women. Both should not steal.) Amen.

Instead…Seek to Make an Honest Living

In the beginning, when God planted a garden in Eden, and after God created man on the sixth day [Gen. 1:26–31], God placed man in the garden and told man to tend (work) it and keep it [Gen. 2:15].

From the very beginning God has ordained work, and since the beginning man is commanded by God to do so. Amen.

In the end, **good honest work** has always been commanded by God. Amen.

Whatever you do, work wholeheartedly, as for the Lord and not for man [Col. 3:23].

"I can do all things through Christ who strengthens me." [Phil. 4:13 NKJV].

"rendering service (work) with a good will (kindness) as to the Lord and not to man," [Eph. 6:7 ESV].

"And whatever you do, in word or deed, do everything in the name of the Lord Jesus, giving thanks to God the Father through him." [Col. 3:17 ESV].

Speak and claim (receive) these scriptures above for yourself. Amen.

May you seek to do well in all things. Amen.

Say to yourself, "I will seek to make an honest living." Say this over and over again, to yourself repeatedly, and seek to do so. Amen.

How?

If you are under the age of sixteen (the legal age to start working), you can participate in the following work activities as long as you have parental/guardian permission or supervision:

1. Yard work (charging a small fee)
2. Bake sales (charging a small fee)
3. Babysitting (charging a small fee)
4. Housework (charging a small fee)

You can perform good honest work for a small fee.

Important note: Before you go to perform any one of these (or any other) work duties, <u>always</u> let a parent/guardian know, and if you don't feel comfortable going alone, bring someone with you such as a parent, guardian, sibling, friend, or someone else.

If you are sixteen and above, you can legally join the workforce. For example you can work at the following:

1. Restaurant
2. Any store in the mall (unless they tell you otherwise)
3. Clothing store
4. Food store or market
5. Babysitting

Many of the jobs listed above require job interviews, résumés, references, and so on. To learn more about each of them please do the following web searches:

Job Interviews	Résumés	References
Go to www.google.com and search job interviews (research what to bring, how to dress, and so on).	Go to www.google.com and search résumés.	Go to www.google.com and search references for jobs.

Keep in mind that continuing your education beyond high school (such as at a trade school, community or technical college, college, or university) can better prepare/equip you for a future profession. "**Commit** your way to the LORD, Trust also in Him, And He shall bring *it* to pass." [Ps. 37:5 NKJV]. Amen.

Trust in God. When you do your part, God will do His. My pastor, Pastor Terry L. Harris, taught on this. Amen.

How to do your part to continue your education:

1. **Do well in school**. Don't skip class or get involved with the wrong people. Pay attention, be in class, study, turn in your homework on time, work hard to get good grades, and if you need help, don't feel ashamed or hesitate to ask for a tutor to help you achieve higher grades. This is *your* education and *your* life. Amen.
2. **Complete** any tests, such as the SAT and ACT.
3. **Get involved** in sports or clubs that can help you receive scholarships.
4. **Graduate** from high school.
5. **Look around**, talk with your family, and pray *before* applying for colleges, technical or community colleges, universities, and trade schools.
6. If you apply for college, trade school, or some other institution and don't receive any scholarships, **that's okay**; apply for loans, grants, work study, and other forms of financial aid. See your high school for details. They will gladly give you all the information you need.
7. In the end, **work with God** to choose your school, seeking to do His will. Amen.

Entrust your work to the Lord, and your plans will succeed [Prov. 16:3].

Once accepted into your choice of school, college, trade school, or university, seek to do well and graduate. Amen.

God will do His part, but you must do yours. Amen.

For I know the plans I have for you, says the Lord, plans to prosper you and not to harm you, plans to give you a future and a hope [Jer. 29:11].

You are destined for greatness!

(The Lord revealed.) Amen.

Tithes and Offerings

Once you begin to work, don't forget to tithe, and remember to bring your tithe to your local church.

"Bring all the tithes into the storehouse (the local church), That there may be food in My house," [Mal. 3:10 NKJV].

Tithes	Offerings
The tithe is 10 percent of your gross income. Every time you get paid, 10 percent belongs to God. The tithe goes to the church you attend.	The offering is any amount you give after you tithe. The offering can go to your local church, TV ministries, charities, and so on.

The tithe is the first fruits of your labor, according to the word of God; the first fruits (the tithe) belong to God [Exod. 34:26].

The tithe (first fruits) comes with a blessing. The blessing, according to Malachi 3:10–11, is that God will open up the windows of Heaven and pour you out a blessing, you won't have room enough to receive it all, and the Lord will rebuke the devourer for your sake, so that he will not destroy the fruit of your ground or field.

This means you will be blessed with more than enough when you tithe. Amen.

Not tithing (giving your first fruits) comes with a curse. The curse comes because you have robbed God [Mal. 3:8–9]. The only way to break the curse is to tithe. Amen.

Remember to give your first fruits (tithe) to God. Amen.

To learn more about tithes and offerings, please view Pastor Robert Morris's teaching *The First Open Door*, from his Free Indeed series. You can purchase this CD or DVD on www.theblessedlife.com.

The Purpose of Tithes and Offerings

My pastor, Terry L. Harris, taught his congregation about tithes and offerings, and his message inspired me to write about them. Amen.

The purpose of tithes and offerings is to keep up and repair the house of the Lord [2 Chron. 24:8–14].

Uses for Tithes and Offerings			
Pay bills	Pay rent	Pay the mortgage	Pay the staff
Pay electric bills	Pay insurance	Pay for upkeep	Pay for repairs
Emergency funds	Pay for outreach programs	Pay for missionary trips	Pay for community programs
Funds for different ministries			

This is the importance of tithes and offerings. Amen.

Street Gangs

'I'm in a gang. Why would you care?'

I care because you **belong** to God, not a gang.

You belong to Me, says the Lord [Isa. 43:1].

"casting all your anxieties on him, because he cares for you." [1 Pet. 5:7 ESV].

"I will betroth you to Me forever; Yes, I will betroth you to Me In righteousness and justice, In lovingkindness and mercy;" [Hosea 2:19 NKJV].

"I have called *you* by your name; You *are* Mine." [Isa. 43:1 NKJV].

I have loved you with an everlasting love; therefore I have drawn you with lovingkindness [Jer. 31:3].

Peace I leave with you; My peace I give to you, I do not give as the world gives. Let not your heart be troubled, neither let it be afraid [John 14:27].

You <u>don't</u> have to join a gang to belong. If you are a child of God, you already belong to God. If you aren't a child of God, you can become one and belong to God. Amen. ☺

Reasons Youth Join Gangs	What God Has to Say (Please look up each verse.)
To belong	You belong to God; He has called you by name; you are His [Jer. 3:14; Isa. 43:1]
To survive (food, money, clothing, shelter, etc.)	God will supply all your needs; you need not worry [Phil. 4:19; Matt. 6:25–34; James 4:2]
For protection	God will shelter you under the shadow of His wings, [Ps. 91:4] [also read Isa. 41:10; Ps. 23:4; Deut. 31:8; Ps. 40:1–2; Prov. 18:10.]

For a sense of purpose	I have a plan for your life, says the Lord [Jer. 29:11], [also read Rom. 8:28].
Look cool	You are a chosen generation, a royal priesthood, a holy nation [1 Pet. 2:9] [also read Ps. 45:13; Judg. 6:2.]
Pressured by peers or family members (want to fit in, not feel left out; threatened, forced, dared, begged, etc.)	Do not be misled, Bad company corrupts good habits [1 Cor. 15:33]. Though you walk in the midst of trouble, the Lord will revive you. You will stretch Your hand against the wrath of my enemies and your right hand will save me [Ps. 138:7; Rom. 8:31; Ps. 143:11.]
Family tradition (in their family's history)	"We ought to obey God rather than men." [Acts 5:29 NKJV]. My son, if sinful man entice you, do not consent [Prov. 1:10], [also read 1 Cor. 10:13; James 1:11–15; Matt. 5:16; Matt. 15:3.]
By force	God has given every man free will [Gen. 2:15–16; Gen. 3]. "The fear of man brings a snare, But whoever trusts in the LORD shall be safe." [Prov. 29:25 NKJV]; [also read Ps. 1:1–3; Prov. 1:10–15; Ps. 56:11].
By accident	Do not be deceived [James 1:16]. "He who walks with wise *men* will be wise, But the companion of fools will be destroyed." [Prov. 13:20 NKJV]. [also read Prov. 1:10–15; 1 Cor. 15:33; Ps. 1:1–3].
Violence in the home (abuse, domestic disputes, violence, etc.)	"When my father and mother forsake me, Then the LORD will take care of me." [Ps. 27:10 NKJV]. The Lord will shelter me under the shadow of His wings [Ps. 91:4]. [also read Isa. 49:15; Ps. 69:8; Jer. 1:4–5].
Poverty	God will take care of you [1 Pet. 5:7]. "And God *is* able to make all grace abound toward you, that you, always

	having all sufficiency in all *things*, may have an abundance for every good work." [2 Cor. 9:8 NKJV] [also read Ps. 34:8–10; Eph. 3:20].
No parental involvement; absence of the father in the home or one-parent home	I, God, am your Father. Turn to Me, says the Lord [Rom. 8:15]. [also read Ps. 27:10; Rom. 8:14–16; Gal. 4:5–7].
School dropout (harder to find a job, etc.)	I have a plan for your life. **Turn to Me, says the Lord** [Jer. 29:11]. I am everything you need. Amen [Phil. 4:13]. [also read Prov. 3:5–6; Matt. 6:33; Prov. 16:3; Isa. 41:10].
Easy money	I (God) shall supply all your needs according to My riches and glory [Phil. 4:19]. Worry for nothing [Matt. 6:25–34].
Isolation from peers, family, friends, society, etc.	You are not alone [Matt. 28:20]; [also read Eccles. 4:12].
TV, society showing gangs in a positive light, etc.	Be not conformed to this world, but be transformed by the renewing of your mind [Rom. 12:2]. Do I persuade men or God? Or do I seek to please men? For if I still pleased men, I would not be a bondservant of God [Gal. 1:10]. Obey God rather than men [Acts 5:29]. For what does it profit a man to gain the whole world and lose his soul? [Matt. 16:26]. Please go to the **Battle of the Mind** strategy on page 58.

(Reasons why the youth join gangs acquired from: www.gangfree.org)

Now that you've learned what God has to say, what say you? Will you choose to obey God or man?

If you are in a gang, **repent**, and turn to God.

In this manner, pray with faith:

"Heavenly Father, I confess I have joined a gang because (tell God the reason why). Forgive me for doing so. I believe You are my Father, I believe You have a plan for my life, I believe I am not alone, and I believe that I belong to You. I am Your daughter (or I am Your son). In Jesus name, amen."

"Or do you not know that your body is a temple of the Holy Spirit within you, whom you have from God? You are not your own, for you were bought with a price. (the **blood of Jesus**) So glorify God in your body." [1 Cor. 6:19–20 ESV].

You belong to God and God loves you! Amen.

Instead of joining a gang, seek to make an honest living. See page 163. Amen.

Involved in a Gang? Speak Up and Speak Out!

Speak up and speak out, let your voice be heard!

If you are involved in a gang (and if you are seeking a way out), **tell** a parent, teacher, counselor, youth pastor, or other trusted adult who will be able to provide you with all the help and assistance you need.

Keep in mind, you might have to conduct spiritual warfare. If so, please see pages 340–410.

Turn to the word of God. Begin to develop a habit of reading the word of God daily. His word provides peace, stillness, hope, strength, deliverance, healing, and love, and reveals the promises of the word of God. Amen.

Jesus is the Word, and the Word is life. Amen.

Believe His word, speak His word, receive His word, think on His word, and apply the word of God to your life and you will see a change in your life and results. (The Lord revealed.) Amen.

Renew your mind using the **Battle of the Mind** strategy on page 58 and by asking the Holy Spirit to replace your thoughts with His.

Pray with faith: "Holy Spirit, think through me. In Jesus name, amen."

The Holy Spirit needs your cooperation in this massive effort to renew your mind, so do your part by renewing your mind with the word of God and He will do His. Amen.

Let not your heart be troubled, neither let it be afraid.

Open up your mouth and speak. Amen.

Homosexuality

'Men with men, and women with women...Is that wrong?'

Yes, it is wrong.

"Therefore God also gave them up to uncleanness, in the lusts of their hearts, to dishonor their bodies among themselves," "For this reason God gave them up to vile passions. For even their women exchanged the natural use for what is against nature. Likewise also the men, leaving the natural use of the woman, burned in their lust for one another, men with men committing what is shameful, and receiving in themselves the penalty of their error which was due." [Rom. 1:24, 26–27 NKJV].

Romans 1:24, 26–27 defines homosexuality, and homosexuality is a **sin**. Amen.

"Or do you not know that your body is a temple of the Holy Spirit within you, whom you have from God? You are not your own, for you were bought with a price. (the **blood of Jesus**) So glorify God in your body." [1 Cor. 6:19–20 ESV].

"You shall not lie with a male as with a woman. It *is* an abomination" [Lev. 18:22 NKJV].

"Do you not know that the unrighteous will not inherit the kingdom of God? Do not be deceived. Neither fornicators, nor idolaters, nor adulterers, nor homosexuals, nor sodomites, nor thieves, nor covetous, nor drunkards, nor revilers, nor extortioners will inherit the kingdom of God. And such were some of you. But you were washed, but you were sanctified, but you were justified in the name of the Lord Jesus and by the Spirit of our God." [1 Cor. 6:9–11 NKJV].

"But from the beginning of creation, God 'made them male and female.' 'For this reason a man shall leave his father and mother and be joined to his wife, and the two shall become one flesh'; so then they are no longer two, but one flesh. Therefore what God has joined together, let not man separate." [Mark 10:6–9 NKJV].

"as Sodom and Gomorrah, and the cities around them in a similar manner to these, having given themselves over to sexual immorality and gone after strange flesh, are set forth as an example, suffering the vengeance of eternal fire." [Jude 1:7 NKJV].

The world legalizes, recognizes, and encourages abominations such as homosexuality. **God does not!**

God's word **never** changes [Rom. 1:24, 26–27; Jude 1:7; Lev. 18:22].

What was true yesterday [Lev. 18:22] is still true today [Rom. 1:24, 26–27; 1 Cor. 6:19–20; Jude 1:7].

The word of God is true [John 17:17], and the word of God still stands; it will never pass away [Luke 21:33], and the word of God will never change. Amen.

Why do people choose homosexuality?

The eyes and the ears:

Be careful what your little eyes see. The eyes are a window to the soul, and if the eye is bad, the whole body will be filled with darkness [Matt. 6:22–23].

Be careful what your little ears hear. Take care how you listen, for whoever has, more will be given to him, and whoever does not have, even what he has will be taken from him [Luke 8:18]. Amen.

Both the eyes and the ears can influence a person into a life of homosexuality. This reveals how homosexuality is a choice; you are not born this way [Rom. 1:24, 26–28]. Amen.

How can the eyes and the ears influence a person into this lifestyle?

Below is a true story of how a young man turned to a life of homosexuality because of what he heard:

On Christian TV (I believe it was the *700 Club*), a young man shared his story. This young man used to live a gay lifestyle, and he shared with the host of the show how he became homosexual. He revealed that when he was a young boy, he overheard two men talking sexually to each other in the men's restroom. (I'm not sure if he saw something too.) The young man said that after he heard the men's conversation, he couldn't get it out of his mind. He kept replaying their words over and over in his head. It was there in the men's restroom after dwelling on the men's conversation (who were gay) that his homosexual lifestyle began.

His story reveals how homosexuality is influenced by what one sees and hears, not by genes. No one is born that way.

A person can also turn to the homosexual lifestyle because of rape, molestation, abuse, incest, inappropriate relationships, being touched inappropriately or in a sexual manner, pornography, and more.

This too reveals how a person chooses the homosexual lifestyle because of their wounds.

Turn to God instead.

Receive help from these incidents (such as rape, molestation, and so on, listed above) by speaking out to an adult and turning to Jesus Christ. **Jesus loves you!** Amen.

The thief comes to steal, kill, and destroy, but I (**Jesus**), have come to give life and life more abundantly [John 10:10]. Amen.

The Spiritual Side of Homosexuality

Homosexuality is a demonic oppression and/or a demonic possession.

There is a difference between demonic oppression and demonic possession.

Demonic Oppression	Demonic Possession
A demonic oppression is a heavy weight or burden. Use this definition to discover if you are demonically oppressed or possessed.	*Demonic possession*, according to www.dictionary.refrence.com, means "to be controlled or dominated by evil spirits, having ownership." According to www.merriam-webster.com it means "the act of having or taking into control, control or occupancy of property without regard to ownership, domination by something (evil spirit)." Use this definition to discover if you are demonically oppressed or possessed. If you suspect you may be possessed, **immediately seek help** from a pastor, youth pastor, or a ministry that specializes in deliverance and spiritual warfare, and follow their instructions.

A couple who appeared on Sid Roth's *It's Supernatural* Christian TV show revealed this truth:

Homosexuality in **men** is known as feminine demonic oppression or possession. This causes a man to act feminine or take on feminine behaviors. According to www.wikipedia.com, *feminine* means "taking on feminine behaviors." [See Rom. 1:27].

Homosexuality in **women** is known as a masculine demonic oppression or possession. This causes a woman to act like a man [Rom. 1:26].

Both demonic oppressions and demonic possessions are sent by the enemy to trick and fool you, to get you to believe right is wrong and wrong is right, and to get you to believe that you were born that way (when you were not born that way). Amen.

The enemy is wrong!

The couple who appeared on Sid Roth's Christian TV show *It's Supernatural* also **revealed** this truth: Demons can enter into you at birth, in the womb, or even upon conception. Wow!

The Lord revealed to share this **true story**, which the couple also shared on Sid Roth's program:

A man who was homosexual came to the couple because he wanted to be set free from the homosexual lifestyle. He asked the couple to pray for him, and the couple did. They prayed and prayed (many times), but at the time, it seemed there were no results. It felt like their prayers went unanswered. The couple lost contact with the man after their prayers seemed to yield no results. Then the man ended up in the hospital with AIDS, and the couple was notified and went to visit him. He told them that with every breath he had left he would give thanks to God (because he was dying of AIDS). The man kept his word, and with every breath he had, he thanked God. Days, weeks, and months passed, and the man's health recovered miraculously. God healed him and he was able to get up out of his hospital bed (which he had been confined to because of AIDS) and walk. God completely healed the man and set him free from homosexuality. Their prayers were answered! The man told the couple he felt something lift off of him and he felt like a man again. No longer did he desire to act like a woman; he wanted to go out and hang with the guys like a man. It is here that the couple revealed the feminine and masculine demonic oppressions and possessions that influence men and women to be gay. It takes God to lift this demonic being off of you and set you free. Amen.

You can be set free; but first you have to want to be set free [John 8:36]. Amen.

The Choice

Do you want to be set free or do you want to stay demonically oppressed or possessed?

The choice is yours, but the word of God is true [Rom. 1:24, 26–27; Jude 1:7; Lev. 18:22]. Amen.

You just have to believe His word and receive your freedom [Mark 11:24]. Amen.

The choice is up to you.

Free Will

There are many reasons why men or women choose the homosexual lifestyle. However, one must choose to participate in this lifestyle or not, because God has given every man, woman, and child free will.

Freewill is "the ability of acting without the constraint of necessity or fate, the ability to act at one's own discretion. Voluntary choice or decision," (according to www.google.com and www.merriam-webster.com).

Every person has free will. Amen.

For example, the two men possessed by the legion of demons in Matthew 8:28–34 still had free will, because they chose not to kill themselves (when the demons wanted them to), and they were able to run to Jesus (even though they were demonically possessed).

If the two demon-possessed men still had free will, how much more does the person who is fighting the homosexual lifestyle?

You too have **free will**. Therefore, there is no excuse for those who participate in the homosexual lifestyle. For God has given **every** man, woman, and child free will. (The Lord revealed.) Amen.

Freedom

He who the Son sets free, is free indeed [John 8:36].

When and if sexual thoughts or thoughts involving homosexuality try to enter your mind, don't let them in. Cast them down immediately and renew your mind using the **Battle of the Mind strategy** on page 58 and by asking the Holy Spirit to replace your thoughts with His.

Pray with faith: "Holy Spirit, think through me. In Jesus name, amen."

The Holy Spirit needs your cooperation in this massive effort to renew your mind, so do your part by renewing your mind with the word of God and He will do His. Amen.

Turn to the word of God. Begin to develop a habit of reading the word of God daily. His word provides peace, stillness, hope, strength, deliverance, healing, and love, and reveals the promises of God. Amen.

Jesus is the Word, and the Word is life. Amen.

Believe His word, speak His word, receive His word, think on His word, and apply the word of God to your life, and you will see a change in your life and results. (The Lord revealed.) Amen.

Meditate on scripture

Here is a list of scriptures you can meditate on:

Psalm 42	Psalm 43	Psalm 34:17	Romans 8:38–39
John 14:1–2	Isaiah 41:13	Isaiah 41:10	Philippians 4:13
Psalm 118	Romans 5:3–5	Proverbs 3:5–6	Philippians 4:4

Psalm 37:25	Romans 8:26	James 1:2–4	2 Timothy 1:7
Psalm 91	Matthew 11:28–30	Romans 8:28	Jeremiah 29:11
Romans 10:17	Psalm 40:1–3	Psalm 9:9	Deuteronomy 31:8
Psalm 46:10	Matthew 28:20	Deuteronomy 33:27	Romans 12:2
Philippians 4:8	Isaiah 26:3	2 Corinthians 10:3–6	
2 Timothy 1:7	Philippians 2:5	Colossians 3:1–2	1 Corinthians 6:18

Pray

In this manner, pray with faith:

"Heavenly Father, release me from the homosexual lifestyle. Release me from this bondage, and this heavy weight. Save me, O my God, and deliver me. Forgive me for living this way. I receive Your freedom and deliverance now. In Jesus name, amen."

It may take time, but you will see the results of God delivering you and setting you free from the homosexual lifestyle. Amen.

Walk by faith, not by sight [2 Cor. 5:7]. Amen.

In the meantime, continue to **praise and thank** God for your freedom and deliverance. This pleases God, and God will come through for you [Ps. 37:5]. Amen.

Learn how to plead the **blood of Jesus** over yourself daily, by going to page 365 of the spiritual warfare section.

If you still need more help, use the strategies outlined in the section on spiritual warfare on pages 340–410.

If you suspect you may be possessed, immediately <u>seek help</u> from a pastor, youth pastor, or ministry that specializes in deliverance and spiritual warfare and follow their instructions.

Overcome in Christ Jesus! Amen.

Struggling with Homosexuality? Speak Up and Speak Out!

Let your voice be heard!

Talk to a counselor, teacher, or other adult if you're struggling with homosexuality. Listen to their response, and see what you can do to make a change in your life and overcome the homosexual lifestyle.

Pour out your heart to God too, who can also help you overcome the homosexual lifestyle. Amen.

"Let not your heart be troubled, neither let it be afraid." [John 14:27]

Open up your mouth and speak. Amen.

Lust, Sexual Immorality, and Adultery

'We're in love so it's okay...We don't need to get married...Marriage is old-fashioned...'

Sex before marriage is never okay, whether you believe you are in love or claim to be a Christian or not. Marriage is ordained by God, and the **marriage covenant** should be **honored**. Keep the marriage bed undefiled. Amen.

"Flee from sexual immorality. Every other sin a person commits is outside the body, but the sexually immoral person sins against his own body. Or do you not know that your body is a temple of the Holy Spirit within you, whom you have from God? You are not your own, for you were bought with a price. (the **blood of Jesus**) So glorify God in your body." [1 Cor. 6:18–20 ESV].

"My son, if sinners entice you, do **not** consent." [Prov. 1:10 ESV].

"No temptation has overtaken you that is not common to man. **God is faithful**, and he will not let you be tempted beyond your ability, but with the temptation he will also provide the way of escape, that you may be able to endure it." [1 Cor. 10:13 ESV].

Do not be conformed to this world, but be transformed by the renewal of your mind, that by testing you may discern what is the will of God, what is good, and acceptable, and perfect [Rom. 12:2].

"Whoever walks with the wise becomes wise, but the companion of fools will suffer harm." [Prov. 13:20 ESV].

"Do not be deceived: "Bad company ruins good morals." [1 Cor. 15:33 ESV].

"But Peter and the apostles answered, "We must obey God rather than men." [Acts 5:29 ESV].

"The fear of man lays a snare, but however trusts in the LORD is safe." [Prov. 29:25 ESV].

"For in that He Himself has suffered, being tempted, He is able to aid those who are tempted." [Heb. 2:18 NKJV].

"Blessed is the man who walks not in the counsel of the wicked, nor stands in the way of sinners, nor sits in the seat of scoffers;" [Ps. 1:1 ESV].

"delivering you from the way of evil, from men of perverted speech," [Prov. 2:12 ESV].

Please read Ephesians 5:1–21.

Lust, according to www.google.com, is "a very strong sexual desire toward someone."

Sexual immorality is any form of sex outside of marriage this includes pornography, sexual fantasies, sexual perversion, sexual intercourse, adultery, and so on.

Adultery, according to www.google.com, means "voluntary sexual intercourse between a person who is married and a person who is not their spouse."

All three are sins. Amen.

Scriptures on Lust, Sexual Immorality, and Adultery			
James 1:14–15	2 Corinthians 5:10	Jude 1:4	Romans 12:1
Ephesians 2:1–3	1 Corinthians 6:18	1Thessalonians 4:3–5	1 Corinthians 10:13
Matthew 5:27–28	Hebrews 13:4	1 Corinthians 7:2	Ephesians 5:3
	James 1:12–15	Proverbs 6:32	Exodus 20:14
Galatians 5:19–21	Ephesians 5:5	James 4:17	2 Peter 2:14
Proverbs 6:24–29			

Keep the marriage bed pure and undefiled. Amen.

The word of God is pure and righteous altogether. The word of the Lord is true and stands forever. More to be desired than gold, yes more than fine gold, is the word of God [Ps. 19:8-10]. Amen.

Flee sexual immorality; flee from the lust of the eyes, the lust of the flesh, adultery, and the pride of life. Amen.

Please read **the Story of David**.

The Story of David

To God give all the honor, all the glory, all the credit, and all the praise. Bless His holy name. Amen.

The Mistakes, Lust, and Adultery of David Study

"Create in me a clean heart, O God."

The Story of David

We first hear of David in 1 Samuel 16. This is where one finds the prophet Samuel mourning after God's rejection of King Saul, because of his continuous disobedience in 1 Samuel 15. The Lord wanted the prophet Samuel to rise again (stop mourning for King Saul), and to anoint another as king over all of Israel. In the end, the prophet Samuel ended up anointing a small shepherd boy, the youngest of his father Jesse's sons. For the Lord was not looking at the outward appearances as man does; God looks at the heart and called David **a man after My own heart** [1 Sam. 13:14].

After David's many encounters with King Saul [1 Sam. 18–31], David's triumph over Goliath [1 Sam. 17], and his continuous triumph over the Philistines and his enemies, he was finally able to establish his kingdom after Saul's death, in 1 Samuel 31. (The Lord just revealed Saul was a man who went after David. His intent was to kill David, and Saul killed righteous people. Was not Saul who later became Paul in the book of Acts, the same type of murderer who went after the righteous to slaughter them? What's in a name? Both Sauls had been killers of righteous men, until God Himself intervened. God intervened for David, because of Saul in 1 Samuel; and in the book of Acts God redeemed Saul on a street called Straight. The Lord revealed.) Amen. Just a little gold nugget for further study in the future of what's in a name. Amen. ☺

After David established his kingdom [1 Chron. 14:2], all went well, right? He no longer had to fight any more Philistines or enemies of Israel, right? Was there peace? No. David continuously fought the Philistines and other foreign enemies that came against Israel during the time of his established kingdom [2 Sam. 5]. The kingdom also remained divided until the tragic murder of King Saul's son Ishbosheth, who reigned over Israel for just two years [2 Sam. 2:8–11; 4]. It wasn't until after Ishbosheth's death that the people united and made David their king [2 Sam. 5]. So David ruled as King (and he was mighty), and God was with him, before him, and against his enemies [2 Sam. 5–7].

Above is a small account of David's life: where he came from, how he became king of all Israel (undivided and united), his enemies, and when he ruled over Israel.

So...how does someone on top end up in the miry clay? [Ps. 40:2].

Where did David slip up? Why did he have to beg God's forgiveness? Why did he have to ask God for a clean heart and a renewed spirit within him? Why did he incur the consequences of disobedience? Where did David go wrong?

David fell. Fell where? Fell into sin.

How did he fall? Through the lust of the eyes, the lust of the flesh, and the pride of life—the same three sins that led to the fall of man in the garden [Gen. 3:1–24]. These same three began David's fall as well. (The Lord revealed.) Amen.

How? Where did he fall? How did he fall? Who did he fall by? When did he fall? Why did he fall?

During the spring, when all kings should have gone off to war. Instead, David sent another commander (Joab) to lead his soldiers to war, and they, in turn, conquered the Ammonites and surrounded the city of Rabbah.

In the meantime, David decided to remain in Jerusalem [2 Sam. 11:1], this was his **first** mistake.

One evening, David arose from his bed and walked on the roof of the King's house.

He decided to go for a walk on the palace roof. Did he know this was a time of bathing? Who knows? Only God knows. It was here on the roof during the evening that he spotted a woman bathing. The woman was said to be very beautiful to behold [2 Sam. 11:2]. David saw a woman bathing; he saw and fell into sin—the lust of the eyes. (To see means: to look at, to gaze upon something with one's eyes. To lust is to desire.) (God revealed.) Amen.

This was the **second** mistake David made: he looked upon a woman in an indecent manner and lusted after (desired) her.

The **third** mistake: David inquired after the woman; he sent someone to find out who the woman was. In response, someone told David that she was the daughter of Eliam, the wife of Uriah, a Hittite, and her name was Bathsheba [see 2 Sam. 11:3].

The **fourth** mistake: David knew the woman was married. And yet, he still desired (*desire* means "to long for/after") her anyway. David had knowledge of Bathsheba's marriage status, and yet he still sent for her and ended up lying with her [see 2 Sam. 11:4]. He gratified (surrendered to) the lust of the flesh and fell into iniquity (*iniquity* means "to sin knowingly" and according to google.com means: "immoral or grossly unfair behavior").

Here we see that David sins twice: once for looking upon the woman (lusting) and again by lying with her carnally (committing adultery). David sinned and fell miserably. These were his mistakes.

Did it end there?

No. Bathsheba conceived, and found out she was pregnant (with child), and sent word to David upon discovering the news [2 Sam. 11:5]. David sent for Uriah, her husband (who had been fighting in battle with his fellow soldiers), to come home, that he might sleep with his wife and fool others into believing that it was Uriah and not David who impregnated her [2 Sam. 11:6–8]. Thus, Uriah came home from the battlefield, but to David's dismay he never made it into bed with his wife, because he was too worried about his commander and fellow soldiers who were left behind on the battlefield [see 2 Sam. 11:9–11].

Keep in mind: God sees all, knows all, and hears all, and He sees everything unfolding (everything that David has done; his thoughts, his plans, and everything David would do) and bears witness to it. **There is nothing that is hidden from God.** (The Lord revealed.) Amen.

We find David still trying to fool Uriah into sleeping with his wife, but again Uriah failed to do so [2 Sam. 11:12–13]. Here lies David's **fifth** mistake: impregnating

Bathsheba and trying to force her husband to sleep with her to cover up his hidden sin.

The **sixth** mistake, and the cruelest of them all, was when David sent word to Joab, who served as the commander of the battlefield, to place Uriah on the front lines, where he would surely be killed, because he never slept with his wife, Bathsheba, to cover up David's crime [2 Sam. 11:14–15].

Joab received David's letter and did as King David requested, placing Uriah on the front lines, and sure enough, Uriah was killed in battle. A messenger sent word to King David to reveal all that had occurred, but the King was not remorseful at all about his sin, and told Joab (the commander of the army) not to mourn, saying death in battle happened all the time. (Joab thought the King would be upset, but to his surprise he was not.) Moreover, King David encouraged Joab to keep fighting until the city was taken and the battle won [see 2 Sam. 11:22–25]. Afterward, word was sent to Uriah's wife, Bathsheba, and she mourned for her husband, Uriah, for a period of time. Later on David brought Bathsheba into his own house, and she became his wife, carrying his child, but God was displeased [2 Sam. 11:25].

Here we witness the pride of life: David lifted himself up and believed his plan had succeeded. David thought he'd gotten away with something...but he was sadly mistaken.

He forgot One person: the One who knows everything, sees everything, and is ever present. King David forgot about God.

David forgot about the Creator of the universe, the One who established the law and testimonies, the One who established the monarch within Israel, the One who anointed him King over all Israel, the One who gave him triumph over all his enemies, and the One who would have given him anything, if he had only asked [2 Sam. 12:7–8].

David forgot about God, the One who loved him dearly, the One whose heart he sought after.

But God did not forget about David.

Before David confessed to his wrongdoings, God sent Nathan the prophet to expose the sins of David the King, using a parable. The parable was about a rich man who had everything, a poor man who had nothing, and a lamb. It was in his own anger, after hearing the parable, that David pronounced his own judgment upon himself. David said that not only should the rich man die (the one who took the lamb from the poor man to eat), but he should restore fourfold the value for the lamb that had been taken and killed [see 2 Sam. 12:1–6].

It was then that Nathan proclaimed, 'You, King David are that man.' (He was the rich man who had taken and killed the lamb of the poor man.)

In his own anger, King David had pronounced death upon himself, by pronouncing death upon the rich man in the parable, and the restoring of fourfold for the lamb. Also King David was shocked to hear that he was the rich man. However, the Lord God loved David and would not let him die. Instead, the Lord pronounced this judgment upon King David and his household: The Lord would raise up adversity against the house of David, and his wives would be taken and gone into by other men before all (in public). Also the child conceived between him and Bathsheba would surely die. (One reason for this was that the enemies of God would blaspheme His name because of the child born out of David's affair.) In the end the sword would never leave David's house [2 Sam. 12:10–15].

What did David do? Read Psalm 51, a psalm created after David had gone into Bathsheba and was confronted by Nathan the prophet.

Did David repent? Yes, he did. [See 2 Samuel 12:13].

Did God spare the child in Bathsheba's womb, conceived during their affair? No. Read 2 Samuel 12:15–23 to see God's reasons for doing so. However, this does not mean it's okay to abort any child born out of an affair. God gives life, and He can take it away. Amen.

Be at peace. The child went to heaven, because David told his servants he could go to the child, but the child couldn't return to him [2 Sam. 12:23].

Keep in mind that all children who die in the womb, miscarry, or live up to a certain age go to heaven. However, after you reach a certain age, you must choose to receive Christ or not to get into heaven, [John 3:16]. Amen.

Do lust, adultery, pornography, sexual fantasies, stinking thinking, and any form of sex outside of marriage have consequences?

Yes.

For David the consequences were the following:

1. The death of his unborn child he conceived in an affair with Bathsheba [2 Sam. 12:15–23].
2. His wives being disgraced in public [2 Sam. 12:11–12].
3. Conflict (the sword never leaving his house—[see 2 Sam. 12:10]).

Do lust, adultery, pornography, sexual fantasies, stinking thinking, and any form of sex outside of marriage have consequences for us today?

Yes, they do. God's word **does not** change. He is the same yesterday, today, and forever, and so is His word [Heb. 13:8]. The Ten Commandments of the Old Testament are repeated in the New Testament [Rom. 13:8–10; Matt. 22:37; 1 Cor. 8:3], and one must keep them in order to walk in righteousness.

Some of the consequences of lust, adultery, pornography, and any form of sex outside of marriage are the following:

1. Loss of innocence (this should be kept until one is married). Keeping the marriage bed undefiled [Heb. 13:4].
2. Sexually transmitted diseases
3. Addictions, bondage, oppression (pornography, drugs, and so on)
4. Pregnant at a young age
5. Defiling oneself (through committing sexual immorality; [1 Cor. 6:18.])
6. Disobeying God [1 Thess. 4:3–5; for it is God's will for you to be kept pure or refrain from sexual immorality]
7. Hurting your relationship with God and others
8. Breaking your fellowship with God
9. Perishing (separation from God; [Eph. 5:5])

Contrary to what the world wants you to believe, **lust cannot be satisfied.**

Just like needing a higher dosage to get the same effect each time a person shoots up drugs, lust works the same way. You need more and more, and more and more, to satisfy you, each time you surrender to lust, until your sin consumes you, and you no longer control your appetite; it controls you. You'll need a bigger amount (of lust through pornography, sexual immorality, etc.) just to satisfy your need, when it only took a small amount (dosage) before. **This is lust, a pleasure seeker, a soul defiler, and soul devourer.** (The Lord revealed.) Amen.

One needs to be careful and **repent**. (*Repent* means to change your thinking, turn from your wicked ways, and ask God for forgiveness. In Jesus name, amen.)

In the end, lust (one's appetite, carnal desire) is something that cannot be satisfied, and ends up consuming anyone who repeatedly gives into it. If not repented of, the one who continuously gives into their carnal lusts and worldly desires (appetites) will perish (be separated from God forever). (The Lord revealed.) Amen.

God has spoken, He has seen, He watches, He knows, He intervenes, and David (being held accountable by God for his wrongdoing) received the punishment and consequences for his sins.

In the end, David repented, turned from his wicked ways, and was gifted a promise [see 2 Sam. 12:24–25]. So must we repent. Amen.

Pure Heart Prayer

This prayer can be prayed each day or whenever one is facing temptation.

Just like any other prayer, one must have faith and believe that what you are saying, you will receive. This is not just a saying, nor is this an "out" every time you sin. You have to really mean what you pray (the author's mother taught her).

You have to mean what you say; you cannot just mouth empty words you neither believe nor care for. You must mean it with all your heart, before you see the results. (The Lord revealed.) Amen. ☺

I pray this prayer below helps you along your journey as you learn more of Jesus, and seek to be more like Him daily. In Jesus name, amen.

Here is the pure heart prayer:

"Create in me a clean heart, O God, and keep my thoughts and heart pure and my mind stayed on you. In Jesus name, amen."

If you have not received Jesus Christ as your Lord and Savior or if you wish to rededicate your life to Him, please read the prayer below aloud, believe, and receive it in your heart [1 John 1:7, 9]

"Lord, I come before you today at the cross to confess to You that I'm a sinner in need of a Savior. Lord, please forgive me of all my sins, and cleanse me of all unrighteousness, wash me with Your blood that I may be forgiven, cleanse me so that I may be whiter than snow. Come into my heart today, as I acknowledge You as my Lord and Savior. I thank You for all that You have done for me on the cross. I thank You for receiving me. I'm now Your child, a new creation. In Jesus holy name, amen."

To maintain living the victorious Christian life, Jesus died for you to live. Seek to learn and practice spiritual warfare to help you endure temptation, overcome the flesh, and fight/war against the enemy when needed. Please see pages 340–410 on spiritual warfare. Amen.

To God give all the honor, all the glory, all the credit, and all the praise. Bless Your holy name. In Jesus name, amen.

My Body—The Temple of the Holy Spirit

The Lord revealed this title. Amen.

Temple? A temple? As you ponder this word, what comes to mind? Are you thinking of the temple of Solomon? What a temple it was, filled with grandeur, beauty, worship, sacrifice, and praise. No other temple can be compared to the one King Solomon built for the Lord [2 Chron. 3–6]. (The floor plan of Solomon's temple is found on www.templemount.org.)

Within the temple of Solomon sat three chambers. The first was called the Outer Court. The second one was the Inner Court, and the third one was named the Holy of Holies. Each court told you how far you could go.

The **Outer Court** was where the people could dwell to witness the sacrifice to the Lord. The **Inner Court** is where the priests dwelled, offering sacrifices and prayers (into the heart) and incense as a sweet-smelling aroma, into the nostrils of God. The last chamber was the **Holy of Holies** where God dwelled. Only the High Priest of Israel could enter into this chamber once a year to make atonement for his sins and the sins of Israel.

How does the temple of Solomon tie in with our human bodies? Do you not know that your body is the temple of the Holy Spirit? [1 Cor. 6:19] Then your body, being a temple, has three chambers too.

How?

First is the Outer Court, or what we call the flesh.

The flesh (the Lord revealed) is: the sinful nature of man.

This part of the human body is tempted, and easily falls into sin. Amen.

Second is the Inner Court, or what many call the soul.

The soul, (the Lord revealed), is: where our thoughts, intentions, heart, and motives lie.

This part of man is easily deceived and where sin and corruption begin. Amen.

The last chamber is the Holy of Holies, or what we call the Spirit.

The Spirit, (the Lord revealed), is: where the perfection of God dwells. Amen.

Upon receiving Christ as Lord and Savior, the Holy Spirit indwells you, and the Spirit part of man becomes whole (perfect), holy (set apart), and sacred to the Lord. This is where the Holy Spirit (dove) dwells. (The Lord revealed.) Amen.

(On the next page is a diagram of the tabernacle of Moses. The temple of Solomon was patterned after this. Amen.)

The Tabernacle of God

Exodus 26

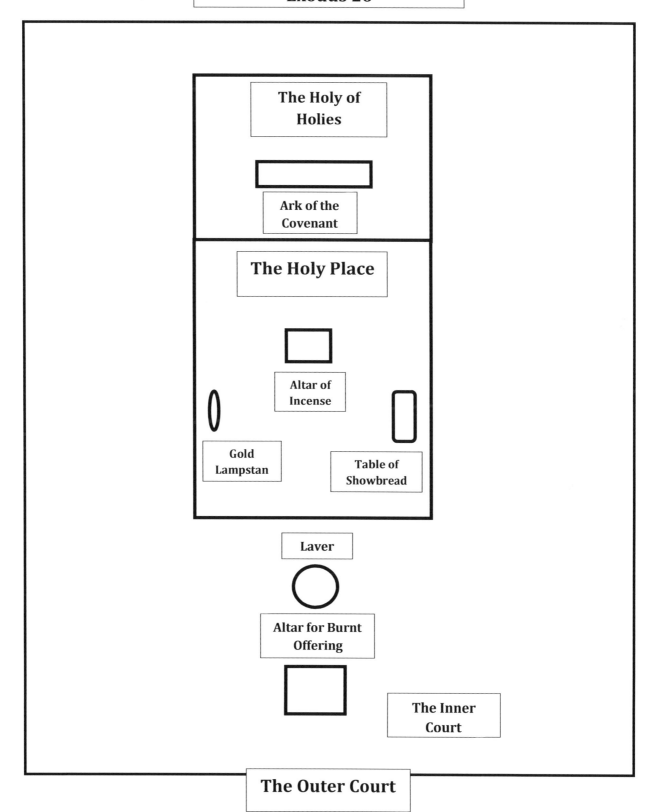

The Holy of Holies

Ark of the Covenant

The Holy Place

Altar of Incense

Gold Lampstan

Table of Showbread

Laver

Altar for Burnt Offering

The Inner Court

The Outer Court

The Lord revealed to draw the Tabernacle of God and pair it with this activity. Amen.

The Body—The Temple of the Holy Spirit

Draw the body. Draw the soul, and draw the Spirit. (The Lord revealed for you to draw the body, soul, and Spirit. Amen.)

Compare the tabernacle of God [Exodus 26] to the human body (which is the temple of the Holy Spirit). What stands out to you? How are they similar? How are they different?

_____

_____

_____

_____

_____

_____

_____

_____

_____

_____

_____

_____

_____

_____

_____

_____

_____

Does God dwell in your spirit (the Holy of Holies)? If not, would you like for Him to? Repeat aloud and believe this short prayer:

"Lord, I come before you today to confess to You that I'm a sinner in need of a Savior. Lord, please forgive me of all my sins, and cleanse me of all unrighteousness, wash me with Your blood that I may be forgiven, cleanse me so that I may be whiter than snow. Come into my heart today, as I acknowledge You as my Lord and Savior. I thank You for receiving me. I'm now Your child, a new creation. In Jesus holy name, amen."

The Temple, the Courts, the Heavens, the Ark, and God

Three Chambers—Three Floors

(The Lord revealed this to the author during prayer on October 7, 2014.) Amen.

The **Outer Court** symbolizes the earth, the lowest heaven, or the first heaven. The first heaven or earth is where the people dwell. (People outside the priesthood remained in the Outer Court and could not enter the inner court of the temple.) This also represents the first floor or chamber in the temple of Solomon and the first floor of the Ark Noah built.

The **Inner Court** symbolizes the second heaven or parts of space. This is the place where fallen angels and principalities try to take control and battle with the armies (angels) of the living God. The Inner Court is also the place where incense were set up to false gods or idols (during the time of idolatry in Israel), near the altar of incense to the **true God** that sits within the holy place of the temple of God. Amen. Behind every idol or false god is a demon. Amen. (The Lord revealed.) Wow! What do you see in any pagan country today where they worship false gods or idols? Incense being burned. Wow! (The Lord revealed.) Amen. This floor also represents the second chamber or floor in the temple of Solomon and the second floor of Noah's Ark.

The **Holy of Holies** represents the third heaven, the highest heaven; the place where God dwells. Before Jesus's finished work on the cross, no man could enter into the third heaven. Similarly, no man, except the High Priest, could enter the Holy of Holies until the Day of Atonement. On the Day of Atonement only the High Priest could enter this chamber, but before he entered, he had to cleanse himself from all sin, through an atoning sacrifice, [see Leviticus 16]. (The Lord revealed.) Amen.

Now the veil [Exodus 26:33; Matthew 27:51] that separated man from God has been torn down by the **blood of Jesus**, and all mankind are welcome into this chamber (the Holy of Holies) when we receive Jesus Christ as Lord and Savior. [John 3:16] (The Lord revealed.) Amen. This last chamber represents the third chamber or floor of the temple of Solomon and the third floor of the Ark of Noah.

The first, second, and third floor of Noah's Ark symbolizes the first, second, and third heaven and the Father, Son, and Holy Spirit. The Lord revealed. Amen.

To get man from the lowest heaven or earth to the highest heaven or third heaven, **Jesus**, Who lived in the third heaven or highest heaven, had to become man and come down to the lowest heaven or earth. Then He had to pass through the second chamber or Inner Court through the priesthood, to tear down the wall of separation that kept us out of the third heaven. Wow! Amen!

The Outer Court, Inner Court, and the Holy of Holies

The **Outer Court** symbolizes the Holy Spirit (the Holy Spirit moves throughout the earth), and it is the Holy Spirit who convicts man of sin, leading man to receive Jesus Christ as Lord and Savior [John 16:8].

The **Inner Court** symbolizes Jesus, because He is our High Priest, Who daily makes intercession for us [Heb. 4:14–16; Heb. 7:25].

The **Holy of Holies** is the Father, because no man can come to the Father except through Jesus Christ [John 14:6]; Jesus is the Inner Court, and one has to pass through the Inner Court to get to the Holy of Holies. There is no other way in, just like there is no other way into heaven or to the Father, but through Christ Jesus. (The Lord revealed.) Amen.

His Word Never Changes

Do not compromise!

Do not throw away your morals, your values, your convictions, and the truth of God's word for the sake of pleasure, lust, or sin.

Too many Christians are compromising their morals and values for the sake of sin (having sex outside of marriage and defiling the marriage bed). Not so with you!

Too many people and Christians are addicted to porn (this is sin). Not so with you!

Sin is still sin. Repent, **honor God**, and honor the marriage bed.

God's word **never** changes! God's word still stands! God's word is true! And what was true then is true now. Amen.

Remember Who You Are in Christ			
Dwell; meditate on the word of God. (Please look up each scripture. Amen.)			
2 Corinthians 5:17, 21	John 1:12	Romans 12:2	Romans 6:18
1 Peter 2:9	John 15:5	Ephesians 2:10	Colossians 3:12
1 Corinthians 6:20	1 Peter 2:5	2 Corinthians 2:15	1 Corinthians 3:16

Overcome

The consequences of sin are too great. Amen.

Overcome lust, sexual immorality, and adultery.

Pray in this manner with faith:

"Heavenly Father, give me more passion for you. In Jesus name, amen."

(Pastor Robert Morris revealed in one of his sermons that one way to overcome lust, sexual immorality, and adultery is to have more passion for God. This drives out the lust for other things. Amen.)

Pray this prayer with faith:

"Heavenly Father, I confess that I'm a sinner. I confess I have [tell God what you have done]. Forgive me. Cleanse me with your blood and make me a new person. Give me more passion for you. In Jesus name, amen."

Turn to the word of God. Begin to develop a habit of reading the word of God daily. His word provides peace, stillness, hope, strength, deliverance, healing, and love, and reveals the promises of God. Amen.

Jesus is the Word, and the Word is life. Amen.

Believe His word, speak His word, receive His word, think on His word, and apply the word of God to your life, and you will see a change in your life and results. (The Lord revealed.) Amen.

Renew your mind using the **Battle of the Mind** strategy on page 58 and by asking the Holy Spirit to replace your thoughts with His.

Pray with faith: "Holy Spirit, think through me. In Jesus name, amen."

The Holy Spirit needs your cooperation in this massive effort to renew your mind, so do your part by renewing your mind with the word of God and He will do His. Amen.

Overcome with **praise and worship**

Praise lifts your focus off the problem and onto the presence of God. Learn more about worship and what true worship is by reading **"The Art of Worship"** on page 48. Amen.

Overcome by **speaking** in your prayer language (tongues). Speaking in tongues builds you up [1 Cor. 14:4]. Amen.

If you need more help, use the strategies outlined in the section on spiritual warfare on pages 340–410.

Do not internalize your struggles, troubles, or hardships when you are struggling with lust, sexual immorality, or adultery. Seek help immediately and tell a parent, teacher, youth counselor, youth pastor, or other trusted adult what you are struggling with. They can provide you with any help or assistance you need.

Also, confess your heart to God and receive His love and healing. Amen.

Open up your mouth and speak. Amen.

If you have overcome adultery and are wondering what to do next, talk with your spouse, and consider marriage counseling and other options to help reconcile your marriage and to help your family heal. (The Lord revealed.) Amen.

Overcome pornography

If you are addicted to pornography or someone you know is, please visit www.drdougweiss.com to purchase the book *Born for War* and to receive advice, counseling, downloads, and intensives that can help you overcome it.

Do not internalize your struggles with pornography. Seek help immediately and tell a parent, teacher, youth counselor, youth pastor, or other trusted adult what you are struggling with. They can provide you with the help and assistance you need.

Cherish Your Body

You are a chosen generation, a royal priesthood, His holy nation, and precious in the sight of God [1 Pet. 2:9]. Amen.

Cherish your body. Do not defile yourself with lust, sex outside of (or before) marriage, or pornography. Treasure yourself, and honor your body—the temple of the Holy Spirit—whom you have from God. You are not your own [1 Cor. 6:18–20]. Amen.

Treasure yourself. Amen.

What if I messed up? Is it too late?

Certainly not!

When you confess your sins, God is faithful and just to forgive your sins and cleanses you from all unrighteousness. [1 John 1:9] Amen.

In this manner pray with faith:

"Lord, I come before you today to confess to You that I'm a sinner in need of a Savior. Lord, please forgive me of all my sins, and cleanse me of all unrighteousness, wash me with Your blood that I may be forgiven, cleanse me so that I may be whiter than snow. Come into my heart today, as I acknowledge You as my Lord and Savior. I thank You for receiving me. I'm now Your child, a new creation. In Jesus holy name, amen."

Receive Christ today, and change, and grow into the likeness of Christ daily. Amen.

Become a new creation in Christ daily [2 Cor. 5:7]. Amen.

Accountability

Hold yourself accountable.

Accountability means holding yourself responsible.

Set up boundaries (rules or guidelines, according to www.wikipedia.com) and list them. Here are a few examples:

1. Not getting involved sexually with another person before marriage.
2. Not viewing inappropriate conduct on television, in movies, and so on.
3. Not going out alone with a significant other.
4. Not replaying inappropriate thoughts or images in your mind.

Setting up boundaries can help you overcome any temptations you might be facing in the present or in the future.

Ask a close friend, parent, counselor, or youth pastor (pick someone you trust) to hold you accountable to help you overcome temptations as well. Talk with them, come up with a list of boundaries together, and check in with them each week or each month to see your progress. They can help encourage you, advise you, answer any questions, pray with you, join in and set up boundaries for themselves too, and become a listening ear. Knowing that someone else is holding you accountable (not just yourself) can help you further overcome sins such as lust, sex before marriage, and pornography.

Do your part to overcome. Amen.

Heart Issues

Self-Examine

It is your responsibility to examine your own heart and ask yourself why. Why are these issues in my heart?

After you ask yourself why and examine yourself; **repent, change, and grow**. Amen.

(This section was revealed by the Lord and inspired by Kevin Harney's book *Leadership from the Inside Out. Amen.*)

Heart Issues, Part 1

Guard your heart with all diligence, for out of it issues the wellsprings of life [Prov. 4:23].

Heart Issues			
Hatred	Anger/rage	Prejudice/racism	Murder in the heart
Boastful	Brutal	Unloving	Despiser of God
Without self-control	Treacherous	Rash (stubborn)	Deceptive
Corrupt	Filled with carnal desires, appetites (lusts)	Led by the flesh (does what is right in one's own eyes)	Unholy
Unrighteous	Violent	Quarrelsome	Gossiper (slanderer)
Foolish	Wicked	Evil-minded	Unmerciful
Untrustworthy	Inventor of evil things	Backbiters	Haters of God
Unthankful	Undiscerning	Covetousness	Divisions
Enmity/conceit	Impurities	Sorcery	Rivalries, pride, arrogance

Heart issues are the issues that defile the heart. (The Lord revealed.) Amen.

"For out of the heart proceed evil thoughts, murders, adulteries, fornications, thefts, false witness, blasphemies. These are *the things*, which defile a man," [Matt. 15:19–20 NKJV].

Defilement comes from within. Amen.

Examine yourself; repent, change, and grow.

Ask yourself, are one or more of these heart issues in my heart? If so, **confess** them to God by praying this prayer with faith:

"Heavenly Father, I confess I have [tell God what heart issue(s) are in your heart] in my heart. Forgive me, for I have sinned against you. Remove these heart issues from me and cleanse my heart of all defilement. In Jesus name, amen."

It takes time, but you will see the results of God delivering you from each heart issue. Amen.

When and if the enemy tries to attack or trick you into believing you have not been forgiven (doubt) or that you will never be set free from your heart issues, immediately cast down his lies. Put on the helmet of salvation (see the "**Whole Armor of God**" in the section on spiritual warfare, on page 353), and seek to renew your mind daily (use the **Battle of the Mind** strategy on page 58.)

Have faith, trust, and believe that God will come through for you. Always remember, **Jesus loves you**! Amen.

Keep your heart cleansed from defilement.

Turn to the word of God. Begin to develop a habit of reading the word of God daily. His word provides peace, stillness, hope, strength, deliverance, healing, and love, and reveals the promises of the word of God. Amen.

Jesus is the Word, and the Word is life. Amen.

Believe His word, speak His word, receive His word, think on His word, and apply the word of God to your life, and you will see a change in your life and results. (The Lord revealed.) Amen.

Renew your mind by using the **Battle of the Mind** strategy on page 58 and by asking the Holy Spirit to replace your thoughts with His.

Pray with faith: "Holy Spirit, think through me. In Jesus name, amen."

The Holy Spirit needs your cooperation in this massive effort to renew your mind, so do your part by renewing your mind with the word of God and He will do His. Amen.

Praise and worship. Praise lifts your focus off the problem and onto the presence of God. Learn more about worship and what true worship is by reading **"The Art of Worship"** on page 48. Amen.

Begin **speaking** in your prayer language (tongues). Speaking in tongues builds you up [1 Cor. 14:4]. Amen.

If you need more help, use the strategies outlined in the section on spiritual warfare on pages 340–410.

Do not internalize your struggles, troubles, or hardships when you are struggling with any heart issue. Seek help immediately and tell a parent, teacher, counselor, youth counselor, youth pastor, or other trusted adult what you are struggling with. They can provide you with any help or assistance you need.

Also, confess your heart to God and receive His love and healing. Amen.

Open up your heart and speak. Amen.

Heart Issues, Part 2

Guard your heart with all diligence, for out of it issues the wellsprings of life [Prov. 4:23].

Heart Issues			
Resentment	Bitterness toward God and/or man	Self-pity/victim mentality	Feel unworthy
Feel worthless	Feel unloved or unwanted	Lost	Unforgiveness
Loneliness	Feel rejected	Feel ugly, poor self-image, low self-worth or low self-esteem	Feel betrayed
Feel ashamed	Wounded	Insecurities	Full of fear
Troubled	Strife or malice	Emptiness	Feel unaccepted or isolated
Envy or jealousy	Selfishness	Feel trapped or vulnerable	Etc.

These heart issues pollute the soul. (The Lord revealed.) Amen.

Let go. Let go of all the troubles, the fears, the wounds, the insecurities, the low self-esteem, the low self-worth, the selfishness, vulnerability, envy, and strife. Let it all_go. Amen.

"Cast your burden on the LORD, And He shall sustain you;" [Ps. 55:22 NKJV].

Come to Me, all who are weary and heavy laden and I will give you rest [Matt. 11:28].

Rest from your troubles, your strife, your hurt, your pain, your fear, your insecurities, your suffering, your sorrow, your wounds and more...

In this manner pray with faith:

"Heavenly Father, I confess I have these heart issue(s) in my heart. [Tell God what they are.] Forgive me for holding them in my heart so long. I let it all go, believing that You will deliver me, sustain me, and cleanse my heart of all pollutants. In Jesus name, amen."

It takes time, but you will see the results of God delivering you from each heart issue. Amen.

When and if the enemy tries to attack or trick you into believing you have not been forgiven (doubt) or you will never be set free from your heart issues, immediately cast down his lies. Put on the helmet of salvation (see the "**Whole Armor of God**," in the section on spiritual warfare on page 353), and seek to renew your mind daily (use the **Battle of the Mind Strategy** on page 58).

Don't take back any heart issues you have already let go to God.

Have faith, trust, and believe that God will come through for you. Always remember **Jesus loves you**! Amen.

Keep your heart cleansed from pollutants.

Turn to the word of God. Begin to develop a habit of reading the word of God daily. His word provides peace, stillness, hope, strength, deliverance, healing, and love, and reveals the promises of God. Amen.

Jesus is the Word, and the Word is life. Amen.

Believe His word, speak His word, receive His word, think on His word, and apply the word of God to your life, and you will see a change in your life and results. (The Lord revealed.) Amen.

Renew your mind using the **Battle of the Mind** Strategy on page 58 and by asking the Holy Spirit to replace your thoughts with His.

Pray with faith: "Holy Spirit, think through me. In Jesus name, amen."

The Holy Spirit needs your cooperation in this massive effort to renew your mind, so do your part by renewing your mind with the word of God and He will do His. Amen.

Praise and worship. Praise lifts your focus off the problem and onto the presence of God. Learn more about worship and what is worship is by reading **"The Art of Worship"** on page 48. Amen.

Begin **speaking** in your prayer language (tongues). Speaking in tongues builds you up [1 Cor. 14:4]. Amen.

If you need more help, use the strategies outlined in the section on spiritual warfare on pages 340–410.

Do not internalize your struggles, troubles, or hardships when you are struggling with any heart issue. Seek help immediately and tell a parent, teacher, counselor, youth counselor, youth pastor, or other adult what you are struggling with. They can provide you with any help or assistance you need.

Also, confess your heart to God and receive His love and healing. Amen.

Open up your heart and speak. Amen.

Overcome Heart Issues, Parts 1 and 2

If you are still struggling with any heart issue...

Overcome and stand!

Take a stand. Even when you see those around you participating in sinful or harmful behavior (such as heart issues), regardless of whether they are your family members, friends, or peers, you don't have to!

Take a stand [Gal. 5:1], and overcome [Rom. 12:21].

Overcome by doing right and being an example for others to follow.

- Live in such a way that many will see and know that you are a follower of Christ [1 Pet. 2:12, 15; 3:15–16]. "Let your light so shine before men, that they may see your good works and glorify the Father in heaven." [Matt. 5:16 NKJV].

Overcome by speaking positively:

- "Death and life *are* in the power of the tongue," [Prov. 18:21 NKJV]. Speak life, speak positively, even when loved ones, friends, or peers speak against you, talk bad about you, and speak down or negatively toward you. Continue to speak life, cast down word curses, bless those who curse you, do good to those who wrong or hate you and pray for those who mistreat you [Luke 6:27–28, 35–36; Rom. 12:14–21]. Amen.

Remembering this:

- All things will work out for the good, to those who love God and are called according to His purpose [Rom. 8:28].
- Have faith in God, trust and receive that He will come through for you. Amen.
- **Jesus loves you!**

Use these strategies to overcome and stand. Use them as often as you need to, **never give up**, and you will receive the victory. Amen.

If you need more help, use the strategies outlined in the section on spiritual warfare on pages 340–410.

If you still need help or suspect there's demonic activity involved in your situation, please **speak** to your pastor, youth pastor, or someone who specializes in deliverance and spiritual warfare, and follow their instructions.

Never give up, stand, and overcome! Amen.

Having done all, to stand [Eph. 6:13].

Overcome

Overcome heart issues with **love.**

Choose to love your neighbor as yourself.

Love covers all sins [Prov. 10:12]. Amen.

This love is accomplished through you, with the help of the Holy Spirit.

Ask the Holy Spirit to love through you daily, in Jesus name; ask Him with faith, so you can learn to love your neighbor as yourself. Amen.

Overcome heart issues with **confession and prayer.**

Use the prayers outlined in each section on heart issues. Keep in mind, you only need to pray once; after you pray, praise and thank God that you believe He will answer your prayers. This pleases God. Amen.

Overcome heart issues with the **name of Jesus.**

Please refer to the section on spiritual warfare on page 374 to see how to use the name of Jesus and to learn about the power that's in the name of Jesus [Hebrews 2:5–8; Matthew 28:18]. Amen.

Overcome heart issues with the **word of God.**

The word of God will not return void [Isa. 55:11]. Once you speak the word and believe what you say, you will have what you say. Amen.

Overcome heart issues with **service.**

Begin to see how you can meet the needs of others. Volunteer your time and service for others (with adult supervision and/or permission). Give back to those in need and make a difference. Amen.

Have faith in God [Mark 11:22, 24]. Amen.

Bitterness; Resentment

Do not keep hold of bitterness or resentment in your heart. Get rid of it. Amen.

Bitterness, according to www.merriam-webster.com, is a state of feeling "angry and unhappy, because of unfair treatment; causing painful emotions felt or experienced in a strong and unpleasant way."

Resentment, according to www.merriam-webster.com, is "a feeling of indignant displeasure or persistent ill will at something regarded as a wrong, insult, or injury."

Scriptures on Resentment

"Get rid of all bitterness, rage and anger, brawling and slander, along with every form of malice." [Eph. 4:31 NIV].

"And whenever you stand praying, if you have anything against anyone, forgive him, that your Father in heaven may also forgive you your trespasses." [Mark 11:25 NKJV].

"looking carefully lest anyone fall short of the grace of God; lest any root of bitterness springing up cause trouble, and by this many become defiled;" [Heb. 12:15 NKJV].

"Pursue peace with all *people*, and holiness, without which no one will see the Lord:" [Heb. 12:14 NKJV].

Scriptures on Bitterness

"Let all bitterness, wrath, anger, clamor, and evil speaking be put away from you, with all malice. And be kind to one another, tenderhearted, forgiving one another, even as God in Christ forgave you." [Eph. 4:31–32 NKJV].

"For if you forgive men their trespasses, your heavenly Father will also forgive you. But if you do not forgive men their trespasses, neither will your Father forgive your trespasses." [Matt. 6:14–15 NKJV].

"Do not say, "I will recompense evil"; Wait for the LORD, and He will save you." [Prov. 20:22 NKJV].

"So then, my beloved brethren, let every man be swift to hear, slow to speak, slow to wrath; for the wrath of man does not produce the righteousness of God." [James 1:19–20 NKJV].

"Hatred stirs up strife, But love covers all sins." [Prov. 10:12 NKJV].

"For I see that you are poisoned by bitterness and bound by iniquity." [Acts 8:23 NKJV].

"Be angry and do not sin; do not let the sun go down on your anger," [Eph. 4:26 ESV].

Romans 12:17–21 says; Live peaceably with all men... do not be overcome by evil, but overcome evil with good. [Please read the rest of Romans 12:17–21.] Amen.

Examine yourself; repent, change, and grow. Amen.

To rid yourself of bitterness or resentment, **pray** this prayer with faith:

"Heavenly Father, keep my heart from all defilement and do not allow the root of bitterness to take hold of it. Do not allow resentment to take hold of my heart. I confess I have held bitterness and resentment toward [tell God who] in my heart. Forgive me and save me, O Lord. I need You today. I release it all to You. Set me free. In Jesus name, amen."

Receive His freedom from bitterness and resentment, and do not allow it to return to your heart. Amen.

To keep your heart free from defilement (bitterness or resentment):

Turn to the word of God. Begin to develop a habit of reading the word of God daily. His word provides peace, stillness, hope, strength, deliverance, healing, love, and reveals the promises of God. Amen.

Jesus is the Word, and the Word is life. Amen.

Believe His word, speak His word, receive His word, think on His word, and apply the word of God to your life and you will see change in your life and results. (The Lord revealed.) Amen.

Renew your mind using the **Battle of the Mind** strategy on page 58 and by asking the Holy Spirit to replace your thoughts with His.

Pray with faith: "Holy Spirit, think through me. In Jesus name, amen."

The Holy Spirit needs your cooperation in this massive effort to renew your mind, so do your part by renewing your mind with the word of God and He will do His. Amen.

Praise and worship. Praise lifts your focus off the problem and onto the presence of God. Learn more about worship and what true worship is by reading **"The Art of Worship"** on page 48. Amen.

Begin **speaking** in your prayer language (tongues). Speaking in tongues builds you up [1 Cor. 14:4]. Amen.

If you need more help, use the strategies outlined in the section on spiritual warfare on pages 340–410.

Do not internalize your struggles, troubles, or hardships when you are struggling with bitterness or resentment. <u>Seek help</u> immediately and tell a parent, teacher, counselor, youth counselor, youth pastor, or other trusted adult what you are struggling with. They can provide you with any help or assistance you need.

Also, confess your heart to God and receive His love and healing. Amen.

Open up your heart and speak. Amen.

Covetousness

"You shall not covet your neighbor's house; you shall not covet your neighbor's wife, nor his male servant, nor his female servant, nor his ox, nor his donkey, nor anything that *is* your neighbor's." [Exod. 20:17 NKJV].

To **covet** means "to strongly desire what belongs to someone else."

Covet, according to www.biblehub.com, means "in a bad sense of ordinate, ungoverned selfish desire."

"You desire but you do not have, so you kill. You covet but you cannot get what you want, so you quarrel and fight. You do not have because you do not ask God." [James 4:2 NIV].

Look to Me, says the Lord. I am everything you need, you need not desire nothing else. **Look to Me**, says the Lord. Amen.

Ask of Me, ask Me anything in My Name, with faith, and I will do it [John 14:14]. Amen.

You do not have, because you do not ask. Ask God with faith. Amen.

Be careful you do not ask amiss [James 4:3].

Do not lash out and attack others, because of your unmet needs or desires (lusts).

Release them to Me; all your needs, all your unmet needs, all your unmet desires, and all your hidden secrets of the heart. Give them to Me, **says the Lord**. Amen.

In this manner pray with faith:

"Heavenly Father, I give you all my unmet needs, I give you all my unmet desires, and I disclose these secrets of my heart [tell God all that's on your heart]. Forgive me for having covetousness in my heart. I give it all to You now. In Jesus name, amen."

Ask, believe, and receive [Mark 11:22]. Amen.

Overcome Covetousness

When you strongly desire what belongs to someone else, turn that desire over to God by asking Him to take it instead. He is everything you need. Amen.

Discover the promises of God, one promise is: "And my God shall supply all your need according to His riches in glory by Christ Jesus." [Phil. 4:19 NKJV].

Worry for nothing;

"Therefore I say to you, do not worry about your life, what you will eat or what you will drink; nor about your body, what you will put on. Is not life more than food and the body more than clothing? Look at the birds of the air, for they neither sow nor reap nor gather into barns; yet our Heavenly Father feeds them. Are you not more of value than they? Which of you by worrying can add one cubit to his stature?

"So why do you worry about clothing? Consider the lilies of the field, how they grow; they neither toil nor spin; and yet I say to you that even Solomon in all his glory was arrayed like one of these. Now if God so clothes the grass of the field, which today is, and tomorrow is thrown in the oven, will He not much more clothe you, O you of little faith?

"Therefore do not worry saying, 'what shall we eat?' or 'what shall we drink?' or 'what shall we wear?' For after all these things the Gentiles seek. For your Heavenly Father knows that you need all these things. But seek thee first the kingdom of God and His righteousness, and all these things shall be added unto you. Therefore do not worry about tomorrow, for tomorrow will worry about its own things. Sufficient for the day is its own trouble." [Matt. 6:25–34 NKJV].

Overcome with **love**

Choose to love your neighbor as yourself. Love covers all sins [Prov. 10:12]. Amen. This love is accomplished through you, with the help of the Holy Spirit. **Ask the Holy Spirit to love through you daily, in Jesus name**; ask Him with faith, so you can learn to love your neighbor as yourself. Amen.

Overcome with **confession and prayer**

Use the prayer above. Keep in mind that you only need to pray once; after you pray, praise and thank God that you believe that He will answer your prayers. This pleases God. Amen.

Begin **speaking** in your prayer language (tongues). Speaking in tongues builds you up [1 Cor. 14:4]. Amen.

Overcome with the **name of Jesus**

Please refer to the section on spiritual warfare on page 374 to see how to use the name of Jesus and to learn about the power that's in the name of Jesus [Hebrews 2:5–8; Matthew 28:18]. Amen.

Overcome with **praise**

Praise lifts your focus off the problem and onto the presence of God. Learn more about worship and what true worship is by reading **"The Art of Worship"** on page 48. Amen.

Overcome with the **word of God**

The word of God will not return void [Isa. 55:11]. Once you speak the word of God and believe what you say, you will have what you say. Amen.

Turn to the word of God. Begin to develop a habit of reading the word of God daily. His word provides peace, stillness, hope, strength, deliverance, healing, and love, and reveals the promises of God. Amen.

Jesus is the Word, and the Word is life. Amen.

Believe His word, speak His word, receive His word, think on His word, and apply the word of God to your life, and you will see a change in your life and results. (The Lord revealed.) Amen.

Renew your mind using the **Battle of the Mind** strategy on page 58 and by asking the Holy Spirit to replace your thoughts with His.

Pray with faith: "Holy Spirit, think through me. In Jesus name, amen."

The Holy Spirit needs your cooperation in this massive effort to renew your mind, so you do your part (renewing your mind with the word) and He will do His. Amen.

If you need more help, use the strategies outlined in the section on spiritual warfare on pages 340–410.

Overcome with **service**

Begin to see how you can meet the needs of others. Volunteer your time and service for others (with adult supervision and/or permission). Give back to those in need and make a difference. Amen.

Overcome with **thanksgiving**

Giving thanks brightens your day and your outlook on life. Amen.

Whenever covetousness tries to enter your heart, overcome it.

All of these strategies listed can help you **overcome** covetousness. Amen.

Do not internalize your struggles, troubles, or hardships when you are struggling with covetousness. **Talk** to a parent, teacher, counselor, youth counselor, youth pastor, or other trusted adult about what you are struggling with. They can provide you with any help or assistance you need.

Jealousy and Envy

Jealousy stems from covetousness. Envy surpasses jealousy. Amen.

Jealousy, according to www.merriam-webster.com, is "an unhappy or angry feeling of wanting to have what someone else has."

Envy, according to www.google.com, is "a feeling of discontented or resentful longing aroused by someone else's possessions, qualities, or luck. Desire to have quality, possession, or other desirable attribute belonging to someone else."

"But if you have bitter envy and self-seeking in your hearts, do not boast and lie against the truth. This wisdom does not descend from above, but *is* earthly, sensual, demonic." [James 3:14–15 NKJV].

"For where envy and self-seeking *exist*, confusion and every evil thing are there." [James 3:16 NKJV].

"A sound heart *is* life to the body, But envy *is* rottenness to the bones." [Prov. 14:30 NKJV].

"For love *is* as strong as death, Jealousy as cruel as the grave; Its flames *are* flames of fire, A most vehement flame." [Song of Sol. 8:6 NKJV].

"Do not fret because of evildoers, Nor be envious of the wicked; For there will be no prospect for the evil *man*; The lamp of the wicked will be put out." [Prov. 24:19–20 NKJV].

"You lust and do not have. You murder and covet and cannot obtain. You fight and war. Yet you do not have because you do not ask." [James 4:2 NKJV].

"Wrath *is* cruel and anger a torrent, But who *is* able to stand before jealousy?" [Prov. 27:4 NKJV].

"Do not be overcome by evil, but overcome evil with good." [Rom. 12:21 NKJV].

Reasons People Can Become Jealous or Envious of Others			
The success and achievements of others	Excessive praise of someone else	Material items	Believing your spouse or significant other is giving attention to someone else
Beauty	Insecurities	Fears	Doubting yourself or your abilities
Others flirt with your spouse, or your boyfriend or girlfriend	Lack of attention	Possessiveness	Rejection (lack of acceptance)
Feel threatened	Desiring what someone else has	Unmet needs or desires	

Love is not jealous, nor does it envy [1 Cor. 13:4–8].

Love covers a multitude of sins [1 Pet. 4:8] and overcomes jealousy.

How?

In this manner, pray with faith:

"Heavenly Father, forgive me for being envious and jealous of others. I confess I became envious or jealous because [tell God why]. Deliver me, O Lord, and remove any envy or jealously from my heart. Help me love others, like I love myself. In Jesus name, amen."

Love one another, as **I (Jesus) have loved you** [John 13:34]. Amen.

Insecurity is one of the root causes of jealousy. Unmet needs and desires are two of the root causes of envy. Confess each in the prayer above, seeking to overcome them. Amen.

Free yourself from envy and jealousy. (The Lord revealed.) Amen.

Overcome Jealousy and Envy

Overcome with **love**

Choose to love your neighbor as yourself. Love covers all sins [Prov. 10:12]. Amen. This love is accomplished through you, with the help of the Holy Spirit.

Ask the Holy Spirit to love through you daily, in Jesus name; ask Him with faith so that you can learn to love your neighbor as yourself. Amen.

Overcome with **confession and prayer**

Use the prayer above. Keep in mind, you only need to pray once; after you pray, praise and thank God that you believe He will answer your prayers. This pleases God. Amen.

Begin **speaking** in your prayer language (tongues). Speaking in tongues builds you up [1 Cor. 14:4]. Amen.

Overcome with the **name of Jesus**

Please refer to the section on spiritual warfare on page 374 to see how to use the name of Jesus and to learn about the power that's in the name of Jesus [Hebrews 2:5–8; Matthew 28:18.] Amen.

Overcome with **praise**

Praise lifts your focus off the problem and onto the presence of God. Learn more about worship and what true worship is by reading **"The Art of Worship"** on page 48. Amen.

Overcome with the **word of God**

The word of God will not return void [Isa. 55:11]. Once you speak the word of God and believe what you say, you will have what you say. Amen.

Turn to the word of God. Begin to develop a habit of reading the word of God daily. His word provides peace, stillness, hope, strength, deliverance, healing, love, and reveals the promises of God. Amen.

Jesus is the Word, and the Word is life. Amen.

Believe His word, speak His word, receive His word, think on His word, and apply the word of God to your life, and you will see a change in your life and results. (The Lord revealed.) Amen.

Renew your mind using the **Battle of the Mind** strategy on page 58 and by asking the Holy Spirit to replace your thoughts with His.

Pray with faith: "Holy Spirit, think through me. In Jesus name, amen."

The Holy Spirit needs your cooperation in this massive effort to renew your mind, so do your part by renewing your mind with the word of God and He will do His. Amen.

If you need more help, use the strategies outlined in the section on spiritual warfare on pages 340–410.

Overcome with **service**

Begin to see how you can meet the needs of others. Volunteer your time and service for others (with adult supervision and/or permission). Give back to those in need and make a difference. Amen.

Overcome with **thanksgiving**

Giving thanks brightens your day and your outlook on life. Amen.

Overcome with **wisdom**

Overcome jealousy by coming to the knowledge that we're all on the same team and we're all in this together. There's nothing to be jealous about (God loves each of us equally); we all have different gifts to be used for the glory of God. **Be confident in who <u>you</u> are in Christ. Amen.**

Don't be envious or jealous of someone else who gets blessed with something you wanted or who has the favor of God upon them. Learn how to wait on your blessing and ask God for more of His favor. He will come through for you. Always remember **Jesus loves you!** Amen.

Whenever envy or jealousy tries to enter your heart, overcome it.

All of these strategies can help you overcome jealousy and envy. Amen.

Do not internalize your struggles, troubles, or hardships when you are struggling with jealousy and envy. **Talk** to a parent, teacher, counselor, youth counselor, youth pastor, or other trusted adult about what you are struggling with. They can provide you with any help or assistance you need.

Guilt

This teaching is inspired by Pastor David Kolenda.

Forgive yourself. (The Lord revealed.) Amen.

Cast all your burdens (cares), on Him, because He cares for you [1 Pet. 5:7].

And whenever you stand praying, if you have anything against anyone (or yourself), forgive him (forgive yourself), that your Father in Heaven may also forgive you your trespasses. [Mark 11:25]. Amen.

Guilt, according to www.merriam-webster.com means "responsibility for a crime or for doing something bad or wrong; a bad feeling caused by knowing or thinking that you have done something bad or wrong."

What do you feel guilty about? Is it a past mistake? A failed relationship? Something you believe you've done wrong to someone?

What is keeping you from forgiving yourself?

Let it go. Let go of past hurts, past failures, past wrongs, and past sins. Forgive yourself and turn over whatever is keeping you from doing so to God.

Jesus says, I have borne your griefs and I have carried your sorrows [Isa. 53:4]. You need not hold on to the past. Give everything to Me, says the Lord. Amen.

Come to Me, all who are weary and heavy laden and I will give you rest [Matt. 11:28].

Rest from your troubles, your past hurts, your pain, your guilt, your suffering, your sorrow...

Pray this prayer with faith:

"Heavenly Father, I lay all my feelings of guilt, past hurts, pain, rejection, trouble, wrongs, worries, turmoil, loneliness, emotional suffering, and mental torment at your feet. I believe you bore my griefs and carried my sorrows. Forgive me, as I forgive myself. I receive your freedom and rest. In Jesus name, amen."

Keep everything at His feet, believe, and receive your rest and freedom from guilt. Amen.

It may take some time to heal, but you will see the results of God healing you of your guilt, suffering, pain, and mental torment.

Put your faith in God and receive that He will come through for you. Always remember **Jesus loves you**. Amen.

You are forgiven! Amen.

Continue to say, **"I am forgiven!"** anytime guilt tries to creep back into your thoughts or your heart. Believe what you're saying and receive the word of God [1 John 1:9]. Amen.

Do not internalize your struggles, troubles, or hardships when you are struggling with guilt. **Talk** to a parent, teacher, counselor, youth counselor, youth pastor, or other trusted adult about what you are struggling with. They can provide you with any help or assistance you need.

Unforgiveness

Unforgiveness in the heart is sin.

Unforgiveness, according to www.merriam-webster.com, refers to a state in which you are "unwilling or unable to forgive."

"And whenever you stand praying, if you have anything against anyone, forgive him, that your Father in heaven may also forgive you your trespasses." [Mark 11:25 NKJV].

"Let all bitterness, wrath, anger, clamor, and evil speaking be put away from you, with all malice. And be kind to one another, tenderhearted, forgiving one another, even as God in Christ forgave you." [Eph. 4:31–32 NKJV].

"For if you forgive men their trespasses, your heavenly Father will also forgive you. But if you do not forgive men their trespasses, neither will your Father forgive your trespasses." [Matt. 6:14–15 NKJV].

"Then Peter came to Him and said, "Lord, how often shall my brother sin against me, and I forgive him? Up to seven times?" Jesus said to him, "I do not say to you, up to seven times, but up to seventy times seven. Therefore the kingdom of heaven is like a certain king who wanted to settle accounts with his servants." [Matt. 18:21–23 NKJV].

"Confess *your* trespasses to one another, and pray for one another, that you may be healed. The effective, fervent prayer of a righteous man avails much." [James 5:16 NKJV].

"Now whom you forgive anything, I also *forgive.* For if indeed I have forgiven anything, I have forgiven that one for your sakes in the presence of Christ, lest Satan should take advantage of us; for we are not ignorant of his devices." [2 Cor. 2:10–11 NKJV]. (The *I* in these verses refers to Paul the apostle).

Here are some of the consequences of unforgiveness:			
God will not listen to your prayers	Envy or jealousy	Strife or malice	Health issues
Heart issues	Resentment	Bitterness	Anger or rage
Uncontrollable (unrestrained) tongue	A Hardened Heart	Hinders your blessings	Hinders your prayers
Hinders your spiritual growth	Hinders your walk with God	Keeps you from being forgiven of your sins	Broken fellowship with God
Giving the person you won't forgive control over you	Hatred	Hurting others	Etc.

Get free. Free yourself from any unforgiveness in your heart. Amen.

Examine yourself; repent, change, and grow.

How? Confess any unforgiveness to God and receive His forgiveness and freedom. Amen.

You may be thinking, why? Why should I forgive them when they harmed me, harassed me, or wronged me? Why should I forgive those who trespassed against me? Why? It's simple...Because while you were still a sinner, Christ demonstrated His love for you and died for you [Rom. 5:8], that you might be forgiven, and so that you might be saved [John 3:16].

When we were still in darkness and sin, Jesus died for us; how much more should we forgive someone who has wronged us, when Christ forgave us when we were still in darkness (sin) and considered the enemies of God [Rom. 5:10].

We must forgive our enemies. Amen.

This doesn't mean you are saying their behavior is okay. You forgive them so that you may be forgiven [Matt. 6:14]. Forgiving someone releases their control from over you. Not forgiving someone allows a person to keep their control over you, by keeping you angry and bitter at them. Lastly, you forgive to receive the blessings of

God; no longer being hindered in your walk with Him because of unforgiveness. Amen.

In the end, forgiving those who have trespassed against you blesses you. Amen.

Forgive

In this manner pray with faith:

"Heavenly Father, I forgive [name(s)] for trespassing against me. In Jesus name, amen."

Truly mean it in your heart when you seek to forgive someone. Amen.

If you still need help forgiving someone, **pray** the following prayer with faith:

"Heavenly Father, help me forgive [name(s)]. In Jesus name, amen."

In the end, forgiving those who have wronged you and caused you harm makes you more like Christ, who forgave those who wronged Him [Luke 23:34]. Forgiving is hard, but the benefits outweigh the process. You will be blessed for doing so. Amen.

The benefits of forgiveness are the following: freedom, peace, joy, life, favor, and more. Amen.

I have forgiven them. Now what?

Keep unforgiveness from returning to your heart.

How?

<u>Remain free</u> (from unforgiveness) through the following:

Love

Love your neighbor as yourself [Mark 12:31].

Love is patient, love is kind; loves does not envy; love does not parade itself, is not puffed up, does not behave rudely, does not seek its own, is not provoked, thinks no evil, does not rejoice in iniquity, but rejoices in the truth...love never fails [1 Cor. 13:4–6, 8].

This love is accomplished through you, with the help of the Holy Spirit.

Ask the Holy Spirit to love through you daily, in Jesus name; ask Him with faith, so you can learn to love your neighbor as yourself. Amen.

This will help you: "Love your enemies, do good to those who hate you, bless those who curse you, and pray for those who spitefully use you." [Luke 6:27–28 NKJV].

It may take some time to heal, but you will see the results of God setting you free from unforgiveness. Amen.

Service

Begin to see how you can meet the needs of others. Volunteer your time and service for others (with adult supervision and/or permission). Give back to those in need and make a difference. Amen.

The word of God

The word of God will not return void [Isa. 55:11]. Once you speak the word of God and believe what you say, you will have what you say. Amen.

Turn to the word of God. Begin to develop a habit of reading the word of God daily. His word provides peace, stillness, hope, strength, deliverance, healing, love, and reveals the promises of God. Amen.

Jesus is the Word, and the Word is life. Amen.

Believe His word, speak His word, receive His word, think on His word, and apply the word of God to your life, and you will see a change in your life and results. (The Lord revealed.) Amen.

Renew your mind

Use the **Battle of the Mind** strategy on page 58 and ask the Holy Spirit to replace your thoughts with His.

Pray with faith: "Holy Spirit, think through me. In Jesus name, amen."

The Holy Spirit needs your cooperation in this massive effort to renew your mind, so do your part by renewing your mind with the word of God and He will do His. Amen.

If you need more help, use the strategies outlined in the section on spiritual warfare on pages 340–410.

Praise

Praise lifts your focus off the problem and onto the presence of God. Learn more about worship and what true worship is by reading **"The Art of Worship"** on page 48. Amen.

Using these strategies can help you overcome unforgiveness and keep it out of your heart. Amen.

Do not internalize your struggles, troubles, or hardships when you are struggling with unforgiveness. **Talk** to a parent, teacher, counselor, youth counselor, youth pastor, or other trusted adult about what you are struggling with. They can provide you with any help or assistance you need.

Loneliness

'I feel lonely…'

You are not alone. I am with you, says the Lord. Amen.

"Do not be frightened, and do not be dismayed, for the LORD your **God is with you** wherever you go." [Josh. 1:9 ESV].

"for he has said, "I will **never** leave you nor forsake you." [Heb. 13:5 ESV].

"It is the LORD who goes before you. **He will be with you**; he will not leave you or forsake you. Do not fear or be dismayed." [Deut. 31:8 ESV].

"casting all your anxieties on him, because he cares for you." [1 Pet. 5:7 ESV].

"and lo, I am with you always, *even* to the end of the age." Amen." [Matt. 28:20 NKJV].

"So we may boldly say: "The LORD is my helper; I will not fear. What can man do to me?" [Heb. 13:6 NKJV].

"Fear not, for I *am* with you; Be not dismayed, for I *am* your God, I will strengthen you, Yes, I will help you, I will uphold you with My righteous right hand."" "For I, the LORD your God, will hold your right hand, Saying to you, 'Fear not, I will help you.'" [Isa. 41:10, 13 NKJV].

"And David said to his son Solomon, "Be strong and of good courage, and do *it*; do not fear nor be dismayed, for the LORD God—my God—*will* be with you. He will not leave you nor forsake you, until you have finished all the work for the service of the house of the LORD.'" [1 Chron. 28:20 NKJV].

"Therefore I will look to the LORD; I will wait for the God of my salvation; My God will hear me." [Mic. 7:7 NKJV].

"Nevertheless I *am* continually with You; You hold *me* by my right hand. You will guide me with Your counsel, And afterward receive me to glory." [Ps. 73:23–24 NKJV].

Please read Psalm 91.

I am with you, says the Lord. Receive My word. **You are never alone**. Amen.

Whenever you feel alone, **remember My word** and receive it into your heart as truth. I am with you. I will never leave you nor forsake you. You are mine! **Says the Lord.**

You belong to Me, and **I love you** with an **everlasting love**, **says the Lord.**

Receive Me. (The Lord revealed.) Amen.

Pray this prayer with faith:

"Lord, I come before you today to confess to You that I'm a sinner in need of a Savior. Lord please forgive me of all my sins, and cleanse me of all unrighteousness, wash me with Your blood that I may be forgiven, cleanse me so that I may be whiter than snow. Come into my heart today, as I acknowledge You as my Lord and Savior. I thank You for receiving me. I'm now Your child, a new creation. In **Jesus holy name**, amen."

You have Me, you are never alone. I will never leave you nor forsake you, says the Lord. Amen.

Turn to the word of God. Begin to develop a habit of reading the word of God daily. His word provides peace, stillness, hope, strength, deliverance, healing, love, and reveals the promises of the word of God. Amen.

Jesus is the Word, and the Word is life. Amen.

Believe His word, speak His word, receive His word, think on His word, and apply the word of God to your life and you will see a change in your life and results. (The Lord revealed.) Amen.

Call on the **name of Jesus**. This will increase your awareness of His presence. He is always there [Matt. 28:20]. Amen.

Renew your mind

Use the **Battle of the Mind** strategy on page 58 and ask the Holy Spirit to replace your thoughts with His. **Pray with faith: "Holy Spirit, think through me. In Jesus name, amen."**

The Holy Spirit needs your cooperation in this massive effort to renew your mind, so do your part by renewing your mind with the word of God and He will do His. Amen.

Turning to the word of God, spending time in His presence, and renewing your mind can help you overcome loneliness whenever you start to feel alone. Amen.

Do not internalize your struggles, troubles, or hardships when you are struggling with loneliness. **Talk** to a parent, teacher, counselor, youth counselor, youth pastor, or other trusted adult about what you are struggling with. They can help you. Amen.

Grief

"To everything *there* is a **season**, A time for every purpose under heaven:" [Eccles. 3:1 NKJV]. A time of sorrow…a time of pain…

"A time to weep, And a time to laugh; A time to mourn, And a time to dance;" [Eccles. 3:4 NKJV].

Grief is a normal part of life. (The Lord revealed.) Amen.

Grief is caused by loss, certain events that have occurred during the past, sickness, certain trials, mishaps, mistakes, miscarriages, and more.

However, **grief is for a season**.

Grief should be short-lived; one shouldn't take up residency (remain) in grief. Amen.

Enjoy your life now!

Get fully committed about **Jesus** and live life now to the fullest. Don't get caught up in the things from the past that keep you from enjoying the present. (The Lord revealed.) **Move forward!** (The Lord revealed.) Amen.

God doesn't want you to be sorrowful all the time. He wants you to enjoy your life on this earth. You must move forward. I know it's hard to let go of things from the past, but if you do, you'll enjoy life more. Amen.

Don't let your emotions control you. Gain control over your emotions, and head toward your victory by surrendering your emotions to God.

You must choose to move forward and never give up!

Try not to get bitter, angry, or annoyed over things you cannot undo. Do not get stuck in the past; move forward.

Grief is not meant to remain a part of your life. Grief is for a season. Amen.

Having sorrow in your heart continually is the spirit of grief. The spirit of grief is not sent by God, it's from the devil.

Let go and live! Amen.

Pastor Joyce Meyer said, **"God doesn't want you to waste your life on something you can't do anything about. It's time to go forward."**

Choose to move forward. (The Lord revealed.) Stop remembering what God has forgotten (your past failings, mistakes, and so on). Press on and receive His joy! Amen.

"In this manner, pray with faith:

Heavenly Father, remove this grief and pain from my heart. I give it all to you. I believe you have borne my griefs and carried my sorrows, and I receive your joy. In Jesus name, amen."

It may take some time to heal, but you will see the results of God relieving you from the spirit grief and from your suffering. Amen.

To further overcome grief, please read Sarah Young's devotional book *Jesus Today.*

He has borne your griefs and carried your sorrows [Isa. 53:4].

Hope in God. Amen.

Do not internalize your struggles, troubles, or hardships when you are struggling with grief. Talk to a parent, teacher, counselor, youth counselor, youth pastor, or other trusted adult about what you are struggling with. They can help you. Amen.

Five Ways to Overcome Discouragement

"Hope deferred makes the heart sick," [Prov. 13:12 NKJV].

Discouragement, according to www.google.com, means "a loss of confidence or enthusiasm; dispiritedness."

Discouragement is one of the favorite tools of the enemy. The enemy tries to use discouragement against us to hinder our faith, hinder us from our calling and our blessings, get us to give up, keep us from fulfilling our purpose on earth, get us to lose faith in God, and so on. (The Lord revealed.) Amen.

Not so with you!

Here are five ways to help you overcome and defeat discouragement:

1. **Pour out your heart to God** [Ps. 62:8; Ps. 34:4].
   Disclosing to God everything that's on your heart can help you feel better, build your faith, relieve stress, and more. Even if you don't get an answer right away, it helps to know the matter is laid at God's feet and is in His hands. Amen.

2. **Rest in God** [Matt. 11:28].
   Taking the time to sit and dwell in the presence of God blesses you.

In his sermon on stress, Dr. Charles Stanley lists the benefits of solitude with God, some of which are the following:

- Repairs the damage of stress
- Equips a person to face tough or hard days
- Develops and deepens one's relationship with God
- Protects one's health
- Makes one's busy days more fruitful
- Answers are given
- Strength from God
- Deeper trust in God

- Gives one a sense of peace, joy, and confidence
- It lets one know that God hears and understands
- Remembering what God has done for one in the past can encourage one now and in the future. (The Lord revealed.) Amen.

These are some of the benefits of spending quiet time alone in the presence of God.

3. **Speaking in tongues** (prayer language)
   Speaking in tongues builds you up [1 Cor. 14:4]. Amen. My pastor, Pastor Harris, revealed that speaking in tongues (your prayer language) is God's stimulus, because speaking in tongues energizes you and is an instant lifter of your mind, will, and emotions that you can use 24/7, regardless of your situation. Amen.

4. **Praise and worship** [Ps. 34:4; Ps. 145:1; Luke 19:38-40]
   Praise lifts your focus off the problem and onto the presence of God. Learn more about worship and what true worship is by reading **"The Art of Worship"** on page 48. Amen. This pleases God and blesses you. Amen.

5. **Optimistic thinking** [Rom. 12:2]
   Renew your mind by using the **Battle of the Mind** strategy on page 58 and by asking the Holy Spirit to replace your thoughts with His.

   Pray with faith: "Holy Spirit, think through me. In Jesus name, amen."

   The Holy Spirit needs your cooperation in this massive effort to renew your mind, so you do your part; (renewing your mind with the word) and He will do His. Amen.

   You can destroy and overcome any discouragement that comes against your mind when you begin to focus your thoughts on the things of God. Amen.

These five strategies can help you overcome and defeat discouragement. (The Lord led me to use five for this teaching, because *five* means "grace," according to the Bible.)

May you be blessed and receive God's grace and peace today. In Jesus name, amen.

"Grace be unto you, and peace, from God our Father and from the Lord Jesus Christ." [Phil. 1:2 KJV].

When and if you feel discouraged, **talk** to someone about it. Amen.

Low Self-Esteem; Low Self-Worth

'When I look in the mirror, I see…'

Self-esteem, according to www.google.com, refers to having "confidence in yourself (your own self-worth) or abilities."

Self-worth, according to www.google.com, refers to "one's own value or worth (how you see yourself)."

"I will praise You, for I am fearfully *and* wonderfully made;" [Ps. 139:14 NKJV].

Scriptures to Boost Your Self-Esteem	Scriptures to Boost Your Self-Worth
"You are altogether beautiful, my love; there is no flaw in you." [Song of Sol. 4:7 ESV]. "For you formed my inward parts; You covered me in my mother's womb. I will praise You, for I am fearfully *and* wonderfully made; Marvelous are Your works, And *that* my soul knows very well." [Ps. 139:13–14 NKJV]. "Do not let your adornment be *merely* outward—arranging the hair, wearing gold, or putting on *fine* apparel—rather *let it* be the hidden person of the heart, with the incorruptible *beauty* of a gentle and quiet spirit, which is very precious in the sight of God." [1 Pet. 3:3–4 NKJV]. "Since you were precious in My sight, You have been honored, And I have	"Therefore do not cast (throw) away your confidence, which has great reward. For you have need of endurance, so that after you have done the will of God, you may receive the promise:" [Heb. 10:35–36 NKJV]. Do not be conformed to this world, but be transformed by the renewal of your mind, that by testing you may discern what is the will of God, what is good, and acceptable, and perfect [Rom. 12:2]. You are a chosen generation, a royal priesthood, His holy nation, and precious in the sight of God [1 Pet. 2:9]. "For the LORD sees not as man sees: man looks on the outward appearance, but the LORD looks on the heart." [1 Sam. 16:7 ESV].

loved you;" [Isa. 43:4 NKJV].

For I know the plans I have for you, says the Lord, plans to prosper you and not to harm you, plans to give you a future and a hope [Jer. 29:11].

"So God created man in His *own* image; in the image of God He created him; male and female He created them." [Gen. 1:27 NKJV].

"Behold what manner of love the Father has bestowed on us, that we should be called children of God! Therefore the world does not know us, because it did not know Him." [1 John 3:1 NKJV].

"For we are His workmanship, created in Christ Jesus for good works, which God prepared beforehand that we should walk in them." [Eph. 2:10 NKJV].

"Charm *is* deceitful and beauty *is* passing, But a woman *who* fears the LORD, she shall be praised." [Prov. 31:30 NKJV].

"I have been crucified with Christ; it is no longer I who live, but Christ lives in me; and the *life* which I now live in the flesh I live by faith in the Son of God, who loved me and gave Himself for me." [Gal. 2:20 NKJV].

"All that the Father gives me will come to me, and whoever comes to me I will never cast out." [John 6:37 ESV].

"Truly I understand that God shows no partiality," [Acts 10:34 ESV].

"'You shall love your neighbor as yourself.'" [Mark 12:31 NKJV]. (First you have to love yourself. Amen.)

"Be still, and know that I *am* God;" [Ps. 46:10 NKJV].

"You shall be a crown of beauty in the hand of the LORD, and a royal diadem in the hand of your God." [Isa. 62:3 ESV].

"The Spirit himself bears witness with our spirit that we are children of God, and if children, then heirs—heirs of God and fellow heirs with Christ," [Rom. 8:16–17 ESV].

Meditate on all these scriptures, and begin to see yourself the way God sees you: precious, beautiful, handsome, and beloved. Amen.

Every day both boys and girls are bombarded with the media, billboards, TV ads, movies, computer games, models in magazines and books, friends, peers, models, actors/actresses, singers, and so on, constantly reminding them what the (ever changing), definition of beauty is. This causes them to feel bad about the way they look and lowers their self-esteem and self-worth.

It doesn't have to be that way for you!

Begin to **see yourself the way God sees you**, not the way the world defines beauty.

How? By being transformed by the renewing of your mind. (The Lord revealed.) Amen.

If you can change the way you think, you can change the way you see yourself, and your outlook on life. Amen.

Accept yourself, **love** yourself, and begin to **see** yourself the way God sees you. Amen.

Renew your mind by using the **Battle of the Mind** strategy on page 58 and by asking the Holy Spirit to replace your thoughts with His.

Pray with faith: "Holy Spirit, think through me. In Jesus name, amen."

The Holy Spirit needs your cooperation in this massive effort to renew your mind, so do your part by renewing your mind with the word of God and He will do His. Amen.

Instead of thinking, *I wish I looked like him or her,* say, ***I am fearfully and wonderfully made* [Ps. 139:13].**

Instead of thinking, *I'm not beautiful* or *I'm not handsome,* say, **"For we are His workmanship, created in Christ Jesus for good works, which God prepared beforehand that we should walk in them." [Eph. 2:10 NKJV].**

Instead of thinking, *I'm worthless*, say, **For I know the plans I have for you, says the Lord, plans to prosper you and not to harm you, plans to give you a future and a hope [Jer. 29:11].**

Believe His word, speak His word, receive His word, claim His word, carry His word close to your heart, and stand on His word daily. Amen.

Self-worth is "the sense of one's own value or worth," according to dictionary.com.

Self-worth is essential to man's emotional, spiritual, and social well-being. It is also the driving force for the human spirit. In light of all this, how can one boost one's individual self-worth? By discovering what hinders it. (The Lord revealed.) Amen.

According to Aubrey Malphurs in the book *Developing a Vision for Ministry*, these are the driving factors that hinder an individual's self-worth:

- **Performance:** 'the belief that you must perform to a certain degree or meet a certain standard to feel good about yourself. This is normally fueled by fear of losing, fear of failure, not meeting a person's standards, fear of disappointing those who are counting on you, being a perfectionist, manipulation, an intense desire for success, and the avoidance of risks.'

    One must realize that their value is <u>not</u> based on their performance or performing to a certain degree or a certain standard or criteria of their own or another's.

- **Acceptance:** 'the belief that to feel good about oneself, one must be accepted by others. This includes appearance; we want to look a certain way or act a certain way, to feel accepted by our peers. This stems from a fear of rejection, the desire to be popular or a people pleaser (regardless of the cost), fear of criticism, and so on.'

    One must realize that one's worth and value is **not** dependent upon the acceptance of others or one's appearance. We have already been fully accepted just as we are by God. It is through Christ Jesus that we have the Father's complete and total acceptance [2 Cor. 5:18]. Amen.

    Our true value is based on the **finished work of the cross by Christ Jesus**, remembering that it is His righteousness, not our own, that keeps us in right standing with God.

    The perfect standard (the Law or Torah required) has already been met by **Jesus**, who has met the criteria of **the Father** for our justification (making us right in the sight of God). Through His sacrifice on the cross, we have the Father's complete and total acceptance, and are now reconciled with God the Father [Rom. 5:10]. Amen.

We no longer have to try to meet a certain standard or perform to a certain degree to find our own self-worth, nor is our value dependent upon the acceptance of others or our appearance. That is fruitless (meaningless), because this standard many strive for and the acceptance many desire has already been met through **Christ Jesus**, and now we can see ourselves and value ourselves the way Christ does...priceless. You are so precious to Him that your value is immeasurable. (This definition of *priceless* was inspired by google.com/priceless.) Look to God's word. Amen. Our value is immeasurable because the cost of sin was the **blood of Jesus**, and the **blood of Jesus is priceless.** Amen.

Look to the cross, where Jesus gave His life for you. That is where you will find your **true** value and self-worth. (The Lord revealed.) Amen.

1 John 3:16 says, "By this we know love, because He laid down His life for us." [NKJV]

1 Peter 2:9 says, "But you are a chosen people, a royal priesthood, a holy nation, God's special possession, that you may declare the praises of him who called you out of darkness into his wonderful light." [NIV]

(This information was inspired by Aubrey Malphurs book *Developing a Vision for Ministry*.)

Have faith in God. Amen.

Are you suffering from Low Self-Esteem?

Begin to see yourself the way God sees you. (The Lord revealed.) Amen.

Below is how God sees you:

Redeemed	Forgiven	Chosen	Beloved
Highly favored	Beautiful	Handsome	Transformed
Covered	Blessed	Protected	Kind
Comforted	Faithful	Giving	Mine (says the Lord)
Good	Self-Controlled	Gentle	Tenderhearted
Brave	Clothed in His righteousness		Accepted
Conformed in the likeness of Christ daily			Loved

And more…

That is how Christ sees you. Will you begin to see yourself in the same way?

In this manner, pray with faith:

"Heavenly Father, help me to see myself the way You see me. In Jesus name, amen."

If you are suffering from low self-esteem and low self-worth, begin to **love yourself**.

God commands you to love your neighbor as yourself [Mark 12:31]. Before you can love your neighbor, you first have to love yourself.

Do you love yourself? If not, ask God to help you.

Pray this prayer with faith:

"Heavenly Father, help me to love myself. In Jesus name, amen."

You are fearfully and wonderfully made [Ps. 139:14]. Believe and receive it. Amen.

Overcome

Overcome low self-worth and low self-esteem

You can use the strategies below to help you overcome low self-worth and low self-esteem and keep it out of your heart. Amen.

The word of God

Turn to the word of God. Begin to develop a habit of reading the word of God daily. His word provides peace, stillness, hope, strength, deliverance, healing, love, and reveals the promises of God. Amen.

The word of God will not return void [Isa. 55:11]. Once you speak the word of God and believe what you say, you will have what you say. Amen.

Jesus is the Word, and the Word is life. Amen.

Believe His word, speak His word, receive His word, think on His word, and apply the word of God to your life, and you will see a change in your life and results. (The Lord revealed.) Amen.

Service

Begin to see how you can meet the needs of others. Volunteer your time and service for others (with adult supervision and/or permission). Give back to those in need and make a difference. Amen.

Praise

Praise lifts your focus off the problem and onto the presence of God.

Learn more about worship and what true worship is by reading **"The Art of Worship"** on page 48. Amen.

If you need more help, use the strategies outlined in the section on spiritual warfare on pages 340–410.

Do not internalize your struggles, troubles, or hardships when you are struggling with low self-worth and low self-esteem. **Talk** to a parent, teacher, counselor, youth counselor, youth pastor, or other trusted adult about what you are struggling with. They can provide you with the help and assistance you need.

Encouragement

Life can sometimes feel dull, boring, or as if there's nothing new under the sun [Eccles. 1:9]. **But God has given each of us a plan, a purpose, a future, and a hope for our lives [Jer. 29:11]. He** is the main reason life is worth living. Amen. ☺

Instead of dreading tomorrow, **wake up each day and say, This is the day the Lord has made, I will rejoice and be glad in it [Ps. 118:24].** (The Lord revealed.) Amen.

Four Steps to Overcome Fear

For God has not given us a spirit of fear, but of power, love, and a sound mind [2 Tim. 1:7].

Fear is bondage—a bondage that must be broken. (The Lord revealed.) Amen.

Bound, according to www.dictionary.refrence.com, refers to "the state of being bound by or subjected to external power or control; being tied up, chained."

To be bound is to be subject to control. Do not allow fear to control you. (The Lord revealed.) Amen.

Overcome!

Four steps to overcoming fear:

1. **Identify the problem.**
   What do I fear? Why do I fear it? Where is this fear from? Why?
   For example, does your fear come from a past experience, fear of rejection, fear of the future, or fear of the unknown? Identifying your fear is the first step needed to overcome it.

2. **Confess your fear(s) unto God.**
   Once you have identified your fear, confess it unto God.

   In this manner, **pray** with faith:
   "Heavenly Father, I confess my fear(s) of [tell God your fear(s)]. I believe You have not given me a spirit of fear, but of power, love, and a sound mind. I receive Your freedom from fear today. In Jesus name, amen."

3. **Receive by faith.**
   Once you have confessed your fear(s) unto God, receive your freedom from fear by faith [Mark 11:24].

4. **Turn to the word of God.**
   Spend time reading the Bible, believe what you are reading, and begin to meditate on the scriptures to renew your mind and change your thinking. Changing how you think can help you get rid of fear. Amen.

Trust in God [please read Psalm 56]. Amen.

When and if fear tries to rise against you:

- Use the four-step strategy outlined above to get rid of fear.
- Overcome fear with the word of God.
- Use the **Battle of the Mind** strategy on page 58.
- Use the **spiritual warfare tactics** on pages 340–410.

Do not internalize your struggles, troubles, or hardships when you are struggling with fear. **Talk** to a parent, teacher, counselor, youth counselor, youth pastor, or other trusted adult about what you are struggling with. They can provide you with any help or assistance you need.

Four Ways to Overcome Anger

Be slow to anger, slow to speak, and quick to listen [James 1:19].

Here are the four ways you can overcome anger:

1. **Meditate**
   Begin to meditate on the word of God whenever anger arises within you. ***Meditation*** means "to ponder, dwell on, and to speak aloud repeatedly."

   A few scriptures you can meditate on are the following:
   Psalm 46:10   Philippians 4:13   James 1:19

2. **Praise**
   Praise lifts your focus off the problem and onto the presence of God. Break out in praise whenever you feel anger rising within you. "Set your minds on things above, not things on the earth." [Col. 3:2 NKJV]. Amen.

3. **Talk to God and man**
   Talk to God when you are angry. Tell Him why you are angry, with whom, and what for. God hears you and He will answer you. You just have to take the time to listen for His voice. Amen.

   Talking with God and a youth counselor or youth pastor about your problems (when you are angry) helps to defuse the problem and overcome anger. Talk; do not shout, fight, kick, scream, or yell. Talk with God and man. Amen.

   Pour out your heart to God [Ps. 62:8] and man. Amen.

4. **Lay it all at God's feet and pray in tongues**
    Prayer helps you let go of things and helps you give all your worries, fears, or anger over to God (by laying it at His feet), helping you overcome them. Amen. Praying in tongues builds you up. Amen.

In this manner, pray with faith:

"Heavenly Father, I confess I'm angry at [tell God who you're angry at], because [tell God what you are angry at and why]. I lay all my anger at Your feet. Help me to be slow to anger, slow to speak, and quick to listen. In Jesus name, amen."

You can also pray in your prayer language. Amen.

These are four ways you can overcome anger.

In all these things we are more than conquerors through Christ Jesus! [Rom. 8:37].

Rejection

To **reject**, according to www.dictionary.refrence.com, means "to refuse to accept (someone or something)."

Have you been rejected? Rejected by your parents? Rejected by your peers? Rejected by your friends? Rejected by someone you love? Or rejected by society?

Rejection is a powerful response, with devastating grief, long-lasting effects, and heart-wrenching pain. One of the worst things anyone can experience is rejection. If you have felt rejection, you may have wondered how it can be overcome.

Turn to Me, says the Lord. I bore your griefs and suffered your sorrows [Isa. 53:4].

I have suffered your abandonment, your rejection, your loneliness, your troubles, your emotional suffering, your mental torment... <u>On the Cross</u> I was forsaken by God and man for you, **says the Lord**.

"He is despised and rejected by men, A Man of sorrows and acquainted with grief." [Isa. 53:3 NKJV].

On the cross I (Jesus) cried out, "My God, My God, why have You forsaken Me?" [Matt. 27:46 NKJV].

"Yet it pleased the LORD to bruise Him; He has put *Him* to grief. When You make His soul an offering for sin, He shall see *His* seed, He shall prolong *His* days, And the pleasure of the LORD shall prosper in His hand." [Isa. 53:10 NKJV].

"But He *was* wounded for our transgressions, He *was* bruised for our iniquities; The chastisement for our peace *was* upon Him, And by His stripes we are healed." [Isa. 53:5 NKJV].

I was wounded for you, beaten for you, tried for you, forsaken/rejected for you. And by My stripes, you are healed. (The Lord revealed.) Amen.

Each of My stripes represents an area of healing for your life. One stripe represents suffering. If you are suffering from rejection, emotional suffering, mental suffering or torment; I already bore it all for you, **says the Lord**.

Come to Me, all who are weary and heavy laden and I will give you rest [Matt. 11:28].

Rest from your troubles, your hurt, your pain, your rejection, your suffering, your sorrow…

Pray this prayer with faith:

"Heavenly Father, I lay all my feelings of rejection, emotional suffering, and mental torment, at your feet and receive Your rest. I receive Your acceptance, I receive Your love, and I receive Your healing by Your stripes for my suffering. In Jesus name, amen."

Keep everything at His feet, believe, and receive. Always remember **Jesus loves you!** Amen.

It may take some time to heal, but you will see the results of God healing you of your rejection, wounds, scars, negative emotions, feelings, mental scars, suffering, pain, torment, and more.

Put your faith in God and receive that He will come through for you.

Trust and **believe** His word, and you will see results. Amen.

(The section on seeing results in prayer was inspired by Pastor Terry L. Harris's sermon "Prayer Tips for More Results." Amen.)

Overcome Rejection

Turn to the word of God. Begin to develop a habit of reading the word of God daily. His word provides peace, stillness, hope, strength, deliverance, healing, and love, and reveals the promises of God. Amen.

Jesus is the Word, and the Word is life. Amen.

Believe His word, speak His word, receive His word, think on His word, and apply the word of God to your life, and you will see a change and results. (The Lord revealed.) Amen.

Meditate on scripture

Here is a list of scriptures you can meditate on, to overcome rejection:

Psalm 42	Psalm 43	Psalm 34:17	Romans 8:38–39
John 14:1–2	Isaiah 41:13	Isaiah 41:10	Philippians 4:13
Psalm 118	Romans 5:3–5	Proverbs 3:5–6	Philippians 4:4
Psalm 37:25	Romans 8:26	James 1:2–4	2 Timothy 1:7
Psalm 91	Matthew 11:28–30	Romans 8:28	Jeremiah 29:11
Romans 10:17	Psalm 40:1–3	Psalm 9:9	Deuteronomy 31:8
Psalm 46:10	Matthew 28:20	Deuteronomy 33:27	

Renew your mind

Use the **Battle of the Mind** strategy on page 58 and ask the Holy Spirit to replace your thoughts with His.

Pray with faith: "Holy Spirit, think through me. In Jesus name, amen."

The Holy Spirit needs your cooperation in this massive effort to renew your mind, so do your part by renewing your mind with the word of God and He will do His. Amen.

Overcome rejection with praise and worship

Praise lifts your focus off the problem and onto the presence of God. Learn more about worship and what true worship is by reading **"The Art of Worship"** on page 48. Amen.

Overcome rejection by speaking in your prayer language (tongues).

Speaking in tongues builds you up [1 Cor. 14:4]. Amen.

"As you come to him, a living stone rejected by men but in the sight of God chosen and precious," [1 Pet. 2:4 ESV].

Do not internalize your struggles, troubles, or hardships when you are struggling with rejection. **Talk** to a parent, teacher, counselor, youth counselor, youth pastor, or other trusted adult about what you are struggling with. They can provide you with any help you need.

Popularity

Be not conformed to this world, but be transformed by the renewing of your mind [Rom. 12:2].

You are a chosen generation, a royal priesthood, His holy nation, and precious in the sight of God [1 Pet. 2:9].

"For we are His workmanship, created in Christ Jesus for good works, which God prepared beforehand that we should walk in them." [Eph. 2:10 NKJV].

"I have been crucified with Christ; it is no longer I who live, but Christ lives in me; and the *life* which I now live in the flesh I live by faith in the Son of God, who loved me and gave Himself for me." [Gal. 2:20 NKJV].

"Do not be unequally yoked together with unbelievers. For what fellowship has righteousness with lawlessness? And what communion has light with darkness?" [2 Cor. 6:14 NKJV].

In the end, "If you were of the world, the world would love you as its own; but because you are not of the world, but I chose you out of the world, therefore the world hates you." [John 15:19 ESV].

Popularity, according to www.google.com, means "the state of being like; admired; or supported by many people."

How does being popular differ from the scriptures provided above?

To be popular is the state of being liked by many people; the scriptures are **setting you apart for Christ.** Amen.

Why is being popular so important to you and to others?

Reasons why (some believe) popularity is so important:

Liked	Accepted	Special	Fit in
Looked up to	Embraced	Respected	Status
Feel appreciated	Wanted	A part of something	Catered to
Admired	Important	To be somebody	Identity
On-Top	Loved		

And more…

Hasn't God already said you are all these things and that you don't need popularity to feel this way?

Picture popularity as a ladder that you are climbing up. Every time you climb up a step, you sacrifice one thing. For example, you climb one step up the popularity ladder and in order to be liked, you have to sacrifice certain friendships because according to some people, they don't "fit in." You comply and get rid of certain friends for the sake of popularity. The next step you climb, you sacrifice godly morals, to feel "accepted." Now right is wrong and wrong is right, for the sake of popularity.

On the next step up the ladder of popularity, you sacrifice relationships "to be somebody." The fourth step up the ladder of popularity you sacrifice your relationship with God to be "liked" or "looked up to." The fifth step up the ladder you sacrifice your character to be "on top," the sixth step up the ladder you sacrifice this and that, and so on and so on, until you've come to the top of the ladder and have nothing else left to sacrifice.

You have come to the point where you have traded who you really are for the sake of being popular.

Once you've reached that point, you feel a void, emptiness, meaninglessness, because with no more steps to climb, and no more sacrifices to make, you wonder how you can find meaning in life. (The Lord revealed.) Amen.

You might be saying or thinking, *I feel as though I've reached my end, and everything is utterly meaningless, meaningless. Where can I turn?*

Some turn to:

suicide	drugs	alcohol	harmful relationships
bitterness	crime	envy	pessimistic thinking
resentment	malice	theft	victim mentality
sinful living	hatefulness	jealousy	ways to get more popular
depression	wrong crowd	covetousness	thinking "woe is me"

Not so with you!

Turn to Me instead, **says the Lord.**

Come to Me, all who are weary and heavy laden, and I will give you rest [Matt. 11:28].

Rest from your troubles, your hurt, your pain, your rejection, your suffering, your sorrow…

Pray this prayer with faith:

"Heavenly Father, I confess I have sacrificed [tell God everything that you sacrificed] for the sake of being popular. Forgive me for doing so. Help me to reconcile with those I've mistreated, and please restore to me everything that I've lost. Fill my void and take away my emptiness. I receive Your rest now. In Jesus name, amen."

"Behold, I stand at the door and knock. If anyone hears My voice and opens the door, I will come in to him and dine with him, and he with Me." [Rev. 3:20 NKJV].

All the time, you were taking steps up the ladder of popularity, sacrificing this and that, reaching the top, only to feel a void and emptiness, I was knocking on the door of your heart. Waiting for you to answer **Me**. You may have turned to harmful choices, and nearly gave up on yourself, but I never gave up on you, **says the Lord**.

Turn to Me instead. Only I can fill your void and emptiness. In Me you'll find everything popularity couldn't give you and everything popularity made you sacrifice to receive, **says the Lord.**

If you haven't already, receive Jesus as your Lord and Savior:

"Lord, I come before you today to confess to You that I'm a sinner in need of a Savior. Lord, please forgive me of all my sins, and cleanse me of all unrighteousness, wash me with Your blood that I may be forgiven, cleanse me so that I may be whiter than snow. Come into my heart today as I acknowledge You as my Lord and Savior. I thank You for receiving me. I'm now Your child, a new creation. In Jesus holy name, amen."

You don't need the world's approval to be somebody. You are already somebody in Christ Jesus! Always remember **Jesus loves you!** Amen.

Meditate on these scriptures to transform and renew your mind:

Romans 12:2   1 Peter 2:9   1 Corinthians 6:19–20

Ephesians 2:10   1 Peter 5:8   Romans 8:28–29

Ephesians 4:24   Galatians 2:20   John 15:19

To further renew your mind, use the **Battle of the Mind** strategy on page 58 and ask the Holy Spirit to replace your thoughts with His.

Pray with faith: "Holy Spirit, think through me. In Jesus name, amen."

The Holy Spirit needs your cooperation in this massive effort to renew your mind, so do your part by renewing your mind with the word of God and He will do His. Amen.

If you need more help, use the strategies outlined in the section on spiritual warfare on pages 340–410.

Dare to Be Different!

Instead of climbing the steps of popularity, seek to begin and develop a relationship with God, through prayer, spending time in His word, spending time in His presence, supervised fasting, praise and worship, and attending a Bible-believing, Spirit-filled church.

Don't try to fit in; you are uniquely created and uniquely different from any other person on the face of the earth. (The Lord revealed.) Amen. Wow! That's something to praise God for!

Turn to the word of God. Begin to develop a habit of reading the word of God daily. His word provides peace, stillness, hope, strength, deliverance, healing, and love, and reveals the promises of God. Amen.

Jesus is the Word, and the Word is life. Amen.

Reading and studying the word of God, and applying it to your life, brings change and growth.

Believe His word, speak His word, receive His word, think on His word, and apply the word of God to your life and you will see a change in your life and results. (The Lord revealed.) Amen.

"that you put off, concerning your former conduct, the old man which grows corrupt according to deceitful lusts, and be renewed in the spirit of your mind, and that you put on the new man which was created according to God, in true righteousness and holiness." [Eph. 4:22–24 NKJV].

Dare to be different! Amen.

Do not internalize your struggles, troubles, or hardships when you are struggling with popularity. **Talk** to a parent, teacher, counselor, youth counselor, youth pastor, or other trusted adult about what you are struggling with. They can provide you with the help, advice, and assistance you need.

Doubt

Evangelist Perry Stone reveals four reasons why Christianity is true.

Read 1 Kings 18 (a powerful encounter between the true God and the fake idol Baal). This distinguishes the true Christian faith from fake religions.

Our God answers the prayers of His people [John 16:24]. He answers the prayers of His people to:

- prove He is God;
- that our joy may be full.

Our God is still a miracle-working God!

Here are the four reasons why we believe and know that Jesus is our Savior, His word is true, and Christianity is true:

1. **The power of change** [Heb. 4:12]
   This starts when one becomes convicted by the Spirit of God when you hear a message preached and you are unsaved (living in sin). When someone asks you to pray the sinner's prayer, you pray this prayer of repentance with faith and receive Jesus into your heart.

   After receiving **Jesus,** a <u>change</u> takes place in you.
   Acts 8:1–3; Acts 9, (you see the change that took place in Saul.)
   - Something happens to a person who receives Christ, called the power of change.
   - The power of change works within every country of the world.
   - People who believe the gospel see their lives transformed. Amen.

2. **The power and authority in the name of Jesus**
    Great men and women of faith throughout history have used the name of Jesus to heal the sick, and when they'd pray in the name of Jesus with faith, healings and miracles would take place.

    - The power and influence of the name of Jesus is universal.
      No matter what country you're in, you can use the name of Jesus with faith and receive results.
      You can reach people who know nothing about the Bible. They go to crusades and events and hear the name of Jesus, and suddenly miracles begin to happen and deliverances take place.

      This is the universal power of the name of Jesus.
      This is proof and evidence that the power of the gospel and the power of Christ is ultimately real. In any country you go to, demons recognize the power and the name of Jesus; they know Who you are talking about [see Matthew 28:18; Acts 4:12; Romans 14:11; Romans 10:13; Acts 3; Acts 4:10–12]. Amen.

    Faith is the key to activating the power within the name of Jesus. Amen.

3. **The power of the word of God** [Ps. 119:50; Heb. 4:12]
    The word of God *quickens*, which means "to make alive." In Hebrew, it means the same as it does in the Greek: "to make alive." This reveals that the word of God has energy. It's quick and powerful. It's alive and energized. Amen.

    See Joshua 6. Why is it that preaching the word brings a quickening to people?
    People start to feel something after they hear the word, even if they heard that story of the Bible before.
    These true stories of the Bible are 3,000–4,000 years old.
    [see Genesis; Exodus; Leviticus...]

- We still whoop and holler about these true Bible stories, regardless of when or how often we hear them.

Why? Because the word of God is a living thing. It's not a dead book. **The word of God has life.** Amen. When the word of God is preached at any time, it can produce miracles, signs, and wonders!

4. **The working of the Holy Spirit**
   - We are each given gifts by God and in-filled with the Holy Spirit.
   - Gifts are given by the Holy Spirit to help us work effectively.
   - The Holy Spirit brings faith to the heart.

When the human spirit is taken out of a man, it brings death.

If you take the Holy Spirit out of the church, it's going to be dead, without life, formal, and routine.

The Spirit of God brings life into the church body.

- Likewise, you need the human spirit in your body to continue living.

Jesus sent the Holy Spirit not just as our teacher or our counselor, but as a sign that He was resurrected and alive [John 16:7]. This was proof Jesus was raised from the dead and had gone back to heaven. Without this being done, we wouldn't be able to operate in the gifts of the Spirit. Amen.

These four reasons are absolute proof and evidence, Evangelist Perry Stone provided, that reveals Christianity is true. Amen.

Do not internalize your struggles, troubles, or hardships when you are struggling with doubt. **Talk** to a parent, teacher, counselor, youth counselor, youth pastor, or other trusted adult about what you are struggling with. They can provide you with any help, advice, or assistance you need.

Pride

"Let not the foot of pride come against me," [Ps. 36:11 NKJV].

Pride, according to www.merriam-webster.com, means "a feeling that you respect yourself and deserve to be respected by other people; a feeling that you are more important or better than other people; conceit; boast."

Pride, according to www.dictionary.refrence.com, means "a high or inordinate opinion of one's own dignity, importance, merit, or superiority, whether as cherished in the mind or as displayed in bearing, conduct, etc. To brag on oneself; boastful."

"God resists the proud, But gives grace to the humble." [James 4:6 NKJV].

The serpent deceived Eve in the garden by telling her that if she'd eat from the Tree of Knowledge of Good and Evil, she would be like God. This reveals pride. [Please read Gen. 3:1–6.]

Read about the fall of Lucifer in Isaiah 14:12–15. This reveals pride.

"Everyone proud in heart *is* an abomination to the LORD;" [Prov. 16:5 NKJV].

"Pride *goes* before destruction, And a haughty spirit before a fall." [Prov. 16:18 NKJV].

"Better *to be* of a humble spirit with the lowly, Than to divide the spoil with the proud." [Prov. 16:19 NKJV].

"When pride comes, then comes shame; But with the humble *is* wisdom." [Prov. 11:2 NKJV].

"A man's pride will bring him low, But the humble in spirit will retain honor." [Prov. 29:23 NKJV].

"For all that *is* in the world—the lust of the flesh, the lust of the eyes, and the pride of life—is not of the Father but is of the world." [1 John 2:16 NKJV].

"Be of the same mind toward one another. Do not set your mind on high things, but associate with the humble. Do not be wise in your own opinion." [Rom. 12:16 NKJV].

Love is patient and kind. Love is not jealous or boastful or proud [1 Cor. 13:4].

"A proud *and* haughty *man*—"Scoffer" *is* his name; He acts with arrogant pride." [Prov. 21:24 NKJV].

"A haughty look, a proud heart, *And* the plowing of the wicked *are* sin." [Prov. 21:4 NKJV].

Pride, like lust, has been with us from the beginning. Please read Genesis 3:1–6 and Isaiah 14:12–15. Pride was one of the root causes of man's fall [Gen. 3], and pride is how the devil fell from heaven [Isa. 14:12–15]. Pride was one of the first sins. Amen.

Causes of Pride				
Wealth	Status	Background	Prestige	Power
High achiever	Highly educated	Country of origin	Position; rank	Appearance
Abilities	Believe you're better or higher then someone else	Believe they're holier (without sin)	Good Works	Have everything (not in want or lack)
Never had to struggle in life	Superiority	Career	All about self (selfishness)	High sense of importance; dignity
Popularity (celebrity or royal status)	Believe they deserve respect	Believe they're above others		

Nothing should make you believe that you are better than someone else. (The Lord revealed.) Amen.

Overcome Pride

Overcome pride with humility

Humility, according to www.merriam-webster.com and www.dictionary.refrence.com, means "the state of not thinking you're better than others; modest opinion of one's own importance, rank, etc. Not proud, or arrogant, not thinking yourself better than others, same as humility."

Ask the Holy Spirit to release the fruit of humility (that is already in you, when you receive Christ) into your heart. In Jesus name, amen.

Humility overcomes pride, [1 Pet. 5:6]. Amen

Overcome pride with prayer

Pray this prayer with faith:

"Heavenly Father, I confess I have let the foot of pride come against me. Forgive me, O Lord, and humble me. In Jesus name, amen."

Overcome pride with the name of Jesus

Please refer to the section on spiritual warfare on page 374 to see how to use the name of Jesus and to learn about the power that's in the name of Jesus [Hebrews 2:5–8; Matthew 28:18]. Amen.

Overcome pride with love

"'You shall love your neighbor as yourself.'" [Mark 12:31 NKJV].

Love is patient, love is kind; loves does not envy; love does not parade itself, is not puffed up, does not behave rudely, does not seek its own, is not provoked, thinks no evil, does not rejoice in iniquity, but rejoices in the truth...love never fails [1 Cor. 13:4–6, 8].

This love is accomplished through you, with the help of the Holy Spirit. **Ask the Holy Spirit to love through you daily, in Jesus name**; ask Him with faith, so you can learn to love your neighbor as yourself. Amen.

This will help you; "Love your enemies, do good to those who hate you, bless those who curse you, and pray for those who spitefully use you." [Luke 6:27–28 NKJV].

Overcome pride with service

Begin to see how you can meet the needs of others. Volunteer your time and service for others (with adult supervision and/or permission). Give back to those in need and make a difference. Amen.

Overcome pride with the word of God

The word of God will not return void [Isa. 55:11]. Once you speak the word of God and believe what you say, you will have what you say. Amen.

Turn to the word of God. Begin to develop a habit of reading the word of God daily. His word provides peace, stillness, hope, strength, deliverance, healing, and love, and reveals the promises of God. Amen.

Jesus is the Word, and the Word is life. Amen.

Believe His word, speak His word, receive His word, think on His word, and apply the word of God to your life and you will see a change in your life and results. (The Lord revealed.) Amen.

Renew your mind

Use the **Battle of the Mind** strategy on page 58 and by asking the Holy Spirit to replace your thoughts with His.

Pray with faith: "Holy Spirit, think through me. In Jesus name, amen."

The Holy Spirit needs your cooperation in this massive effort to renew your mind, so do your part by renewing your mind with the word of God and He will do His. Amen.

If you need more help, use the strategies outlined in the section on spiritual warfare on pages 340–410.

Overcome pride with praise

Praise lifts your focus off the problem and onto the presence of God. Learn more about worship and what true worship is by reading **"The Art of Worship"** on page 48. Amen.

Overcome pride with thanksgiving

Giving thanks brightens your day and your outlook on life. Amen.

Also, refer to the **Overcome and Stand** strategy on page 29.

Using these strategies will help you overcome pride and keep it out of your heart. Amen.

Do not internalize your struggles, troubles, or hardships when you are struggling with pride. **Talk** to a parent, teacher, counselor, youth counselor, youth pastor, or other trusted adult about what you are struggling with. They can provide you with any help, advice, or assistance you need.

Selfishness

Loves does not seek its own (no selfish gain); [1 Cor. 13:5].

Selfish and **selfishness**, according to www.merriam-webster.com and www.dictionary.refrence.com, means "concerned excessively with oneself and not concerned for others. Concentrating on one's own advantage, pleasure, or well-being without regard for others, etc. Caring, devoted only for self, concerned about one's own self-interests only. The culture of me, me, me; everything revolves around me."

"even as the Son of Man came not to be served but to serve, and to give his life as a ransom for many." [Matt. 20:28 ESV].

"'You shall love your neighbor as yourself.'" [Mark 12:31 NKJV].

"But if you have bitter envy and self-seeking in your hearts, do not boast and lie against the truth. This wisdom does not descend from above, but *is* earthly, sensual, demonic. For where envy and self-seeking *exist*, confusion and every evil thing *are* there." [James 3:14–16 NKJV].

"*Let* nothing *be done* through selfish ambition or conceit, but in lowliness of mind let each esteem others better than himself. Let each of you look out not only for his own interests, but also for the interests of others." [Phil. 2:3–4 NKJV].

"Let all bitterness, wrath, anger, clamor, and evil speaking be put away from you, with all malice. And be kind to one another, tenderhearted, forgiving one another, even as God in Christ forgave you." [Eph. 4:31–32 NKJV].

Love gives and love serves [John 3:16; Matt. 28:20; Matt. 20:26]. **Love does not take for itself. Amen.**

Causes of Selfishness (These aren't reasons to be selfish.)				
Lack	Fear	Loss of control (fear of losing control, in life)	Lack of self-confidence	Needs not being met
Lack of support (at home, etc.)	Sense of entitlement (the "I deserve it" attitude)	Brokenness	Not getting what you want all the time	Loss
Not used to sharing	Stress, fatigue, worry, anxiety	Empty relationships	Neglect and abandonment; abuse	Emptiness

Put away selfishness. (The Lord revealed.) Amen.

Overcome selfishness with humility

Humility, according to www.merriam-webster.com and www.dictionary.refrence.com, means "the state of not thinking you're better than others; modest opinion of one's own importance, rank, etc. Not proud, or arrogant, not thinking yourself better than others, same as humility."

Ask the Holy Spirit to release the fruit of humility (that is already in you, when you receive Jesus Christ) into your heart. In Jesus name, amen.

Humility overcomes selfishness [1 Pet. 5:6]. Amen

Overcome selfishness with prayer

Pray this prayer with faith:

"Heavenly Father, I confess I have put myself ahead of others. I confess I've had a me, me, me, I deserve it, entitlement attitude. Forgive me, Lord, and help me love my neighbor as myself and serve. In Jesus name, amen."

Overcome selfishness with the name of Jesus

Please refer to the section on spiritual warfare on page 374 to see how to use the name of Jesus and to learn about the power that's in the name of Jesus, [Hebrews 2:5–8; Matthew 28:18]. Amen.

Overcome selfishness with love

"'You shall love your neighbor as yourself.'" [Mark 12:31 NKJV].

Love is patient, love is kind; loves does not envy; love does not parade itself, is not puffed up, does not behave rudely, does not seek its own, is not provoked, thinks no evil, does not rejoice in iniquity, but rejoices in the truth...love never fails [1 Cor. 13:4–6, 8].

This love is accomplished through you, with the help of the Holy Spirit.

Ask the Holy Spirit to love through you daily, in Jesus name; ask Him with faith so you can learn to love your neighbor as yourself. Amen.

This will help you; "Love your enemies, do good to those who hate you, bless those who curse you, and pray for those who spitefully use you." [Luke 6:27–28 NKJV].

Overcome selfishness with service

Begin to see how you can meet the needs of others. Volunteer your time and service for others (with adult supervision and/or permission). Give back to those in need and make a difference. Amen.

Overcome selfishness with the word of God

The word of God will not return void [Isa. 55:11]. Once you speak the word and believe what you say, you will have what you say. Amen.

Turn to the word of God. Begin to develop a habit of reading the word of God daily. His word provides peace, stillness, hope, strength, deliverance, healing, and love, and reveals the promises of God. Amen.

Jesus is the Word, and the Word is life. Amen.

Believe His word, speak His word, receive His word, think on His word, and apply the word of God to your life and you will see a change in your life and results. (The Lord revealed.) Amen.

Renew your mind

Use the **Battle of the Mind** strategy on page 58 and by asking the Holy Spirit to replace your thoughts with His.

Pray with faith: "Holy Spirit, think through me. In Jesus name, amen."

The Holy Spirit needs your cooperation in this massive effort to renew your mind, so do your part by renewing your mind with the word of God and He will do His. Amen.

If you need more help, use the strategies outlined in the section on spiritual warfare on pages 340–410.

Overcome selfishness with praise

Praise lifts your focus off the problem and onto the presence of God. Learn more about worship and what true worship is by reading **"The Art of Worship"** on page 48. Amen.

Overcome selfishness with thanksgiving

Giving thanks brightens your day and your outlook on life. Amen.

Also refer to the **Overcome and Stand** strategy on page 29.

Whenever the enemy tries to use selfishness against you or the flesh rises against you, causing selfishness, use these strategies to help you overcome selfishness and keep it out of your heart. Amen.

Do not internalize your struggles, troubles, or hardships when you are struggling with selfishness. **Talk** to a parent, teacher, counselor, youth counselor, youth pastor, or other trusted adult about what you are struggling with. They can provide you with the help, advice, and assistance you need.

Lying

"You shall not bear false witness against your neighbor." [Exod. 20:16 NKJV].

Lying, according to www.thefreedictionary.com and www.dictionary.refrence.com, means "to be untruthful, or to tell false statements, to fabricate, to mislead; to speak falsehoods; deliberately deviating from the truth."

"Lying lips *are* an abomination to the LORD, But those who deal truthfully *are* His delight." [Prov. 12:22 NKJV].

Do not grieve the Holy Spirit. (Lying grieves the Holy Spirit.) "Therefore, putting away lying, "*Let* each one *of you* speak truth with his neighbor," for we are members of one another." [Eph. 4:25 NKJV].

"The truthful lip shall be established forever, But a lying tongue *is* but for a moment." [Prov. 12:19 NKJV].

Five Reasons Why We Lie
1. **To save face**   To save face means to avoid embarrassment or embarrassing situations, for yourself and others.
2. **To prevent or avoid conflict**   This means a person believes that telling a lie could prevent or avoid a conflict and keeps matters from getting worse.
3. **To smooth out relationships**   This is putting on airs (pretending) to make social events pass quickly (such as at a party or dinner.)
4. **For personal relationships**   To make friends and/or end friendships or other relationships
5. **To gain power**   To feel in control of a situation.

Information on the reasons why we lie acquired from Alder/Proctor's book, *Looking Out/Looking In,* pages 326-327.

Lies keep you from telling the truth. Lies lead to more lies to cover up the lie you already told. Lies bind and breed deceit until everything you say is a lie and nothing you say is the truth. Get rid of lying. Amen.

Know the truth and the truth shall set you free [John 8:36]. Amen.

Get rid of lying. Amen.

Overcome Lying

Step 1: Begin to speak the truth without fear [2 Tim. 1:7].

If you need help doing so, **pray** this prayer with faith:

"Heavenly Father, I confess I lie often. Forgive me for doing so. Help me to be able to speak the truth without fear regularly. Regardless of the reason, help me to avoid lying and deceit. In Jesus name, amen."

Step 2: Acquire God's wisdom and knowledge.

It is written, to anyone who lacks wisdom, let him ask God for it [James 1:5].

Having wisdom and knowledge means knowing when to listen, when to speak, what to say, how to speak, how to use your acquired knowledge, and so on.

Open up your spiritual ears and listen to the voice of God, who will put the right words in your mouth. Amen.

In this manner, pray with faith:

"Heavenly Father, Your word says to anyone who lacks wisdom, let him ask for it. So I ask you for wisdom today. In Jesus name, amen."

"Heavenly Father, give me the words to speak. I need Your help today. In Jesus's name, amen."

Step 3: Listen to the Holy Spirit.

Listen to the still small voice of the precious Holy Spirit, who will give you the words to speak or caution you to be still and listen [John 10:27].

Turn away from lying, and overcome. Amen.

God does not like a lying nor deceitful tongue [Exodus 20:16]. Amen.

Hate; Prejudice

Hate, according to www.dictionary.refrence.com, means "to dislike intensely or passionately; feel extreme aversion for or extreme hostility toward; detest." According to and www.merriam-webster.com, it indicates "Intense hostility and aversion usually deriving from fear, anger, or sense of injury; to feel extreme enmity for; intense dislike for."

Prejudice, according to www.dictionary.refrence.com, means "an unfavorable opinion or feeling formed beforehand or without knowledge, thought, or reason. Unreasonable feelings, opinions, attitudes, especially of a hostile nature, regarding an ethnic, racial, social, or religious group."

"If someone says, "I love God," and hates his brother, he is a liar; for he who does not love his brother whom he has seen, how can he love God whom he has not seen?" [1 John 4:20 NKJV].

Brother, according to www.biblhub.com, in Greek means "a fellow Christian; someone in the same religious community."

"Whoever hates his brother is a murderer, and you know that no murderer has eternal life abiding in him." [1 John 3:15 NKJV].

"Hatred stirs up strife, But love covers all sins." [Prov. 10:12 NKJV].

"Let no corrupt word proceed out of your mouth, but what is good for necessary edification, that it may impart grace to the hearers." [Eph. 4:29 NKJV].

"'You shall not hate your brother in your heart." [Leviticus 19:17 NKJV].

"He who says he is in the light, and hates his brother, is in darkness until now. He who loves his brother abides in the light, and there is no cause for stumbling in him. But he who hates his brother is in darkness and walks in darkness, and does not know where he is going, because the darkness has blinded his eyes." [1 John 2:9–11 NKJV].

"'You shall love your neighbor as yourself.'" [Mark 12:31 NKJV].

Neighbor, in Greek (the original language the New Testament was written in), means "anyone you meet."

"Let all bitterness, wrath, anger, clamor, and evil speaking be put away from you, with all malice. And be kind to one another, tenderhearted, forgiving one another, even as God in Christ forgave you." [Eph. 4:31–32 NKJV].

Reasons Why People Can Feel Hatred or Be Prejudiced Against Others (This doesn't give anyone a reason to hate or be prejudiced. Amen.)				
Jealousy; envy	Lack of understanding	Fear	Stereotypes	Upbringing (raising); what you've been taught to believe
Family members	Different cultures or religions	You are classified as "different" from others	Pride	Lack of trust
Feel they're better than others	Beauty	Not wanting to feel vulnerable	Insecurities	Inferiority
Feel like someone's stealing from you (or sense of entitlement)	Being hurt	Terminated relationships	Anger	Etc.

Hate no one, and don't hold prejudices against anyone. Instead, **love**.

"A new commandment I give to you, that you love one another: just as I have loved you, you also are to love one another." [John 13:34 ESV].

Treat others how you would want to be treated (with love and not hate) [Luke 6:31]. Amen.

"And you shall love the LORD your God will all your heart, with all your soul, with all your mind, and with all your strength.' This *is* the first commandment. And the second, like *it, is* this: 'You shall love your neighbor as yourself.' There is no other commandment greater than these." [Mark 12:30–31 NKJV].

Remember, *Neighbor*, in Greek (the original language the New Testament was written in), means "anyone you meet."

Let no unwholesome words come out of your mouth, but only what is helpful for building others up according to their needs that it may benefit those who listen [Eph. 4:29].

Unwholesome, according to www.biblehub.com, means "worthless, corrupt, bad, and rotten."

Love does **no harm** to their neighbor [Rom. 13:10].

Hate and prejudice are **wrong**, resulting in harm to one's neighbor (who is anyone you meet). Amen.

If you love God, you would love your neighbor. (The Lord revealed.) Amen.

Love is patient, love is kind; loves does not envy; love does not parade itself, is not puffed up, does not behave rudely, does not seek its own, is not provoked, thinks no evil, does not rejoice in iniquity, but rejoices in the truth...love never fails [1 Cor. 13:4–6, 8].

This love is accomplished through you, with the help of the Holy Spirit.

Ask the Holy Spirit to love through you daily, in Jesus name; ask Him with faith so you can learn to love your neighbor as yourself. Amen.

To receive the Holy Spirit's help, first you need to receive Jesus Christ as your Lord and Savior (if you haven't already).

Receive Me, says the Lord.

Pray this prayer with faith:

"Lord, I come before you today at the cross, to confess to You that I'm a sinner in need of a Savior. Lord, please forgive me of all my sins, and cleanse me of all unrighteousness, wash me with Your blood that I may be forgiven, cleanse me so that I may be whiter than snow. Come into my heart today, as I acknowledge You as my Lord and Savior. I thank You for all that You have done for me on the cross. I thank You for receiving me. I'm now Your child, a new creation. In Jesus holy name, amen."

Overcome Hate and Prejudice

Serve

Begin to see how you can meet the needs of others. Volunteer your time and service for others (with adult supervision and/or permission). Give back to those in need and make a difference. Amen.

The word of God

Turn to the word of God. Begin to develop a habit of reading the word of God daily. His word provides peace, stillness, hope, strength, deliverance, healing, and love, and reveals the promises of God. Amen.

The word of God will not return void [Isa. 55:11]. Once you speak the word of God and believe what you say, you will have what you say. Amen.

Jesus is the Word, and the Word is life. Amen.

Believe His word, speak His word, receive His word, think on His word, and apply the word of God to your life and you will see change in your life and results. (The Lord revealed.) Amen.

Renew your mind

Use the **Battle of the Mind** strategy on page 58 and ask the Holy Spirit to replace your thoughts with His.

Pray with faith: "Holy Spirit, think through me. In Jesus name, amen."

The Holy Spirit needs your cooperation in this massive effort to renew your mind, so do your part by renewing your mind with the word of God and He will do His. Amen.

If you need more help, use the strategies outlined in the section on spiritual warfare on pages 340–410.

The name of Jesus

Please refer to the section on spiritual warfare on page 374 to see how to use the name of Jesus and to learn about the power that's in the name of Jesus, [Hebrews 2:5–8; Matthew 28:18]. Amen.

Praise

Praise lifts your focus off the problem and onto the presence of God. Learn more about worship and what true worship is by reading **"The Art of Worship"** on page 48. Amen.

Thanksgiving

Giving thanks brightens your day and your outlook on life. Amen.

Also, refer to the **Overcome and Stand** strategy on page 29.

Using these strategies will help you overcome prejudice and hate and keep it out of your heart. Amen.

Why Hate? Why Be Prejudice?

We all come in different shades, shapes, and sizes, from black to beige, brown, white, or mixed, to big, small, short, or tall. **All** of us are God's creation. (The Lord revealed.) Amen.

Just like the multicolored fish in the sea and different shaped birds of the air, so has God made man, His favorite creation, in many colors, shapes, and sizes.

One should not despise, look down upon, pity, or hate someone for the color of their skin, their shape, or their size. Ultimately hurting someone is hurting God. God literally feels the pain of His people. (The Lord revealed.) Amen.

Instead, seek to love another, as God has loved you. Do good to one another, seek to do no harm to one another, nor speak maliciously or with hate, but be kind to one another in all things. Do as your Heavenly Father commanded you: **love** [Eph. 4:32; Mark 12:31; John 13:34]. (The Lord revealed.) Amen.

Have you suffered from someone being prejudiced or hateful, or have you had hurtful words spoken against you?

Forgive. Forgive those who have wronged you.

Remember, when we were still in darkness (and sinners), Jesus died for us and forgave us of our sins; how much more should we forgive someone who has wronged us, when Christ forgave us when we were still considered enemies of God [Rom. 5:10]. Amen.

We must forgive our enemies. Amen.

This doesn't mean you are saying their behavior is okay. You forgive them, so that you may be forgiven [Matt. 6:14]. Forgiving someone releases their control from over you. Not forgiving someone allows a person to keep control over you by keeping you angry and bitter at them. Forgiving someone helps you receive forgiveness and the blessings of God. Amen.

Forgive those who have trespassed against, and wronged you. Amen.

In this manner pray with faith:

"Heavenly Father, I forgive [name(s)] for trespassing against me, wronging me, and showing prejudice or hatefulness toward me. In Jesus name, amen."

Really mean it in your heart when you seek to forgive someone. Amen.

If you need help forgiving someone, pray the following prayer with faith:

"Heavenly Father, help me forgive [name(s)]. In Jesus name, amen."

In the end, forgiving those who have wronged you and caused you harm makes you more like Christ, who forgave those who wronged Him [Luke 23:34]. Forgiving is hard, but the benefits outweigh the process. You will be blessed for doing so. Amen.

(Forgiveness is key. Amen.)

If **you** were the one who said something that was prejudice or hateful against someone, ask for forgiveness from those you said it against and from God. You will be blessed for doing so. Please see the section on conflict management on page 113 to help you.

It is your responsibility; you must examine your own heart and ask yourself why? Why are these heart issues in my heart?

After you ask yourself why and examine yourself, **repent, change, and grow**. Amen.

May you seek to make your motives pure. This pleases God.

May your motives **not** be filled with selfish gain, lust, ego, pride, self, and so on. Amen.

Always remember **Jesus loves you!**

(The Lord revealed the words above, and it was inspired by Kevin Harney's book *Leadership from the Inside Out.*)

Taming the Tongue

Words

Inspired by Pastor Terry L. Harris

"Death and life are in the power of the tongue, and those who love it will eat its fruits." [Prov. 18:21 ESV]. The fruits are the words of your mouth. (The Lord revealed.) Amen.

Words are important; words bring life or death, blessing or cursing, and every idle word men may speak, they will give account of it in the Day of Judgment [Matt. 12:36]. So let no unwholesome words come out your mouth, but only what is helpful for building others up according to their needs that it may benefit those who listen [Eph. 4:29].

Words can hurt, your words can leave a lasting effect (both negative and positive). Be wise with your words; slow to speak, slow to anger, and quick to listen [James 1:19]. Amen.

"For by your words you will be justified, and by your words you will be condemned." [Matt. 12:37 NKJV]. (The Lord revealed.) Amen.

The Power of the Spoken Word of God

Inspired by Pastor Terry L. Harris

For the **Word of God** is living and active, sharper than any double edged-sword, it penetrates even to dividing soul and spirit, joints and marrow; it judges the thoughts and attitudes of the heart [Heb. 4:12].

Hebrews 4:12 explains some, but not all of the power within God's word, (but to be honest, no one knows the extent of power that is within the word of God.) Amen. ☺

There's power in the spoken word of God.

What does that mean?

It means there is **Dunamis** power within the word of God. (The Lord revealed.) Amen.

Dunamis is a Greek word used for power, especially for the power of God (and according to www.biblestudytools.com/lexicon) means "strength, power, powerful deeds, physical force, power to perform miracles, ability, moral power and excellence of soul, power of influence which belongs to riches and wealth, power to achieve by applying the Lord's inherent abilities, mighty power, power hidden and released within the spoken word of God." Wow!

There truly is power within the spoken word of God! Amen.

With so much power hidden within the word of God, why do so few use it?

It's simple: many do not know of the Bible's awesome power nor do they take the time to read and study God's word or speak it aloud.

Speaking releases the power of the word of God. Amen.

Anyone can read the Word of God, and many read the word of God and call it a good book, but speaking the word of God with faith can release its **Dunamis** power. Amen.

In the end, you have to believe the word of God to see its power manifest (in your life) and the word of God is a weapon that must be spoken to take full effect. Amen.

Will you take the time to read, study, and speak aloud the word of God with faith?

Jesus is the Word, and the Word is life.

Amen.

The Tongue

"Death and life are in the power of the tongue, and those who love it will eat its fruits." [Prov. 18:21 ESV].

According to www.biblehub.com, ***fruit*** in Hebrew means "figurative of actions; their consequences good or bad, speech."

The tongue is mentioned ninety-three times in the Bible (according to www.cru.org). Since it is mentioned so many times, it must be important.

Proverbs reveals how death and life are in the power of the tongue. Proverbs also warns about keeping the tongue out of trouble; to beware of flattery or smooth words, to stay away from gossip and slander, and to turn away from harsh words, deceit, wrath, or anger.

Proverbs also reveals how a wise tongue brings forth healing, and that it is wise to be silent at times; restraining the lips, and more.

The tongue can bring forth both good and bad fruit. The type of fruit the tongue yields is up to each individual.

The tongue can be disrespectful or respectful, hateful or kind, loving or bitter. This is the power of the tongue, and those who love it will eat its fruit. Amen.

What type of tongue do you have? And if you need to, how can you change your fruit (words)?

Turn to the word of God. His word says, "Do not let any unwholesome talk come out of your mouths, but only what is helpful for building others up according to their needs, that it may benefit those who listen." [Eph. 4:29 NIV].

Begin to replace words that are bitter, hateful, unkind, malicious, bad, and bring forth death; with words that are good, kind, loving, uplifting, and bring forth life.

Changing your speech can change your life, and your outlook on life. Amen.

The Consequences of the Tongue

Murmuring and Complaining

Inspired by Pastor Terry L. Harris

Murmur, according to www.biblehub.com, is *diagogguzo* in Greek (the original language of the New Testament) and means "to convey heavy complaining, grumbling, to complain throughout a crow or among one another, constant buzz of negative complaining."

Murmur, according to www.biblehub.com, is *anan* in Hebrew and means "to complain, offer complaint."

Complain, according to www.biblehub.com, is *stenazo* in the Greek and means "to groan, express grief, anger, or desire, to feel pressure from what is coming on—which can be intensely pleasant or anguish (depends on the context); denotes feeling that is internal and unexpressed, groan within oneself; deep sigh."

Complain, according to www.biblehub.com, is *anan* in Hebrew (the same word is used for *murmur*), and means "to murmur, to mourn, offer complaint."

Do all things <u>without</u> murmuring and grumblings [Phil. 2:14].

Let no unwholesome words come out your mouth, but only what is helpful for building others up according to their needs that it may benefit those who listen [Eph. 4:29].

"*Be* hospitable to one another without grumbling," [1 Pet. 4:9 NKJV].

"Neither murmur ye, as some of them also murmured, and were destroyed of the destroyer." [1 Cor. 10:10 KJV].

Please read Numbers 11.

What were the consequences of murmuring and complaining?

According to Numbers 11, the children of Israel started to murmur and complain about eating manna (the substance God supplied for them in the wilderness). Each day the people gathered manna to eat until they grew tired of it and yearned for the meat, leeks, onions, cucumbers, and garlic of Egypt, (instead of being grateful for what God had provided.) It displeased the Lord.

Not only did their murmuring and complaining displease the Lord, but His anger was aroused against them.

Murmuring and complaining causes the Lord to be displeased and His anger to be aroused. Amen.

Displeasure or *charan*, according to www.biblesuite.com, in Hebrew means "fierceness, wrath, fury, burning anger."

Anger or *aph*, according to www.biblesuite.com, in Hebrew means "face, nose, nostril (as an organ of breathing); countenance" and His anger was aroused; *arouse* according to www.biblesuite.com, means "to burn or to be kindled with anger, burn, rage, fire to burn, burned with anger, be wax hot, grieve, be displeased."

This is how the Lord feels when we murmur and complain.

Instead of murmuring seek to be grateful. Instead of complaining rejoice in what you already have and praise and thank God for Who He is, what He has done, what He has already provided for you, and what He will do. Amen.

In all things, give thanks. Amen.

In this manner pray with faith:

"Heavenly Father, forgive me for murmuring and complaining. Help me to be grateful without complaining. Help me rejoice instead of murmuring. May no unwholesome words come out of my mouth, but only what is helpful for building others up. In Jesus name, amen."

"Praise the LORD! Oh, give thanks to the LORD, for *He* is good! For His mercy *endures* forever." [Ps. 106:1 NKJV].

Deceit

To **deceive,** according to www.thefreedictionary.com and www.google.com, means "to cause someone to believe what is not true, to mislead, to ensnare, often times to take advantage or gain some personal advantage over them."

To **deceive**, according to www.biblehub.com, in Hebrew means "deceives, disappoints, and betrays one, fraud, wrong, falsehood, testify falsely, false oath, falsify, or self-deceived prophets, prophesy falsely, lie, false tongue, scheme, shame, liar, vain thing."

In Jeremiah 14:14 NKJV, the Lord says, "The prophets prophesy lies in My name. I have not sent them, commanded them, nor spoken to them;"

Do not say "God said" when God didn't say it. Be silent and hold your peace. It's better to say nothing than to lie on God, deceiving others and yourself. Amen.

The prophets in Jeremiah's time prophesized what is false, deceiving the king and the people, but they could not fool God. The consequence of their deception is found in Jeremiah 14:15–16. In the end, what the false prophets prophesized during the time of Jeremiah didn't come to pass; instead they would be consumed by the famine and sword, and the Lord would pour their wickedness on them. Amen.

To deceive means to lead people astray. Do not lead people astray or yourself by lying to God, speaking what is false, lying, scheming, cheating, committing fraud, betraying others, and so on.

The consequences of deceit are the following: it may come back on you, you will incur consequences, your sins will be found out, and you will be called a liar and untrustworthy. Amen.

Speak the truth. Speak the truth without fear. **Be honest**. **Be truthful** to yourself and others; truth overcomes deceit. Amen.

In this manner pray with faith:

"Heavenly Father, forgive me for being deceitful and leading people astray. I put away all falsehood. Help me to speak the truth. In Jesus name, amen."

"Therefore, having put away falsehood, let each one of you speak the truth with his neighbor," [Eph. 4:25 ESV].

"You shall not take the name of the LORD your God in vain, for the LORD will not hold *him* guiltless who takes His name in vain." [Exod. 20:7 NKJV].

God's name does not begin or end with a cuss word.

Holy does not belong in the phrase that starts with a *c* and ends with a *p*. Nor should the word *holy* be in any sentence that does not pertain to the things of God.

Holy means: "set apart."

God's name is holy, and His name should be respected, revered, and honored.

Do not use the name of the Lord in vain. Putting a cuss word before or after His name is taking God's name in vain.

Vain in Hebrew, according to www.biblehub.com, is *shav* and means "emptiness, nothingness, ineffective, emptiness of speech—lying, false (empty); of conduct—worthless; ruin or morally guile; figurative idolatry, uselessness, etc."

Using God's name in vain includes the following:

1. Putting a cuss word before or after His name
2. Swearing falsely on God
3. Taking an oath using God's name and not keeping your oath
4. Not revering His name
5. Using His name without feeling or meaning it (with empty words).

The consequence of using God's name in vain is that God will not hold you guiltless.

To **not hold you guiltless** in Hebrew, according to www.biblehub.com, means "to not go unpunished." You will not go unpunished if you use God's name in vain. Amen.

Repent and bless the Lord at all times; and with all that's within you bless His Holy name. **Let praise (not cussing) be continually in your mouth** [Ps. 34]. Amen.

In this manner pray with faith:

"Heavenly Father, forgive me for using your name in vain. Let praise be continually in my mouth. In Jesus name, amen."

Bad Words; Cuss Words

Cursing, cuss words, or bad words are all profanity.

To *curse*, in Hebrew, according to www.biblehub.com, means "to bind, curse, bitterly curse, to execrate profanity."

Profanity, according to www.google.com and www.thefreedictionary.com, means "blasphemous or obscene language, dirty words, cursing, swearing, abusive, vulgar."

Profane (the root word of *profanity*) in Hebrew is *chalal*, according to www.biblehub.com, and means "to defile, pollute, desecrate, defile oneself, pollute oneself, make common, violate the honor of, dishonor, to treat as common, to wound, to pierce."

Your words are weapons, and words are powerful. Words have the power to uplift or to tear down. (The Lord revealed.) Amen.

The **consequences of profanity** (this is using bad words or cuss words) are that you **defile yourself**. You pollute your own soul when you use bad words or cuss words. Harsh words also grieve the Holy Spirit. Amen.

Start speaking the word of God (words that bring life), and ask God to cleanse your heart of any defilement caused by cuss words and bad words (profanity). Amen.

Overcome by speaking positively:

- "Death and life *are* in the power of the tongue," [Prov. 18:21 NKJV]. Speak life, and speak positively, even when loved ones, friends, or peers speak against you, talk bad about you, and speak down or negatively toward you. Continue to speak life, cast down word curses, bless those who curse you, do good to those who wrong or hate you and pray for those who mistreat you [Luke 6:27–28, 35–36; Rom. 12:14–21]. Amen.

In this manner pray with faith:

"Heavenly Father, forgive me for speaking bad words that pollute my soul. Create in me a clean heart, O God, and renew a steadfast spirit within me. In Jesus name, amen."

Speak the words that bring life. (The Lord revealed.) Amen.

"Let the words of my mouth, and the mediation of my heart, be acceptable in thy sight, O LORD, my strength, and my redeemer." [Ps. 19:14 KJV].

Blasphemy

Blasphemy in Hebrew is *paats*, and according to www.biblehub.com, it means "to hold contempt, abhor, scorn, despise, spurn, reject, blaspheme, contempt."

To *blaspheme* is to say something that offends God, insults Him, or shows contempt or lack of reverence, according to www.wikipedia.com.

The consequences of blasphemy are the following:

1. What you speak can come back on you.
2. You can receive some form of judgment.
3. You will receive degrees of punishment during judgment day (if you refuse to repent).

Repent and fill your mouth with praise and song. Keep your mouth clean and your heart undefiled. Amen.

In this manner pray with faith:

"Heavenly Father, forgive me for speaking blasphemous things. Let no unwholesome words come out of my mouth, but only what is helpful for building others up. In Jesus name, amen."

"Let the words of my mouth, and the meditation of my heart, be acceptable in thy sight, O LORD, my strength, and my redeemer." [Ps. 19:14 KJV].

Twisting Words and Manipulation

David said, "All day [the whole day; warm hours] they twist [*twist* is *atsab* in Hebrew, meaning 'to distort, fabricate, hurt, grieve, pain, crossed, worry, anger, displease, vex'] my words; (speech, matter, etc.)" [Psalm 56:5 NKJV]. (Hebrew definitions are taken from www.biblehub.com.)

To **twist someone's words** means "to fabricate." To **fabricate**, according to www.google.com, means "to invent or concoct something, typically with deceitful intent." Basically it means to invent a lie about someone or something, (that is what twisting someone's words mean.)

Do not twist someone's words (fabricate) to make yourself look good or someone else look bad. Cease being deceitful. Amen.

Manipulate in Hebrew, according to www.biblehub.com, means "seized, captured, grasp, lay hold of, wield, seize (with the hand), arrest, catch (accusative of the person); terrorize them, stop, grasp in order to wield, caught, etc."

Manipulate in Greek, according to www.biblehub.com, means "touch, handle, injure, harm, manipulatively touch; handle especially to do violence, injure."

Manipulate according to www.idictionary.com, means to "treat or operate with, to control or play upon, by artful, unfair, or insidious means; especially to one's own advantage; to change by unfair means, so as to serve one's purpose."

To manipulate is to operate in a way that works to your advantage.

Being deceitful by twisting words and manipulation are both wrong. Amen.

The consequence of twisting words and manipulation is when someone cries out to God against you for word twisting or manipulation, you are in danger of God's anger being aroused against you.

When God's anger is aroused, punishment ensues (*ensue* means, according to www.google.com, "to occur afterward").

Please read Psalm 56:1–7.

Be wise with your words and refrain your lips from word twisting (deceit), and manipulation.

Speak words that edify (build up), not words that tear down or deceive.

In this manner pray with faith:

"Heavenly Father, forgive me for using manipulation or word twisting to deceive others. Let no unwholesome words come out of my mouth, but only what is helpful for building others up. In Jesus name, amen."

Let no unwholesome words come out of your mouth, but only what is helpful for building others up according to their needs that it may benefit those who listen [Eph. 4:29].

Unwholesome, according to www.biblehub.com, means "worthless, corrupt, bad, and rotten."

Idle Words

"They speak idly everyone with his neighbor; *With* flattering lips *and* a double heart they speak." [Ps. 12:2 NKJV].

Idle words, in Greek according to www.biblehub.com, means "vain speaking, foolish talking, fruitless discussion, empty talk, random talk, babble."

"For out of the abundance of the heart the mouth speaks. A good man out of the good treasure of his heart brings forth good things, and an evil man out of the evil treasure brings forth evil things. But I say to you that for every idle word men may speak, they will give account of it in the day of judgment. For by your words you will be justified, and by your words you will be condemned." [Matt. 12:34–37 NKJV].

The consequence of speaking idly is that you will be held accountable for every word you speak.

Say what you mean and mean what you say. Choose your words wisely, so you might be justified.

Justified, according to www.merriam-webster.com, means "to prove or show to be just, right, or reasonable."

In this manner pray with faith:

"Heavenly Father, forgive me for speaking idle words. Give me wisdom so I might know how to speak and how to listen. In Jesus name, amen."

"And don't say anything you don't mean." [Matt. 5:33, *The Message*]. Amen.

Charm

"Charm *is* deceitful and beauty *is* passing," [Prov. 31:30 NKJV].

Charm, in Hebrew, according to www.biblehub.com, means "pleasant or pleasing, etc."

Charm, according to www.google.com, means "to delight greatly or arouse admiration."

The Bible calls charm deceitful.

Deceit in the Bible, according to www.biblehub.com, means "untruth, by implication, sham, without a cause, falsehood, liar, vain thing; wrongfully, deception, etc."

Charm is pleasing to the ears to hear, and can breed falsehood. (This is how charm can be deceitful.) Amen.

"And her mouth *is* smoother than oil; But in the end she is bitter as wormwood, Sharp as a two-edged sword." [Prov. 5:3–4 NKJV].

One of the consequences of charm is deceit (leading people astray).

The consequences of deceit are the following: it may come back on you, you will incur consequences, your sins will be found out, and you will be called a liar and untrustworthy. Amen.

Keep your mouth from speaking deceit [Ps. 34:13] and your lips from devising lies.

Let no unwholesome words come out of your mouth, but only what is helpful for building others up according to their needs that it may benefit those who listen [Eph. 4:29].

Unwholesome, according to www.biblehub.com, means "worthless, corrupt, bad, and rotten."

Become a man or woman who fears the Lord, and let praise and thanksgiving continually be in your mouth. Amen.

In this manner pray with faith:

"Heavenly Father, forgive me for using charm to deceive others. Help me keep my mouth from speaking deceit. In Jesus name, amen."

Sarcasm and Bitter Words

Inspired by Pastor Terry L. Harris

"Who sharpen their tongue like a sword, And bend *their* bows to shoot their arrows-bitter words," [Ps. 64:3 NKJV].

Sarcasm, according to www.biblehub.com, means "a sharp bitter or cutting remark; a bitter gibe or taunt." Sarcasm comes from the Greek word *sarkoamos*, which is taken from another Greek word and means, according to www.biblehub.com, "to tear flesh, bite the lip in rage, sneer."

According to both www.wikipedia.com and www.dictionary.com, "In sarcasm; ridicule or mockery is used harshly often cruelly and contemptuously, for destructive purposes."

Sarcasm can be cruel to the ear to hear and bitter to the heart. Amen.

Bitter, according to www.biblehub.com, is *mar* or *marah* in Hebrew and means "bitterness, hurtful, angry, grieved, provoked, discontented, great, heavy, bitter chafed."

Bitter, according to www.thefreedictionary.com, means "cutting, sarcastic" (bitter words).

In Psalm 64:3, bitter words are like arrows. (Words are our speech.) The word *arrow* is *chets* in Hebrew, and according to www.biblehub.com, means "dart, shaft, wound."

In the end, both sarcasm and bitter words are arrows sent out from someone's mouth to wound, tear, scar, cut, taunt, destroy, and grieve others.

The consequence of shooting sarcasm and bitter words at the blameless (wounding others), without fear, is that God can suddenly shoot at you with an arrow and you (like those you used your words against) can end up wounded [Ps. 64:4, 7–10]. Harsh words also grieve the Holy Spirit. Amen.

Instead of using sarcasm and bitter words when speaking to others, let no unwholesome words come out of your mouth, but only what is helpful for building others up according to their needs that it may benefit those who listen [Eph. 4:29].

Unwholesome, according to www.biblehub.com, means "worthless, corrupt, bad, and rotten."

Overcome by speaking positively:

- "Death and life *are* in the power of the tongue," [Prov. 18:21 NKJV]. Speak life, speak positively; even when loved ones, friends, or peers speak against you, talk bad about you, and speak down or negatively toward you. Continue to speak life, cast down word curses, bless those who curse you, do good to those who wrong or hate you and pray for those who mistreat you [Luke 6:27–28, 35–36; Rom. 12:14–21]. Amen.

In this manner pray with faith:

"Heavenly Father, forgive me for using sarcasm and bitter words to hurt others. Let no unwholesome words come out of my mouth, but only what is helpful for building others up. In Jesus name, amen."

Let no unwholesome words come out of your mouth, but only what is helpful for building others up according to their needs that it may benefit those who listen [Eph. 4:29].

Gossip

A gossip goes around telling secrets, so don't hang around with chatterers [Prov. 20:19].

Gossip in Hebrew, according to www.biblehub.com, means "talebearer, slanderer, to roll to pieces, whisperer."

Gossip is talking idly or spreading rumors about personal or private matters.

Gossip is spoken of in James 3:5 NIV, which says, "Consider what a great forest is set on fire by a small spark." **Gossip** is the small spark that sets a great forest ablaze. By your words you can ruin and tear down, and by your words you can rebuild or build up. Amen.

"A perverse person stirs up conflict, and a gossip separates close friends." [Prov. 16:28 NIV]; this is the consequence of gossip. Amen.

Instead of spreading gossip, pursue truth, and strive for peace with everyone [Heb. 12:14; John 8:32]. (The Lord revealed.) Amen.

In this manner, pray with faith:

"Heavenly Father, forgive me for spreading gossip and lies. Help me to pursue truth and to strive for peace with everyone. In Jesus name, amen."

Let no unwholesome words come out of your mouth, but only what is helpful for building others up according to their needs that it may benefit those who listen [Eph. 4:29].

Scoffers and Mockers

"knowing this first of all, that scoffers will come in the last days with scoffing, following their own sinful desires." [2 Pet. 3:3 ESV].

Scoffer in Hebrew is *lits*, according to www.bible.com, and means "to scorn, deride, mock, make a mockery, etc." The Greek word for *scoffer* is *emakites* and means "a mocker, false teacher, etc."

Scoffer, according to www.thefreedictionary.com, means "someone who mocks or treats with derision or contempt (ridicule)."

Mocker is the same word as *scoffer* in Greek and has the same meaning. *Mocker* in Hebrew, according to www.biblehub.com, is *hathulim* and means "mockery, deceptions, a derision (ridicule)." **Mock,** according to www.thefreedictionary.com, means "to mimic in sport or derision, to imitate, counterfeit, to frustrate the hopes of, disappoints."

A scoffer sneers at the truth, and a mocker deceives many.

Mockery and scoffing brings a yoke of bondage; that is the consequence [Isa. 28:22].

Their **bonds** are made stronger, (bonds are chains and shackles; making them stronger fastens, tightens, and strengthens them, according to www.biblehub.com), when one mocks or scoffs. Amen.

Instead of binding yourself with scoffing and mocking, be set free by the Spirit [Isa. 10:27], seeking to build others up with your words instead of tearing them down. Amen.

Overcome by speaking positively

- "Death and life *are* in the power of the tongue," [Prov. 18:21 NKJV]. Speak life, speak positively; even when loved ones, friends, or peers speak against you, talk bad about you, and speak down or negatively toward you. Continue to speak life, cast down word curses, bless those who curse you, do good to those who wrong or hate you and pray for those who mistreat you [Luke 6:27–28, 35–36; Rom. 12:14–21]. Amen.

In this manner, pray with faith:

"Heavenly Father, forgive me for scoffing or mocking. Set me free and let no more unwholesome words come out of my mouth, but only what is helpful for building others up. In Jesus name, amen."

Let no unwholesome words come out of your mouth, but only what is helpful for building others up according to their needs that it may benefit those who listen [Eph. 4:29].

Doubt; Unbelief

Doubt in Greek is *distazo*, according to www.biblehub.com, and means "to waver, hesitate, two, double—going two ways, shifting between positions, uncertain at a crossroad, refusing to choose one way over the other, halt between two opinions, duplicate."

Unbelief in Greek is *apistia*, according to www.biblehub.com, and means "distrust, unfaithfulness, betraying trust, want of faith, weakness of faith."

Wavering, shifting between two positions, and weakness of faith all signal doubt or unbelief.

The consequences of doubt and unbelief are the following:

Rejecting or rebelling against God [please read Numbers 14:1–25 and Numbers 13:26–33].

Falling away from the faith

Shifting between following God and following science or idols

Unanswered prayer (caused by unbelief)

Not being able to cast out demons or participate in spiritual warfare (because faith is the key)

Not being able to grow

No results in your life or prayer life

Losing out on your blessings

Etc.

In the end, doubt and unbelief displeases God. Amen.

Overcome with faith! Pray and ask God to help your unbelief in Jesus name, [like the father who brought his mute son to Jesus, he asked Jesus to help his unbelief, please see Mark 9: 14-29], and overcome unbelief. Amen. When you ask God, believe He will do it, and you will see results. Try God and see. (The Lord revealed.) Amen.

In this manner, pray with faith:

"Heavenly Father, help my unbelief and take away my doubt. Reveal yourself to me. In Jesus name, amen."

Jesus says, "If you ask anything in My name, I will do *it*." [John 14:14 NKJV].

Trust and believe God. Amen.

Contentious, Argumentative, and Malicious Words

Inspired by Pastor Terry L. Harris

Contentious in Hebrew is *marah* and *madon*, and according to www.biblehub.com, means "rebellious, disobedience, refractory, unpleasant, bitter, change, provoking, grievously, resist; quarrelsome, strife, discord, brawling" [see Prov. 21:9; 26:21].

Argumentative is *antilego* in the Greek, and according to www.biblehub.com, means "given to expressing divergent or opposite views, tend to disagree, quarrelsome, to speak against, contradict, speak or say something in opposition, resist, oppose, combative, dispute."

The consequences of being contentious and argumentative are the following:

It is written in Romans 2:8–9 KJV, "But unto them that are contentious, and do not obey the truth, but obey unrighteousness, indignation, and wrath, Tribulation and anguish, upon every soul of man that doeth evil,"

Tribulation is one of the consequences of being contentious or argumentative.

Other consequences of being contentious and argumentative are the following:

One can be hard to talk to

One can be hard to deal with or get along with

Pessimistic

Always ready to dispute

Instead of being contentious and argumentative, you should strive to be slow to anger, slow to speak, and quick to listen [James 1:19]. **Control your temper**, hold your tongue, avoid strife, and **seek to make peace with everyone**. Amen.

In this manner, pray with faith:

"Heavenly Father, forgive me for being contentious and argumentative. Help me be slow to anger, slow to speak, and quick to listen. Let no unwholesome words come out of my mouth, but only what is helpful for building others up. In Jesus name, amen."

This doesn't mean that you can't share your opinion (my pastor Terry L. Harris taught his congregation that opinions are healthy), and it doesn't mean you can't get your point across. It means to do so in manner that avoids strife (losing your temper). Amen.

Malicious in Hebrew is *chomos*, and according to www.biblehub.com, means "violence, wrong, harsh treatment, ruthlessness, wickedness of men, cruelty, oppressor, damage, unrighteousness, false, injustice, violent dealing."

The consequences of maliciousness are tearing down others and offending God. Harsh words also grieve the Holy Spirit. Amen.

Put off malice, in the same put off anger, wrath, slander, and abusive (filthy) language and put on the new self [Col. 3:10]. Amen.

Turn away from speaking cruelly, turn away from treating others harshly or doing wrong. Ask God to make you more like Him and He will do it. This is putting on the new self. Amen.

In this manner pray with faith:

"Heavenly Father, forgive me for being malicious toward others. Help me turn away from malice, and make me more like you, Jesus. In Jesus name, amen."

Let no unwholesome words come out of your mouth, but only what is helpful for building others up according to their needs that it may benefit those who listen [Eph. 4:29].

Hurtful Words, Harshness, and Slander

Hurtful words, according to www.thesaurus.com, are "damaging, dangerous, destructive, malicious, unkind, upsetting, nasty, bad, cutting, harmful, distressing, cruel."

Harsh in Hebrew is *chazaq,* and according to www.biblehub.com, means "to fasten upon, hence, to seize, be strong, fortify, obstinate, to bind, restrain, grow firm, strengthen."

One consequence of speaking harsh or hurtful words is stirring up anger [Proverbs 15:1]. Instead of stirring up anger, respond with a gentle answer, because a gentle answer turns away wrath [Proverbs 15:1]. Amen.

Slander in Hebrew is *dibbah*, and according to www.biblehub.com, means "evil report, whispering, defamation, infamy."

Consequences of slandering others are the following: being a fool or silly [Prov. 10:18], hurting others with your words, and displeasing and dishonoring God. Harsh words also grieve the Holy Spirit. Amen.

Avoid being foolish, and restrain your lips, for this is wise [Proverbs 10:19] and **let no unwholesome words come out of your mouth, but only what is helpful for building others up according to their needs that it may benefit those who listen [Eph. 4:29].**

Unwholesome, according to www.biblehub.com, means "worthless, corrupt, bad, and rotten."

In this manner, pray with faith:

"Heavenly Father, forgive me for speaking hurtful, harsh words, or slander. Help me to be slow to anger, slow to speak, and quick to listen. Let no unwholesome words come out of my mouth, but only what is helpful for building others up. In Jesus name, amen."

Ask for forgiveness from the person(s) and God, when you hurt someone with your words. Please see "Conflict Management" on page 113.

Learn how to tame your tongue, because life and death are in the power of the tongue [Prov. 18:21]. Amen.

Spiritual Warfare

This section was inspired by my very own pastor, Pastor Terry L. Harris.

Prelude to Spiritual Warfare

Inspired by Pastor Terry L. Harris

Before you or anyone else can learn and apply the key weapons of spiritual warfare to your life, you must have a relationship with Jesus Christ [Rom. 10:9]. Amen.

In this manner, pray with faith:

"Lord, I come before you today to confess to You that I'm a sinner in need of a Savior. Lord, please forgive me of all my sins, and cleanse me of all unrighteousness, wash me with Your blood that I may be forgiven, cleanse me so that I may be whiter than snow. Come into my heart today, as I acknowledge You as my Lord and Savior. I thank You for receiving me. I'm now Your child, a new creation. In Jesus holy name, amen."

Congratulations. You are now a child of God! Amen.

Secondly, to learn and apply the key weapons of spiritual warfare, you must have **faith.**

Without faith, it's impossible to please God [Heb. 11:6]. Without faith you cannot access any of the spiritual warfare weapons. All things are possible to those who believe [Mark 9:23]. **Have faith in God** and gain access to the weapons of your warfare. Amen.

With God and faith you can now gain access to your spiritual weapons needed for spiritual warfare. Amen.

Overcome Using These Key Weapons

Using these key weapons will help you stand and overcome any attack of the enemy.

Here is a list of the key weapons of our warfare:

1. The Whole Armor of God
2. The Cross
3. The precious Blood of Jesus
4. The Name of Jesus
5. Praise and Worship
6. Prayer and Fasting
7. Angels on assignment
8. Obedience (staying in God's will)
9. The Word

This Is War!

To everything there is a season, a time for every purpose under heaven...There's a time for peace and a time for war [Eccles. 3].

This is war!

When you engage in spiritual warfare, <u>expect</u> the enemy to attack.

My pastor, Pastor Terry L. Harris, taught his congregation the information below from his P.A. (Power and Authority) System, Part 3 sermon.

1. **Evil spirits can talk/communicate with each other.**
   - Keep in mind, you are going up against intelligent beings. You have to know what you're doing, have faith, and be filled with confidence before engaging in spiritual warfare.
   - Fear not! **We have Jesus!** And all demons are under our feet. Amen.

2. **Demons can identify who you are.**
   - When you begin to serve God more, attend church regularly, pray regularly, and so on, demons begin to recognize who you are and where you are. This builds up your reputation in the spiritual realm.
   - Like Jesus and Paul you want to develop a reputation in the spirit realm [Acts 19:11–12], so that when a demon's boss (and there are different ranks in the spirit realm, like there are in the military) sends lower-ranking demons out against you, they will be too afraid to come against you, because you know how to use the name of Jesus (and other spiritual warfare weapons). Amen.

3. **Who are you?**
   - When you begin to serve God, operate in spiritual warfare, and use your spiritual weapons (when needed), you will begin to gain respect in the spirit realm by winning spiritual battles.

- Once your name starts getting out in the spirit realm (because there is a spirit realm and a natural realm, and God, angels, demons, and so on dwell in the spirit realm, whereas you dwell in the natural realm), demons will begin to recognize who you are, and that's a good thing. You shouldn't be moved by what the enemy throws at you. **Stand** and <u>keep on</u> believing God. Amen.

Keep in mind: demons can recognize born-again Christians that just get beat up, don't fight back, and operate in self-pity. Once this happens, more demons will start attacking, because they know when someone is an easy target. **Don't let that be you.** Fight back!

You must discern when something is an attack from the enemy or caused by your own choices, the decisions of others, your own flesh, and so on. You can know when an attack is from the enemy, because of the nature of the attack; it comes unexpectedly and can be bizarre or chaotic.

When you go under attack from the enemy (the enemy is satan and his demons), fight back! All power and authority was given to Jesus. Jesus then gave us power and spiritual authority over Satan and his demons [Luke 9:1; Luke 10:19].

Use the power and spiritual authority Jesus Christ gave you to overcome the attacks of the enemy. Quit talking about the devil and what he is doing to you. Begin to talk about how God is going to bring you out of this and how you will soon gain the victory. Amen.

According to evangelist John Paul Jackson, "power is what produces miracles, open ears, and blind eyes. Authority is the force that removes stuff, and causes demonic spirits, infirmities, and so on to flee, and affects the spiritual and physical world."

Authority, Evangelist Jackson reveals, removes stuff such as illnesses, infirmity, afflictions, demons, and more. Power repairs what is done or replaces what is broken down; power affects the visible realm—the realm you and I live in.

Dunamis power is dynamite—explosive, and creative power that Jesus Christ has given us [Acts 1:8].

Exousia is the Greek word for *authority* and means "the government right over subjects, submission to carry out orders," etc., that Jesus has given to us [see Matt. 8]. Authority trumps darkness. Amen.

Authority is greater than power. Use both against the enemy. Amen.

That is what evangelist John Paul Jackson revealed about power and authority. Amen.

Pastor Terry L. Harris also reveals the information below on spiritual warfare:

Once you start attacking the enemy, stick with it, and don't be surprised if the enemy fires back.

When you fight back (and never give up), you eventually stop the fiery darts of the enemy. When you stop the enemy's attacks, you can send the enemy back to where he came from.

War takes time—not every battle is an overnight thing—but in the end you will see the desired results.

Keep in mind that the enemy attacks you in the natural realm (once again, this is the realm you and I live in) and uses physical things to come against your life such as a person, a thought, emotions, a chaotic situation, a flat tire, a broken window, and so on. The devil is doing all these things to get you to give up and to stop fighting back against him (using your spiritual weapons). The enemy knows that these weapons are mighty and can pull him down [2 Corinthians 10:4]. Amen.

Too many times God gets blamed when we are the ones who give up the fight. Not so with you! **Never give up!** Amen.

There is a thing called **enemy anger**. This happens because you are serving God and drawing closer to Him. In response, the enemy sends fiery darts that manifest in the natural realm. You have the power and authority to overcome it. Even when there is demonic activity involved, you can overcome it with the power and authority Jesus Christ has already given you. The key to tapping into these weapons is faith.

Once you begin the fight, continue to fight until God tells you to stop fighting.

Stick with it, and sooner or later the attacks from the enemy manifesting in the natural realm will stop, and you will receive the **victory** and your blessings. Amen.

Even when things look crazy in the natural realm, keep on fighting, and never give up!

Have faith in God [Mark 11:20–21]. The **key** to victory is your faith. You must have faith to see results and to gain the victory. Amen.

Never give up, speak in Jesus's name, keep using your spiritual weapons, have faith, and you will be victorious! Amen.

Fear no evil, for God is with you [Ps. 23:4]. Amen.

The Purpose of Spiritual Warfare

"For we do not wrestle against flesh and blood, but against principalities, against powers, against the rulers of the darkness of this age, against spiritual *hosts* of wickedness in heavenly places." [Eph. 6:12 NKJV].

The purpose of Spiritual warfare is the following:

- To defeat and overthrow the powers of darkness.
- To cast down high arguments that exalt themselves against the word of God.
- To cast out demons.
- To bind up demons.
- To quench the fiery darts of the enemy.
- To destroy curses and to destroy word curses.
- To expose the wicked plots of Satan.
- To overcome the powers of the enemy.
- To war against the fleshy (carnal) nature of man.
- To cast down wicked imaginations and evil thoughts.
- To expose and repent of (correct), any evil intentions of the heart.
- To see through and cast down deception.
- To break through and destroy mental strongholds.
- To tear down strongholds.
- To overcome lusts and temptations.
- To defeat depression, worry, stress, and discouragement.
- To overcome the negative influence of our peers and others.

- To set the captive free from bondage, to set free those who are oppressed, and so on.

- To defeat and overthrow suicidal thinking, harmful, and negative thinking patterns and taking every thought into captivity, and bringing it into the obedience of Christ Jesus.

- And more!

What Spiritual Warfare Isn't

Caution: Man has dominion only over the earth, not in heaven.

Then God blessed them, and God said to them, Be fruitful and multiply; fill the earth and subdue it, and rule over [Gen. 1:28].

To **rule over** means "to have dominion, to reign over." Amen.

God has given man dominion over the earth and the earth alone.

When you or anyone else engages in spiritual warfare, do not attack a demonic principality over a city or a region.

Evangelist John Paul Jackson was given a dream by God. My (the authors') explanation of the dream was taken from my memory and not from what Evangelist Jackson said word for word. Please see Evangelist Jackson's book *Needless Causalities of War* to find out more. In this dream, there were Christian leaders standing on top of platforms that could be raised up and down, like an elevator. Each leader stood on different platforms. The leaders were facing toward the moon, and were yelling and throwing hatchets at it. The more the leaders yelled, the more the crowd (that stood below them) cheered them on. Whenever the crowd below cheered, the platform each leader stood upon rose higher. Not too long after all their yelling, the Christians leaders grew tired and fell asleep on their platforms. That's when demonic entities came from the direction of the moon and came down and began to attack the Christian leaders. The attack came as a surprise to the leaders, who had been asleep on top of these platforms. All Evangelist John Paul Jackson could hear were their screams as the dream finally faded out.

At the end of this dream, Evangelist Jackson heard God's audible voice (after the dream faded out to white), say, "To attack powers (principalities) over a region or area is as useless as throwing hatchets at the moon."

After the dream, Evangelist Jackson revealed that trying to attack powers/principalities of darkness over a geographical area, region, or city opens one up to unforeseen attacks. He gave examples of ministers who engaged in spiritual warfare over a region or city and of all the attacks and consequences they faced and had to overcome and repent of, (when Evangelist Jackson pointed out what they did wrong).

Why were the pastors opened up to unforeseen attacks? Because the pastors left their God-given region of authority and went up to engage in spiritual warfare in another realm over which they have no authority over. God gave man dominion only over the earth; the heavens belong to God. (Evangelist John Paul Jackson revealed.) Amen.

Evangelist John Paul Jackson revealed that earthly warfare should be the only spiritual warfare you engage in. Geographical entities such as principalities, powers, and so on are not in our area of dominion. Amen.

For example, Leviathan, a creature described in Job 41 (who many believe is either Satan or a demonic entity), can be defeated only by God. No man can defeat him. Leviathan dwells in a region over which we have no dominion or control over, so we are not to engage in spiritual warfare with him.

What does this mean? This means, according to Evangelist Jackson, that you cannot rebuke a principality of abortion over a city; it will remain over the city until the hearts of the people are changed. [Please read Jeremiah 17].

You can only rebuke the spirit of abortion in a person, not over a city or region, because man has been given dominion only over the earth. Amen.

If you believe you have engaged in spiritual warfare over a city or a region, and you have begun to see or face unforeseen attacks, repent, and tell God that you're sorry for engaging in spiritual warfare in a realm over which you have no dominion or power. He will forgive you and lift any demonic attacks against your life and in the lives of those around who may have been affected, because of you engaging in a spiritual warfare battle you shouldn't be in. Amen.

In this manner, pray with faith:

"Heavenly Father, forgive me for engaging in spiritual warfare in a realm over which I have no dominion or power, and lift these unforeseen attacks against my life and others. In Jesus holy, holy, holy name, amen and amen."

Engage in spiritual warfare only on earth, not heaven. Amen.

(To learn more about why man should not engage in spiritual warfare in the heavens, please read Evangelist John Paul Jackson's book *Needless Causalities of War.)*

Put on the Whole Armor of God

"Put on the whole armor of God, that you may be able to stand against the wiles of the devil." [Eph. 6:11 NKJV].

Type of Armor	Type of Weaponry	Scripture Verse	Function
The Belt of Truth	**Defensive**	**Ephesians 6:14**	Gird yourself with the belt of truth. The truth is the word of God [John 8:32; the Lord revealed]. Amen. Your faith and beliefs must be grounded in the word of God. Your hope must be grounded in Christ. Evangelist Perry Stone reveals that just as a belt holds everything up on your armor, the truth of God's word holds everything together. If you are not grounded in the word of God, you will eventually fall apart in battle. Amen. The belt of truth is also to keep (remember/hold) the word of God within oneself (the

			heart and the mind). To have the word in one's heart one must memorize/meditate on it in one's thoughts, using the **Battle of the Mind** strategy on page 58. (The Lord revealed.) Amen.
The Breastplate of Righteousness	**Defensive**	**Ephesians 6:14**	This weapon protects your heart [Prov. 4:23]. This keeps your heart safe from the lies and deception of the enemy. The breastplate of righteousness keeps what Christ has done in remembrance: His life, His works, His power, His authority, His healing, His love, His compassion, His sacrifice, His death and resurrection, and more. You remember the cross and all that it means. (The Lord revealed.) We are

			also reminded that it is His righteousness that keeps us in right standing with God, not our own. This weapon also protects the heart from defilement (such as bitterness, pride unforgiveness, hatred, envy, and boastfulness). Amen.
Feet shod with the Preparation of Peace	**Defensive**	**Ephesians 6:15**	This weapon allows you to walk in the peace of God that surpasses all knowledge and understanding [Phil. 4:7]. Peace is transferable, (Evangelist John Paul Jackson revealed), which means that wherever you tread, you can take peace with you. This enables you to be able to stand in all things. Amen. Peace is transferable to others, according to

			Evangelist Jackson, so you can leave your peace with others, like Jesus did, by saying, **Peace be with you** [John 20:21]. This weapon is also used to tread upon the enemy, to preach the gospel, and to triumph and have dominion over each new territory. Amen.
Shield of Faith	**Defensive**	**Ephesians 6:16**	The shield of faith is used to quench the fiery darts of Satan. This weapon is also used to keep the enemy out of one's heart and mind. (The Lord revealed.) **Faith** comes by hearing and hearing by the word of God [Rom. 10:17]. Praying in the Spirit also builds your faith [1 Cor. 14:15]. Amen.
Helmet of Salvation	**Defensive**	**Ephesians 6:17**	The helmet of salvation protects how you think, reminds you of who

			you are in Christ Jesus, and protects your mind from doubt and the attacks of the enemy. For example, whenever a sinful or carnal thought passes through your mind, cast it down immediately and replace that thought with the word of God. This is using the word of God and putting on the helmet of salvation. Amen.
The Sword of the Spirit	**Offensive**	**Ephesians 6:17**	This weapon is the living word of God [Heb. 4:12] and the quickened word of God (*rhema*) that stands out to you whenever you read the Bible and the Word from God that the Holy Spirit reveals to you when you're in a bind, so you can **defeat** the enemy. Amen.
Bow and Arrows	**Offensive**		This weapon was revealed to me (the author) by God, in a

			dream, and is used to shoot arrows (arrows are the word of God) at the enemy when he sends attacks against your mind. Amen.
Praying in the Spirit (praying in Tongues – your Heavenly Language) Intercession: • This is to pray on behalf of others. • Speaking in tongues allows the Holy Spirit to intercede on our behalf. Warfare tongues: • This is the explosive (*dunamis*) power of the Holy Spirit,	**Offensive**	**Ephesians 6:18**	This weapon is used to defeat the enemy and to release words into the atmosphere to push back against the enemy's attacks [2 Cor. 10:4]. (The Lord revealed.) Amen. Prayer releases your cares to God, as you pour out your heart to Him. There are also prayers of binding and loosing, and intercession. You can pray in agreement. You can pray for your wants and needs to be met. You can pray in the Spirit, and more. Amen. Pastor Terry L.

revealed through speaking in tongues. Warfare tongues are more aggressive tongues, they are louder, and pull down strongholds. Don't just sit there and take it from the enemy, war against him.			Harris revealed warfare tongues in his "P.A. System" sermon. *P.A.* stands for "power and authority."

How to Put on the Whole Armor of God

The whole armor of God should be put on each day.

Put on the **whole armor of God daily** and use your weapons when needed. (The Lord revealed.) Amen.

How? You can put on the whole armor of God (daily) by **speaking** this aloud with faith:

"Heavenly Father, I put on the whole armor of God today. Thank you for my armor that You provided. In Jesus name, amen."

Believe and you shall receive [Mark 11:24].

(Remember, there's power in the name of Jesus! Amen.)

"For we do not wrestle against flesh and blood, but against principalities, against powers, against the rulers of the darkness of this age, against spiritual *hosts* of wickedness in the heavenly *places*. Therefore take up the whole armor of God, that you may be able to withstand in the evil day, and having done all, to stand. Stand therefore having girded your waist with truth, having put on the breastplate of righteousness, and having shod your feet with the preparation of the gospel of peace; above all, taking the shield of faith with which you will be able to quench all the fiery darts of the wicked one. And take the helmet of salvation, and the sword of the Spirit, which is the word of God;" [Eph. 6:12–17 NKJV].

Amen.

(Pastor Terry L. Harris taught on the whole armor of God and how we should wear it daily. Amen.)

Weapons of Our Warfare

The Cross

And Jesus, bearing His own Cross went forth into the place of a skull, which is called in Hebrew Golgotha [John 19:17].

The altar—the cross

The cross symbolized an altar, but unlike an altar of stone, it was made of wood. (The Lord revealed.) Amen.

Is it possible that Isaac, who was Abraham's only son of promise, was the same age as Jesus when he was about to sacrificed on the altar built by his father Abraham [see Gen. 22]. Genesis 22:9, reveals to us a picture of what would happen to Jesus many hundreds of years later. Only this time, God the Father would allow His Only Begotten Son to be sacrificed for the forgiveness of sins [John 3:16].

It is possible that Isaac was the same age (as Jesus) and that the picture of Abraham getting ready to sacrifice his only son of promise is a picture of Jesus getting ready to be sacrificed on the cross.

The cross was an altar. Jesus was the sacrificial lamb, and **His shed blood** was the means of you and I having our sins forgiven and completely washed away [John 1:29].

Abraham's son was human, and what Abraham was about to do (sacrifice his only son of promise) was only showing what God Himself would do to His Son for us [John 3:16].

Only Jesus can forgive you of sin, and only His blood can wash your sins away. Amen.

In the end, the cross was an altar and the means of Jesus carrying our sins and **shedding His blood** upon it, so that you and I could live and be forgiven [1 Pet. 2:24]. Amen.

Where does the power of the cross lie?

It is the **blood of Jesus** that gives the cross its meaning. (The Lord revealed.) Wow! Amen.

One day as I (the author) was looking in the mirror, I looked down and saw my cross necklace hanging around my neck. As I looked at the cross, I asked God about it and He replied, **"The cross is a reflection of Me."**

His answer blew me (the author) away, but as I thought about it, I realized it was true. **He (Jesus) is the reason for the cross**. Amen.

What are some of the benefits of the cross? This is a list of a few of the many benefits of the cross:

- **a place of sacrifice**
- **a place of memorial**
- **a place of offering**
- **a place of remembrance**
- **a place of freedom**
- **a place of victory**
- **a place of release**
- **a place of burden**
- **a place of peace**
- **a place of hope**
- **a place the enemy was defeated!**

What can you do to receive these benefits of the Cross? With faith, claim these benefits in Jesus name. Amen.

In this manner speak aloud with faith:

"Heavenly Father, I **claim** the freedom of the cross. In Jesus name, amen.

"Heavenly Father, I **claim** the victory of the cross. In Jesus name, amen.

"Heavenly Father, I **claim** the release from [tell God what you need release from] by the cross. In Jesus name, amen.

"Heavenly Father, I **claim** that Jesus bore all my burdens while on the cross. In Jesus name, amen.

"Heavenly Father, I **claim** the peace of the cross. In Jesus name, amen.

"Heavenly Father, I **claim** the hope of the cross. In Jesus name, amen.

"Heavenly Father, I **claim** the enemy is defeated in my life, because of what Jesus did on the cross. In Jesus' name, amen."

The cross itself is only a piece of wood, an altar for sacrifice. It's Who was on the cross and what He did that gives the cross its benefits and its meaning.

His Name is Jesus! Jesus is Who was on the Cross. Amen.

Claim these benefits and walk in the freedom and victory Christ gave you on the Cross. Amen.

The Precious Blood of Jesus

"and without the shedding of blood there is no forgiveness of sin." [Heb. 9:22 ESV].

"For the life of the flesh *is* in the blood," [Lev. 17:11 NKJV].

"and the blood of Jesus Christ His Son cleanses us from all sin." [1 John 1:7 NKJV].

"who Himself bore our sins in His own body on the tree, that we, having died to sins, might live for righteousness—by whose stripes you were healed." [1 Pet. 2:24 NKJV]. (The tree is the Cross. Amen.)

"In Him we have redemption through His blood, the forgiveness of sins, according to the riches of His grace" [Eph. 1:7 NKJV].

Isaiah 53's "Suffering Servant" is an account of the suffering of Jesus. Jesus suffered a lot so that you and I could live a victorious, abundant, and blessed life on earth and receive eternal life in heaven. In His suffering, His blood was shed. The blood of Jesus deterred God's wrath against us, the blood of Jesus made it possible for the forgiveness of sin, the blood of Jesus made it possible for us to receive the gift of eternal life, and more.

There's power in the blood of Jesus! Amen.

Here are some of the effects and benefits of the blood of Jesus:

the forgiveness of sin [1 John 1:7; John 3:16]	cleansing power [1 John 1:7, 9]	victory [Rev. 12:11]	nullifying the power of sin— now sin has no more power over us [Rom. 6:14–23]	cleansing us of all unrighteousness [1 John 1:9]
peace with Father God [Col. 1:22]	reconciliation with Father God [2 Cor. 5:18]	abundant life [John 10:10]	eternal life [John 3:16; John 10:10]	a covenant [Matt. 26:28]
a protective hedge [Job 1]	deliverance [Rom. 5:7–11; Col. 1:13–15]	healing (by His stripes) [Isa. 53:5]	freedom [Eph. 2:13–16; John 8:32]	redemption [Eph. 1:7; Heb. 9:11–22; 1 Pet. 1:18–19]
mercy [Rom. 3:25; Heb. 9:23–26]	God's wrath deterred [Isa. 51:10]	The ability to enter freely into God's presence [Heb. 10:19]	defeated Satan, demons, and the power of darkness [Matt. 12:28]	defeated death, hell, and the grave [Rev. 1:18]

His Life—
Jesus Came to Me (the author) in a Dream

In the dream Jesus said, "Do you know there is a life insurance policy on My life?"

No, I didn't know, but I was so shocked that Jesus was before me that I couldn't respond to Him in the dream.

Now, let's start the dream from the beginning…

The night before this dream I cried out to God to please visit me. I yearned for Him to come. That night, He answered my prayer.

In the beginning of my dream I was in the parking lot of a Japanese restaurant. I remember walking up the curb onto the sidewalk and going inside. (In real life I love Asian food and sushi.) Inside the Japanese restaurant were many people. My mom and brother Andrew were already there, so we got a seat together. We all sat down and the place was crowded.

That's when Jesus came out of nowhere. He came and sat at our table close to Andrew and my mom, and I sat across from Him. People all around the restaurant began asking Jesus questions. My mom and others asked Jesus questions too. (I believe Jesus answered each question.) I don't remember the questions people asked Him or how He answered them.

At the table, my mom kept on saying the name Jesus, and Jesus smiled and kept asking my mom to say His name again. She did. Jesus was so overjoyed each time my mom said His name. I just watched and smiled. It was wonderful to see. In the restaurant He showed how He is both God and man. Amen.

Then our food came, even though I don't think anyone ordered anything; the food was a mix of chicken salad, croutons, and salad dressing. It was a perfect blend. Jesus even complimented the food. He really liked it (yes, He ate too). It was the best chicken salad I have ever tasted in my life. We (my Mom, brother, and I) made sure to give Jesus the best pieces of food with our chopsticks (yes, we all ate with chopsticks). We even gave Jesus the last best piece of food and He enjoyed it. In the end it was the greatest salad I've ever tasted, and to this day I've never tasted anything like it.

Others began asking Jesus questions again while I worried about what I should say or ask Him. I felt like other people showed Him more knowledge.

After the food was all gone, Jesus got up, complimenting the once more and how it was the right amount of chicken, sauce, and salad blended together. I used a napkin to clean the table, and then I went to the garbage a few feet away. Jesus came back to sit down at our table as I went to the kitchen of the restaurant to see if there was a towel I could use to wipe the table off or clean our dishes (why, I don't know). The man who worked in the kitchen pointed to where the towel was, and I thanked him in Japanese (*arigato* means "thank you" in Japanese; yes, I know a few words of Japanese ☺). Then I came out of the kitchen back into the restaurant and put the towel in a pot of boiling hot water, which held the rest of the dishes. When I came back out of the kitchen, most of the people in the restaurant were gone (including my mom and my brother). Only Jesus and I were left.

All of a sudden Jesus and I were transported to the old blue house that was my childhood home. The news was on the TV, and the TV sat on top of our big piano that sat in our kitchen/dining room. (This is where the TV had been in our kitchen/dining room in real life.) The newscaster was talking about the military, I think.

I was standing near the stove when I saw Jesus over at the sink in the kitchen. He took a small bowl to dip into a bigger bowl (the bigger bowl was a bowl that we used to wash dishes in; the smaller bowl was a regular bowl that we used for eating). The bigger bowl was sitting in the sink, and Jesus drank the water from the bigger bowl (using the smaller bowl). There were no dishes in the bigger bowl at the time; there was only clean water. I stood still by the stove, staring at Jesus, wondering what I should say and how I should act. (I acted so dumb at that moment.) Jesus knew my thoughts as I looked at Him. He walked over by me and went past me until He stood in front of the TV. Jesus's hair was short and brown, and I saw His face. His nose was a bit sharp, but I couldn't see His eyes. He looked like Akiane's picture. He wouldn't allow me to see the piercings in His hands or feet, although I did see His feet in brown sandals. His mouth was also like Akiane's drawing. To see Akiane's drawing of **Jesus** (which was also featured in the book and movie *Heaven Is For Real* by Todd Burpo*)*, please visit **www.akiane.com**.

After Jesus finished drinking and wiped His mouth, and after he came over to get in front of the TV while reading my thoughts. (I had been washing the dishes in a pot on the stove that had been heated up (don't ask me why.))

Jesus began asking me a series of questions that began with, "Did you know…"

I didn't know the answer to any of His questions.

Jesus was wonderful, and He smiled. It was so beautiful. As we walked through the kitchen toward the back room (where my parents stayed), the talk became more serious.

That's when Jesus said, "Did you know there is a life insurance policy on My life? It would benefit all of you [every Christian]."

With this life insurance policy on Jesus's life, all of us would be taken care of, and it would benefit us all greatly. Amen.

The Lord Jesus also turned to me, and as I stopped to listen, He said, "Do you know the benefits I died for you to receive?" (No, I didn't know).

The benefits of His death are all included in His life insurance policy. Amen.

At the end of our conversation Jesus talked about my dad, the military, and how He knows everything.

As the dream ended, I slowly began fading out of the dream, and the last words I heard Jesus say were **"God the Father, God the Son, and God the Holy Spirit. I AM, that I AM, that I AM."**

Jesus revealed Who He was by saying "**I AM**." Jesus declared that it was really Him in the dream and how He is God. Amen.

I pondered all Jesus said when I woke up, and I immediately wrote it all down, and kept His words in my heart.

That was my dream of **Jesus** and all that He said. Amen.

This dream occurred in February 2013.

The life insurance policy on Jesus's life benefits us all—yes, you and me too. Amen.

Please see the word study called **"The Blood Study"** in the second *Word* book to find out more. Amen.

The Benefits of the Blood of Jesus and His Life Insurance Policy

The benefits of the **blood of Jesus** listed and further listed in the word study **"The Blood Study"** in the second *Word* book reveal some of the many benefits found in Jesus's life insurance policy. Amen.

Apply the blood of Jesus

Claim, believe, and receive the benefits of the **blood of Jesus** over your life and over the lives of others daily. Amen.

How?

In this manner, pray daily with faith:

"Heavenly Father, I **plead the blood of Jesus** over my life, my family [list their names], my friends [list their names], and others, and I claim the effects, power, and benefits of the **blood of Jesus** over us all. In Jesus name, amen."

You can plead the **blood of Jesus** over your life, family, friends, and others daily. Amen.

God will honor your prayers. Amen. ☺

Pleading the blood of Jesus is a powerful weapon of your warfare. Amen.

His Wounds

James Goll, who guest-starred on Sid Roth's *It's Supernatural*, shared this:

Jesus told him, "For every wound I received I obtained a special level of healing for My people."

In a vision Goll saw **Jesus**, and on **Jesus**'s back were thirty-nine stripes. Goll saw the names of every sickness and disease written within each stripe, because each stripe was peeled back for him so that he could see each name written on it.

Goll said that in a vision, he saw **Jesus**'s back laid open, and within every one of **His wounds** was written the name of every sickness and disease.

Jesus obtained healing for every mental disease through the **crown of thorns**.

Most diseases are transferred by touch (the hands). Through the piercing of His hands, **Jesus** obtained healing for **every contagious disease**.

His feet were nailed for **paralysis**.

Jesus has received healing for **every heart condition** (such as a hole in the heart, heart disease, and so on) through the piercing of His side.

That is what James Goll shared with Sid Roth on *It's Supernatural*.

There's healing for your body in the stripes and through the wounds of Jesus! You just have to believe and receive it. (The Lord revealed.) Amen.

As they were eating, Jesus took bread, and blessed it, and broke it, and gave it to the disciples, saying, Take, eat, this is my body, broken for you, [Matt. 26:26; 1 Cor. 11:24].

Apply what Jesus has done through His wounds

In this manner pray with faith:

"Heavenly Father, I'm suffering with [tell God what physical ailment you are suffering from]. I believe by Your stripes, Jesus, I am healed, and I receive my healing today. In Jesus name, amen.

"Heavenly Father, I'm suffering with [tell God what mental disease you're suffering from]. I believe that Jesus obtained healing for every mental disease through His crown of thorns, and I receive my healing today. In Jesus name, amen.

"Heavenly Father, I'm suffering with a disease transferred by touch [tell God which disease]. I believe that Jesus obtained healing for every contagious disease through the piercing of His hands, and I receive my healing today. In Jesus name, amen.

Heavenly Father, I'm suffering with paralysis. I believe that Jesus obtained healing for paralysis through the piercing of His feet, and I receive my healing today. In Jesus name, amen.

"Heavenly Father, I'm suffering from a heart condition [tell God what kind of heart condition you're suffering from]. I believe that Jesus obtained healing for any heart condition through the piercing of His side, and I receive my healing today. In Jesus name, amen."

The Name of Jesus

Inspired by Pastor Terry L. Harris

"Save me, O God, by Your name," [Ps. 54:1 NKJV].

"And she will bring forth a Son, and you shall call His name JESUS, for He will save His people from their sins." "Behold, the virgin shall be with child, and bear a Son, and they shall call His name Immanuel," which is translated, "God with us." [Matt. 1:21, 23 NKJV].

"And being found in appearance as a man, He humbled Himself and became obedient to *the point* of death, even the death of the cross. Therefore God also has highly exalted Him and given Him the name which is above every name, that at the name of Jesus every knee should bow, of those in heaven, and of those on earth, and of those under the earth, and *that* every tongue should confess that Jesus Christ *is* Lord, to the glory of God the Father." [Phil. 2:8–11 NKJV].

There's power in the name of Jesus! (The Lord revealed.) Amen.

Here is a list showing how much power is in the name of Jesus:

- The power to strike fear in the enemy is in the name of Jesus.

- The power to defeat the enemy is in the name of Jesus.

- The power to cause the enemy to flee is in the name of Jesus.

- The power to forgive is in the name of Jesus.

- The power to be forgiven is in the name of Jesus.

- The power of forgiveness is in the name of Jesus.

- The power to save is in the name of Jesus.

- The power to be saved is in the name of Jesus.

- The power to deliver is in the name of Jesus.

- The power to be delivered is in the name of Jesus.

- The power to bring about answered prayer is in the name of Jesus.

- The power to stand is in the name of Jesus.

- The power of peace is in the name of Jesus.

- The power to be set free is in the name of Jesus.

- The power to heal is in the name of Jesus.

- The power to be healed is in the name of Jesus.

- The power of protection is in the name of Jesus.

- The power to activate the things of God is in the name of Jesus.

- The power to release blessings is in the name of Jesus.

- The power to provide is in the name of Jesus.

- Life is in the name of Jesus; *Dunamis* power is in the name of Jesus; joy is in the name of Jesus; mercy is in the name of Jesus; favor is in the name of Jesus; wholeness is in the name of Jesus; strength is in the name of Jesus; love is in the name of Jesus; hope is in the name of Jesus; help is in the name of Jesus; authority is in the name of Jesus.

- The power to love is in the name of Jesus.

- The power to persevere is in the name of Jesus.

- The power to endure is in the name of Jesus.

- The power to win is in the name of Jesus.

- The power to overcome is in the name of Jesus.

- The power to triumph is in the name of Jesus.

- The power to walk uprightly is in the name of Jesus.

- The power to give is in the name of Jesus.

- The power to gain wealth is in the name of Jesus.

- The power to grow is in the name of Jesus.

- The power to restore is in the name of Jesus.

- The power to soar is in the name of Jesus.

- The power to be uplifted is in the name of Jesus.

- The power to know is in the name of Jesus.

- Truth is in the name of Jesus; salvation is in the name of Jesus, redemption is in the name of Jesus; recovery is in the name of Jesus; victory is in the name of Jesus.

- The power to remember is in the name of Jesus.

- The power to convict is in the name of Jesus.

- The power to change is in the name of Jesus.

- The power to be still is in the name of Jesus.

- The power to wait is in the name of Jesus.

- The power to rest is in the name of Jesus.

- The power to cast out, cast down, and bind thoughts or demons are in the name of Jesus.

- The power to take back what the enemy has stolen is in the name of Jesus.

- Awareness of His presence is in the name of Jesus.

- And more!

Everything is under the **name of Jesus**, everything must <u>obey</u> the name of Jesus, and <u>everything</u> is subject to the **name of Jesus**. **His name** is above every name [Phil. 2:9-10]. Amen. ☺

To activate the power in the name of Jesus:

Speak, sing, shout, or whisper the name of Jesus with faith to release the power in His name. Amen.

Watch and see what God will do for you!

In Jesus name, amen.

Praise and Worship

This teaching on praise and worship was inspired by Pastor Terry L. Harris.

Make a joyful shout to the Lord! [Ps. 100:1].

"Shout to God with the voice of triumph!" [Ps. 47:1 NKJV]. My pastor said Psalm 47 is powerful if you put it into practice: speak it aloud with faith and you will see the results from the word of God. God is a God of results! Amen.

"God *is* Spirit, and those who worship Him must worship in spirit and truth." [John 4:24 NKJV].

To praise is to give thanks, to confess and glorify.

To **praise**, according to www.google.com/praise, means "to express warm approval or admiration of, to commend, express admiration for, to applaud, express approval for, appreciate, sing praise for, speak highly of, rave about, heap praises."

Here is a small list of praises you could say to God:

- Praise the Lord!
- Thank You, Jesus!
- I praise You, Father! I glorify Your name!
- I sing praises to Your name O God!
- Thank You, Father. You're so awesome!
- Thank You, Jesus, for what You've done for me!
- Praises to Your name!
- I love You, Jesus! I love You, Father!
- I bless Your name, O Lord!
- And more!

Worship, according to www.google.com/worship, means "the feeling or expression of reverence and adoration for; honor, adore, praise; glorify, exalt, extol."

To learn more about worship please see **"The Art of Worship"** on page 48.

Participating in **praise and worship** in the midst of spiritual warfare, craziness, mess, and troubles with the devil, family members, friends, coworkers, and others **brings results**. Give praises to God! According to my pastor, Pastor Terry L. Harris, giving God praise despite all the craziness and troubles going on in your life <u>impresses</u> Father God. God sees all that's going on in your life and what you're dealing with, and He sees how instead of complaining, murmuring, or self-pity, you are giving praises to Him. That impresses God! Amen.

Praising God when times are bad can move God to fight on your behalf more quickly. Amen.

Your praise and worship becomes a weapon against the enemy. Amen.

Praise and worship should not be conditional (based only upon your circumstances). <u>Regardless</u> of what is going on in your life (good, bad, nothing), **praise God**. Take time out of your schedule to give God praise. It can be a quick "Thank you, Jesus," a quick "I love you, Father," or "Thank you, God, for saving me from making a terrible mistake." God appreciates any time you take time to think about Him and give Him praise and thanksgiving.

Praise God with understanding. Know what you're praising God for, and know what you're worshipping Him for. Praise God because of who He is, praise Him for His sacrifice, worship Him for His goodness, thank Him for His truth, thank Him for His love. Don't just say "Thank you, Jesus" and not know what you're thanking Him for. Praise, worship, and thank God knowing why you're giving Him praise, worship, and thanksgiving. Amen.

Keep this in mind: God inhabits the praises of His people. When you begin to praise and worship God, you will begin to sense His presence drawing near. Amen.

Keep on praising God! Amen.

This is spiritual warfare and My pastor, Pastor Terry L. Harris, revealed how satan attacks us with tangible (physical) things such as a person, a thought, emotions, a chaotic situation, a flat tire, a broken window, and so on. The devil is doing all these things to get you to give up and to stop fighting him back. Even if you get discouraged, do not stop fighting back, use your spiritual warfare weapons such as praise and worship. Quit talking about the devil and what he is doing to you. Begin to talk about how God is going to bring you out of this and how you will soon gain the victory. Walk by faith, not by sight [2 Cor. 5:7]. Amen.

Here is a list of some of the benefits, effects, blessings, and rewards of praise and worship:

- Praise and worship confuses and frustrates the enemy.

- Praise and worship confounds the enemy and defeats the enemy and his plans.

- Praise and worship tears down walls and exposes the devil.

- Praise and worship brings forth victory and brings it sooner.

- Praise and worship moves God and moves God on your behalf.

- Praise and worship releases our faith (believing we have the victory even when we don't see it).

- Praise and worship rains down blessings.

- Praise and worship brings the blessings sooner.

- Praise and worship brings joy!

- Praise and worship brings forth strength.

- Praise and worship uplifts you.

- Praise and worship takes your focus off the problem and into His presence.

- Praise and worship sets you free!

- Praise and worship pleases God.

- Praise and worship ushers in the presence and the anointing of God.

- Praise and worship can break the yoke of bondage.

- Praise and worship can bring deliverance and peace.

- Praise and worship can bring stillness in the midst of a storm.

- Praise and worship ushers in an atmosphere of healing and prophecy.

- Praise and worship changes you.

- Praise and worship changes things.

- Praise and worship defeats fear.

- Praise and worship shows your love for God.

- Praise and worship can reveal God's love for us.

- Praise and worship relieves us from worry, stress, fear, anxiety, sickness, disease, and depression.

- Praise and worship deepens your trust in God.

- Praise and worship forces the enemy to give up and wears him out!

- Praise and worship reveals God!

- Praise and worship declares to people what God is doing!

- Praise and worship brings a change in the atmosphere.

- Praise and worship impresses God.

- Praise and worship boasts about the goodness, love, faithfulness, strength, truth, and all of who God is.

- Praise and worship increases your awareness of God and His presence.

- Praise and worship brings forth miracles.

- Praise and worship deepens your bond with God.

- Praise and worship builds your faith.

- Praise and worship stirs your soul.

- Praise and worship refreshes your soul.

- Praise and worship can bring rest to your soul.

- Praise and worship renews you.

- Praise and worship reveals the mysteries of God.

- Praise and worship stills you.

- Praise and worship reveals your testimony.

- And more!

How to Activate the Spiritual Warfare Weapon of Praise and Worship

Activate this weapon by taking the time to give God praise each day and to set aside a time for worship, to receive all the benefits and rewards of praise and worship. Amen.

Praise God every day!

Amen

"I will bless the LORD at all times; His praise *shall* continually *be* in my mouth." [Ps. 34:1 NKJV].

Prayer and Biblical Fasting

Scriptures on prayer:

"In this manner, therefore, pray: Our Father in heaven, Hallowed by Your name. Your kingdom come. Your will be done On earth as *it is* in heaven. Give us this day our daily bread. And forgive us our debts, as we forgive our debtors. And do not lead us into temptation, But deliver us from the evil one. For Yours is the kingdom and the power and the glory forever. Amen." [Matt. 6:9–13 NKJV].

"Therefore I say to you, whatever things you ask when you pray, believe that you receive *them*, and you will have *them*." [Mark 11:24 NKJV].

"Be anxious for nothing, but in everything by prayer and supplication, with thanksgiving, let your requests be made known to God; and the peace of God, which surpasses all understanding, will guard your hearts and minds through Christ Jesus." [Phil. 4:6–7 NKJV].

Scriptures on Biblical fasting:

"Moreover, when you fast, do not be like the hypocrites, with a sad countenance. For they disfigure their faces that they may appear to men to be fasting. Assuredly, I say to you, they have their reward. But you, when you fast, anoint your head and wash your face, so that you do not appear to men to be fasting, but to your Father who *is* in the secret *place*; and your Father who sees in secret will reward you openly." [Matt. 6:16–18 NKJV]. (Countenance means face).

This scripture reveals the Daniel's fast; "I ate no pleasant food, no meat or wine came into my mouth, nor did I anoint myself at all, till three whole weeks were fulfilled." [Dan. 10:3 NKJV].

"So we fasted and entreated our God for this, and He answered our prayer." [Ezra 8:23 NKJV].

"Then, having fasted and prayed, and laid hands on them, they sent *them* away." [Acts 13:3 NKJV].

Prayer is a two-way open communication system with God.

Biblical Fasting **means to abstain from certain food and/or drink for a period of time, <u>for a spiritual purpose</u>.**

Prayer and Biblical fasting are two effective tools to use for spiritual warfare. Amen.

The Benefits of Prayer	The Benefits of Biblical Fasting
• To see God move in your life and in the lives of others • To intercede for others • To see people get saved • To bind and to loose • To deepen your bond of trust with God • To watch God work • To see your prayers answered • To offer up petitions and requests • To hear from God • To know God's will • To build your faith • To deepen your relationship with God • To receive what you ask for • That your joy may be full	• To break free from bondage and oppression • To defeat the enemy • To expose the works of Satan • To expose the plans of Satan • To expose the enemy • For deliverance • For freedom • To see an unsaved loved one get saved • An act of changing and committing yourself to God • To receive healing for yourself and others • To seek God • To hear from God • To hear God more clearly • When in distress or crying out

(Evangelist Perry Stone revealed)

- To fellowship with God
- To get rid of stress, worry, fear, anxiety, and so on
- To deepen your bond with God
- To appreciate God more
- To appreciate the things God does for you and others
- To give thanks
- To see God move
- To see God move on your behalf and others
- To expose the plans of the enemy
- To expose the enemy
- To defeat the enemy
- To defeat depression
- To overcome sorrow
- To bring forth victory
- To get you through tough times
- To get rid of doubt
- To persevere
- To overcome
- To endure
- To receive help
- To get answers

for mercy (He hears even more)

- To honor God
- To crucify (subdue) the flesh (the carnal nature of man)
- To overcome
- For a heartfelt prayer or sorrowful plea to be met
- To avoid imminent or impending danger (for self, others, nation, etc.)
- To intercede on behalf of others
- To mourn
- To receive a miracle
- To see God move on your behalf or on behalf of others
- To build your faith
- To deepen your bond of trust with God
- To see prayers answered
- To increase your awareness of God
- To activate or operate in your spiritual God-given gifts
- For protection, strength, provision
- To know where you're going
- To see where you're going

- To increase in wisdom and knowledge
- To receive understanding
- To become more like Jesus
- To lay things at His feet
- To learn to trust God
- To learn
- To learn more about God
- To remind God of His word
- To remind God of His promises
- To remember what God has already done for you and for others
- To get through the current situation
- To deepen your faith
- To help you overcome (get through) struggles, troubles, trials, mind battles, situations in life, etc.
- To bring joy!
- To learn to depend (rely) on God
- To receive His peace
- To receive His answers
- To learn His voice
- To call on His name
- To discover His will
- To receive an answer
- To receive vision or dreams
- And more!

- To fill His presence
- To become more aware of His presence
- To begin to recognize where, when, and how God moves
- It brings faithfulness
- To forgive and be forgiven
- It brings contentment
- Changes you from the inside out
- Ushers in the anointing
- Can bring change and growth
- To activate or operate in your gifts
- To speak in tongues
- For protection, provision, and strength
- For direction
- For clarity
- To know where you're going in life
- To increase your awareness of God
- To spend more time with God
- To become more like Jesus
- To receive healing and deliverance
- To receive freedom

- To receive miracles
- To receive an impartation
- To know God's will
- To decree
- And more!

Pastor Terry L. Harris inspired this list of the benefits of prayer, in his teachings on prayer. Amen.

How to Activate the Spiritual Warfare Weapon of Prayer and Biblical Fasting

To activate the spiritual warfare weapon of prayer, simply pray with faith, to the Heavenly Father, and end your prayers in Jesus name. Faith is the key; believe that you will receive what you are praying for and it will be yours [Mark 11:24]. Amen. It is your faith that helps you receive the benefits of prayer. Amen.

To activate the spiritual warfare weapon of Biblical fasting, participate in a fast with adult permission and/or supervision. Biblical fasting means abstaining from certain foods and/or drink for a short period of time for a spiritual purpose. A spiritual purpose includes healing, deliverance, salvation for unsaved loved ones, a miracle, and so on. You can also fast from TV, computer time, negative media, and other activities. To learn more about Biblical fasting please read the second *Word* book. Amen. When you fast, you will receive the benefits of fasting. Amen.

Do all things for the glory of the Father in heaven [1 Cor. 10:31]. Amen.

Angels on Assignment

This teaching is inspired by Pastor Terry L. Harris, who taught on our guardian angels.

Your guardian angels are sent by God to fight for you, protect you, defend you, to keep you in all your ways, help you, and more.

"For he shall give his angels charge over thee, to keep thee in all thy ways." [Ps. 91:11 KJV].

"The angel of the LORD encamps around those who fear him, and delivers them." [Ps. 34:7 ESV].

This verse takes place while John is in heaven: "Then I looked, and I heard the voice of many angels around the throne, the living creatures, and the elders; and the number of them was ten thousand times ten thousand, and thousands of thousands," [Rev. 5:11 NKJV].

"And of the angels He says: "Who makes His angels spirits And His ministers a flame of fire." [Heb. 1:7 NKJV].

"Then an angel appeared to Him from heaven, strengthening Him." [Luke 22:43 NKJV].

This describes an angel: "Above it stood seraphim; each one had six wings: with two he covered his face, with two he covered his feet, and with two he flew. And one cried to another and said: "Holy, holy, holy *is* the LORD of hosts; The whole earth *is* full of His glory!" [Isa. 6:2–3 NKJV].

"Yet Michael the archangel, in contending with the devil, when he disputed about the body of Moses, dared not bring against him a reviling accusation, but said, "The Lord rebuke you!" [Jude 1:9 NKJV].

Angels have many purposes; below is a list of the some of the many purposes of Angels:

- To work on your behalf
- To help you
- To fight on your behalf
- To give you a message
- To defend you
- To keep you in all your ways
- To protect you
- To minister to you and to encourage you
- To report to the heavenly Father on your behalf
- And more

Angels are assigned to you at birth [Matt. 18:10]. However, once you reach a certain age (the age of understanding, when you know right from wrong), keeping your Guardian angels requires you to enter into God's redemptive covenant by receiving Jesus Christ as your Lord and Savior. Amen.

If you have not yet entered into God's redemptive covenant, please pray this prayer with faith:

"Lord, I come before you today to confess to You that I'm a sinner in need of a Savior. Lord, please forgive me of all my sins, and cleanse me of all unrighteousness, wash me with Your blood that I may be forgiven, cleanse me so that I may be whiter than snow. Come into my heart today, as I acknowledge You as my Lord and Savior. I thank You for receiving me. I'm now Your child, a new creation. In Jesus holy name, amen."

Congratulations! After praying this prayer with faith, you are now a part of God's redemptive covenant! Amen.

Testimonies of Angels

The first testimony of angels is by Evangelist Perry Stone, who speaks of his dad Pastor Fred Stone's encounter with angels. Pastor Fred was given a vision by God. In the vision he saw his brother getting into a terrible car accident, an accident that would cost his brother his life. Pastor Fred went into deep intercession for his brother, and after hours of praying, God told him that his brother did not have any protection because he was not under God's redemptive covenant. God also told Pastor Fred that he could send his angel to help save his brother, so Pastor Fred did and prayed for his angel to protect his brother and his brother's wife (who was a passenger in the car). His angel obeyed and his brother's life and his wife's life were spared. To hear the rest of the story and a detailed description, please read Evangelist Perry Stone's book *Opening the Gates of Heaven*.

In the end, hearing what could have happened and why he and his wife didn't end up in a fatal car accident from Pastor Fred, caused his brother to repent and give his life to Christ. Wow! What a powerful testimony. Amen.

The second testimony of angels is a true account from the author's mother. A few years ago, her mother was walking up the front concrete steps of their old blue house. There were quite a few steps to walk up. Her mom was dressed all in white, because they had just come back from church. I think it was the first Sunday of the month (Communion Sunday). She was walking up the steps carrying her Bible, coat, and purse, and the author was behind her. All of a sudden she tripped while walking up the stairs. She should have fallen backward on the author, which would have caused them both to fall down the stairs together. Instead she fell forward and landed on the pavement right before the next flight of stairs, the grass, and the dirt. The author's Dad, who was waiting for them at the door, ran to help her, and so did the author. We helped her up, dusted her off, and helped her up the rest of the stairs and on into the house. She was not hurt, thank God.

Later on the author's mom told her what happened. She said that when she was about to fall, she felt a hand push her forward, and she fell forward instead of backward on the author, or worse, down the steps. The author was shocked. Her mom asked her if I had pushed her forward, and the author said no. Her mom later said she knew then that her angel had pushed her forward to avoid a bad fall (and she wasn't hurt). Wow! The Lord had her angel save her life by helping her avoid a bad fall. Whoa! Amen.

The third testimony of angels is a true account from the author. Back in the summer of 2014, I (the author) was walking outside because I had to take out the recycling. To get to the recycling bin, I had to pass through the courtyard, a place where there were tables and chairs and people could sit and relax. As I was walking, a little girl who lived in our townhome complex was outside with her brothers, playing with her toys. I smiled, said hi, and stopped walking. The little girl looked at me and said something back. Then she looked behind me and tilted her head up and said, "Hi, Pops." I didn't know who she was talking to, because there was no one behind me. Even when I looked, there was no one there. I shrugged it off and began walking again and put the recycling in the recycling bin. When I came back into the house, I told my mom what had happened. Four hours later, the Lord allowed it to dawn on me that the little girl was talking to my angel. I was shocked and in awe that my angel had gone with me when I was taking out the recycling.

To this day that story still amazes me. It's amazing how **a child has eyes to see into the spiritual realm.** It's even more amazing that God allows the angel to be seen by the child and reveals to me how my angel is always with me. Wow! Amen.

These are a few of the many testimonies of angels. Amen.

Do you have a testimony to share of an angel(s) you believe God sent to help you? If so, please share your story in the space provided below.

This spiritual warfare weapon, **angels on assignment**, is already activated when you enter into God's redemptive covenant. Amen.

"For He shall give His angels charge over you, To keep you in all your ways." [Ps. 91:11 NKJV].

Obedience (Staying in God's Will)

"Behold, to obey is better than sacrifice," [1 Sam. 15:22 NKJV].

"But this is what I commanded them, saying, 'Obey My voice, and I will be your God, and you shall be My people. And walk in all the ways that I have commanded you, that it may be well with you.'" [Jer. 7:23 NKJV].

"If you keep My commandments, you will abide in My love, just as I have kept My Father's commandments and abide in His love." [John 15:10 NKJV].

"If you love Me, keep My commandments." [John 14:15 NKJV].

To obey means to follow orders and to do what you are told. When you keep obeying God, you remain in His will. Amen.

Here are some of the blessings of obedience:

- The safest place to be is in the will of God.

- You remain in God's will.

- You learn to trust God more.

- You learn not to question God.

- You learn not to fear the what-ifs.

- You learn to depend on God.

- You learn His will is best.

- You leave the outcome to Him.

- You leave the consequences in His hands.

- You learn not to fear the future.

- You build your faith.

- You learn to walk by faith and not by sight.

- You please God.

- You receive insight and wisdom from Him that His plan is better than your plan.

- You learn what the consequences would have been if you had made that decision.

- You learn His ways are better than your ways.

- You learn His thoughts are higher than your thoughts.

- You learn more about God.

- You learn His voice.

- You learn not to fear.

- You learn not to rely on yourself.

- You learn to obey His voice.

- You learn to trust in Him.

- It brings thankfulness.

- It shows how highly you think of God's word.

- It is a test of faith.

- It requires patience and tests you while you wait.

- You will receive rewards and blessings for your faithfulness and obedience.

- And more!

Activating the Spiritual Warfare Weapon of Obedience

To receive the blessings of obedience and activate the spiritual warfare weapon of obedience, just obey God and do what He says and commands you to. Amen. (Obedience is the key.) Amen.

"If you keep My commandments, you will abide in My love, just as I have kept My Father's commandments and abide in His love." [John 15:10 NKJV].

The Word

"For the word of God *is* living and powerful, and sharper than any two-edged sword, piercing even to the division of soul and spirit, and of joints and marrow, and is a discerner of the thoughts and intents of the heart." [Heb. 4:12 NKJV].

"All scripture *is* given by inspiration of God, and *is* profitable for doctrine, for reproof, for correction, for instruction in righteousness," [2 Tim. 3:16 NKJV].

You can **release** God-given power and authority by speaking the word of God with faith.

"For as the rain comes down, and the snow from heaven, And do not return there, But water the earth, And make it bring forth and bud, That it may give seed to the sower And bread to the eater. So shall My word be that goes forth from My mouth; It shall not return to Me void, But it shall accomplish what I please, And it shall prosper *in the thing* for which I sent it." [Isa. 55:10–11 NKJV].

There is power in the spoken word of God! Amen.

For whatever God speaks, it will come to pass! Amen.

You must **believe** the word of God (His word is true), speak the Word of God with faith, power, and authority, and watch and see what God will do. Amen.

Renewing the Mind with the Word of God

Pastor Terry L. Harris taught his congregation how to renew the mind in his sermon titled "From Saul to Paul."

Do not be conformed to this world, but be transformed by the renewal of your mind, that by testing you may discern what is the will of God, what is good, and acceptable, and perfect [Rom. 12:2].

"casting down arguments and every high thing that exalts itself against the knowledge of God, bringing every thought into captivity to the obedience of Christ," [2 Cor. 10:5 NKJV].

Transforming your mind is a continual (ongoing) process. You must **continue** to allow the word of God and the precious **Holy Spirit** to transform and renew your mind.

Tackle your thoughts by casting down thoughts not of God. Examples of thoughts not of God are lustful thinking, self-pity thinking, victim mentality, carnal thinking, sexually explicit thoughts, malice, pessimistic thinking, crazy thinking, sinful thinking, carnal imaginations, negative thinking, evil thoughts, and so on. **Not every thought that comes to your mind is right.** You must learn when thoughts are not of God and cast them down. Doing this daily will help you transform your mind and change your thinking. Amen.

Keep this in mind: do not assume every sinful or negative thought or carnal/lustful imagination you have comes from the devil. Some thoughts could stem from your own heart or the flesh (the carnal nature of man). Amen. Regardless of where the thoughts come from, cast them down immediately. In Jesus name, amen.

In this manner pray with faith, to cast down thoughts and carnal imaginations not of God:

"In the name of Jesus, I cast down the thought or carnal imagination not of God. You have no place in my thinking; you have no place in my mind. Leave now! Go! Amen."

In this manner speak with power and authority to bring thoughts into captivity to the obedience of Christ:

"In the name of Jesus, I bring every thought into captivity to the obedience of Christ."

Once you bring every thought into captivity, replace the negative, carnal, lustful thought or imagination with the **word of God**.

For example, after you cast down a lustful thought or carnal imagination, you can speak this from God's word, "It is no longer I who live, but Christ who lives in me." [Gal. 2:20 ESV] or Do you not know that your body is the temple of the Holy Spirit within you, who you have from God? You are not your own. You were bought with a price (the **blood of Jesus**). So glorify God in your body [1 Cor. 6:19–20]. Amen.

Use whatever scripture you want to replace negative thoughts with.

Once you speak the word of God, ponder, meditate on the word, and allow the word of God to sink into your heart; your thinking will change and your mind will be renewed. Amen.

Other ways to renew your mind or change your thinking are the following:

Ask the Holy Spirit to think through you daily. In Jesus name, amen.

The Holy Spirit needs your cooperation in this massive effort to renew your mind, so you do your part (renewing your mind with the word) and He will do His. Amen

Use the tools outlined in the **Battle of the Mind** strategy on page 58.

Plead the blood of Jesus over your mind and heart daily. Amen.

In this manner pray with faith:

"Heavenly Father, I plead the blood of Jesus over my mind and heart. In Jesus name, amen." (Do this as many times a day as you need.) Amen.

This may seem hard or difficult at first, but the results are well worth the effort. (The Lord revealed.) Amen.

How to Cast Down Word Curses

"No weapon formed against you shall prosper, And every tongue *which* rises against you in judgment You shall condemn. This *is* the heritage of the servants of the LORD, And their righteousness *is* from Me," Says the LORD." [Isa. 54:17 NKJV].

Every word spoken against you, you can condemn. Amen.

John Paul Jackson further explains word curses below:

Proverbs 26:2 NKJV says, "Like a flitting sparrow, like a flying swallow, So a curse without cause shall not alight."

When someone speaks a word against you or against your life such as "You're stupid, you'll never amount to anything, or you're ugly," counter the word curse immediately with the truth. **Speak** the truth of God's word over yourself.

You are **not** stupid; you are smart and wise in Christ Jesus! You are fearfully and wonderfully made [Ps. 139:14]. Amen.

You **will** amount to something! God has a plan for your life and you will fulfill it! [Jer. 29:11].

You are **not** ugly, you are beautifully and wonderfully made [Ps. 139:14]. Amen.

The easiest time to break a word curse is right after it is administered.

- Speak the truth of God's word immediately and continue to speak the truth of His word over yourself, until you believe it and His word is all you can think of. In the end, this will stop a word curse.
- For example; if someone calls you dumb, cast it down immediately by saying I'm **not** dumb; **I'm smart, for the Lord has blessed me with a sound mind** [2 Tim. 1:7]. Amen.

Stop speaking word curses over yourself or others.

Let every word that comes out of your mouth lift up or bless others. This doesn't mean you can't disagree with someone or discipline them; just speak in a way that is not demeaning. You have the power to bless (wield/create) and the power to curse (destroy and dismantle). Amen.

Speak words of blessing to people, and speak words of life and truth.

You can also use constructive criticism, but do not curse anyone. Amen.

Counter any word curses. Live a lifestyle of speaking blessings, and you will attract the attention of God and heaven. (Evangelist John Paul Jackson revealed.) Amen.

Evangelist John Paul Jackson reveals these truths in God's word:

"Death and life *are* in the power of the tongue, And those who love it will eat its fruit." [Prov. 18:21 NKJV].

"Let the words of my mouth and the meditation of my heart Be acceptable in Your sight, O LORD, my strength, and my Redeemer." [Ps. 19:14 NKJV].

"For out of the abundance of the heart the mouth speaks. A good man out of the good treasure of his heart brings forth good things, and an evil man out of the evil treasure brings forth evil things. But I say to you that for every idle word men may speak, they will give account of it in the day of judgment. For by your words you will be justified, and by your words you will be condemned." [Matt. 12:34–37 NKJV].

In the end, **words are important**, because every idle word men speak, they will give account of it in the Day of Judgment [Matt. 12:36]. So let no unwholesome words come out your mouth, but only what is helpful for building others up according to their needs that it may benefit those who listen [Eph. 4:29]. Amen.

Words have lasting effects (negative and positive), so **be wise** with your words; slow to speak, slow to anger, and quick to listen. Amen.

Binding and Spoiling

"But if I cast out demons by the Spirit of God, surely the kingdom of God has come upon you. Or how can one enter a strong man's house and plunder his goods, unless he first binds the strong man? And then he will plunder his house." [Matt. 12:28–29 NKJV].

"Binding and Spoiling" was inspired by my pastor, Pastor Terry L. Harris, in his sermon "My P.A. System, part 6."

When the enemy is attacking you through situations, people, and so on, and there is demonic activity involved, **bind and spoil**. **Bind** the demons or oppressions and **spoil** (speak destruction to that person's physical actions). That means you can spoil things that are going on in the natural (physical) realm (the realm we live in) Amen. You can spoil the person's fun, lustful behavior, crazy behavior, and so on. In Jesus name with faith, amen. This reveals some of the power and authority God has given you. Amen.

You can also spoil the fruits of depression, anxiety, mental torment, inability to sleep, and so on that go on in your own life, after you bind the demon/oppression. Amen.

To **bind** means "to tie."

Spoiling means "to take; to plunder; to rob; to spoil the goods" (Pastor Terry L. Harris revealed). The goods are all the outward showings of the enemy, (the actions that people are doing), because spiritual warfare sent by the enemy manifests itself in the physical realm. Please see "This Is War!" on page 344.

First you bind, and then you spoil. Amen.

For example, to bind and spoil, speak this aloud with faith:

"In the name of Jesus, I bind up the enemy of fear and spoil the goods of anxiety, stress, mental torment, and so on. Amen."

Use this prayer format anytime you need to bind the enemy and spoil his goods.

You can also use these prayers below too, to bind and spoil (pray in faith):

"In the name of Jesus, I bind up every demon working on assignment against my life and spoil the goods of drug use, suicidal thinking, and depression. Amen."

"In the name of Jesus, I bind up every demon working against my life and spoil the fruits of depression or crazy behavior from people working against my life. Amen."

Pray in this format whenever you need to bind the enemy or oppression (oppression means: heavy weight or burden), and spoil the goods. Amen.

The word is powerful—sharper than any two-edged sword. Use the word whenever you encounter trouble with the enemy, and you will see results. (The Lord revealed.) Amen.

"All scripture *is* given by inspiration of God, and *is* profitable for doctrine, for reproof, for correction, for instruction in righteousness," [2 Tim. 3:16 NKJV].

This Is War

Keep attacking the enemy and stick with it. **Don't give up!**

Results don't happen overnight, but in the end, if you stick with it, you will receive the victory. Amen.

Remember, once you start attacking the enemy, don't be surprised if the enemy fires back. When the enemy attacks you, attack the enemy back. Amen.

When physical things come against your life, sent by the enemy (through the mind the emotions, people, and so on), the devil is just trying to wear you down enough to get you to give up and to stop attacking him (fighting back). The reason the enemy does this, is because he knows the word [2 Cor. 10:4].

This is war; stick with it until God tells you to stop fighting the enemy.

Don't blame God if you give up.

Stick with it, and sooner or later, the attacks from the enemy in the natural will stop.

Even if things look crazy, keep on fighting. **Never give up!**

Have faith, speak with power and authority, use your spiritual warfare weapons, never give up, and God will carry you through to victory. Amen.

[Faith is the key in spiritual warfare battles. Amen.]

"This Is War" was inspired by Pastor Terry L. Harris's teachings on spiritual warfare.

Victory

God will give you the victory; please read about Gideon in Judges 6–8 to learn how God comes through for His people.

Have faith in God! Amen.

Remember

"Remember" was inspired by Pastor Terry L. Harris, who taught his congregation how to go back in their history and remind themselves what God has already done for them in the past. Such reflection was meant to encourage them to remember that God will come through for them again in the present and in the future. Amen.

"Only fear the LORD, and serve Him in truth with all your heart; for consider what great things He has done for you." [1 Sam. 12:24 NKJV].

Remembering what **God** has done for you in the past (and reminding yourself of what God did for His people in the Word of God) is the key to your present and future victories. (The Lord revealed.) Amen.

Remember the things God has done. (The Lord revealed.) Amen.

Go through your history with God and write down all that God has done for you in the space provided below:

_____

_____

_____

_____

_____

_____

_____

_____

_____

_____

_____

List what God has done in His word for His people:

_____

_____

_____

_____

_____

_____

_____

_____

_____

_____

_____

_____

_____

_____

_____

_____

_____

_____

_____

_____

_____

_____

_____

_____

_____

Have faith in God!

God came through for you in the past, and He came through for His people in His word. Rest assured, He will come through for you <u>again</u> in the present and in the future. **Worry for nothing**. Amen.

This is *The Word*

"It is written, 'Man shall not live by bread alone, but by every word that proceeds from the mouth of God.'" [Matt. 4:4 NKJV].

Amen

Always remember Jesus loves you!

About the Author

Storm Marie Rubin

Storm Marie Rubin was born in Nurnberg, Germany. She so happened to be born on Groundhog Day on February 2, 1992, to her dad (Lee Rubin), who was in the military at that time, and her mom (Bridgett Rubin). She is the youngest of four children (and the only girl), and her father named her after the Desert Storm war.

The Church she attends is Tacoma Christian Center in Tacoma, Washington.

She was inspired by God to write this book after being called by God in a dream to reach the youth. She is attending Faith Evangelical College and Seminary in Tacoma, where she expects to graduate in summer 2015 with a bachelor's degree in Leadership. She will be continuing her education at Faith Evangelical College and Seminary to attain her master's degree in Christian counseling.

While continuing her education, she plans to work on many books, activities, and games for the youth and young adults. In the future she will also be working on children's books and other novels.

Her eldest brother, Jeremy Rubin, wrote a book titled ***Have Faith...I Will Wait on You.*** This book is an inspiring story of love and grace and encourages readers to find their purpose in life.

You can contact the Author (Storm M. Rubin) by email at:
TheWordBook@yahoo.com

Printed by CreateSpace, An Amazon.com Company

Available from Amazon.com and other online stores

Available on Kindle and online stores

My eldest brother **Jeremy Rubin's** book *Have Faith...I Will Wait on You* is also
Available on Kindle and online stores

The second volume of *The Word*, by Storm Marie Rubin, is coming soon.

Made in the USA
Middletown, DE
24 May 2015